The Provisions of War

EXPANDING THE BOUNDARIES OF FOOD AND CONFLICT, 1840–1990

EDITED BY JUSTIN NORDSTROM

The University of Arkansas ...
Fayetteville
2021

ISBN: 978-1-68226-196-5 (cloth)
ISBN: 978-1-68226-175-0 (paper)
eISBN: 978-1-61075-750-8

25 24 23 22 21   5 4 3 2 1

Manufactured in the United States of America

♾ The paper used in this publication meets the minimum requirements
of the American National Standard for Permanence of Paper for Printed
Library Materials Z39.48-1984.

Cataloging-in-Publication Data on file at the Library of Congress

CONTENTS

SERIES EDITORS' PREFACE

The University of Arkansas Press series Food and Foodways explores historical and contemporary issues in global food studies. We are committed to representing a diverse set of voices that tell lesser-known food stories and to opening up new avenues for interdisciplinary research. Our strengths are works in the humanities and social sciences that use food as a critical lens to examine broader cultural, environmental, and ethical issues.

Feeding ourselves has long entangled human beings within complicated moral puzzles of social injustice and environmental destruction. When we eat, we consume not only food on the plate but also the lives and labors of innumerable plants, animals, and people. This process distributes its costs unevenly across race, class, gender, and other social categories. The quotidian processes of food production and distribution can obscure the significance of these material and cultural connections, impeding honest assessments of our impact on the world around us. By taking these relationships seriously, Food and Foodways provides a new series of critical studies that analyze the cultural and environmental relationships that have sustained human societies.

The Provisions of War gathers the work of sixteen scholars who consider how food not only shapes the outcome of war but also provides meaning in moments of human conflict that prompt us to reassess the conventional geographical and historical boundaries of modern warfare. The collection approaches the home front and the battlefield as interconnected spaces where the domestic work of preparing and eating food extends to the front lines, and where the violence and mass death of the warzone encompasses the fields, barns, and kitchen tables back home. And by scaling the tempo of war to the pace of agricultural, logistical, and culinary cycles, the collection's authors also reveal how the rhythms of modern conflict have corresponded to broader shifts in the social relationships between food and human identity over the last two centuries.

Spanning the globe, this volume is also unique in its emphasis on studying the roles played by food, agricultural, and nutrition in the myriad conflicts of empire and decolonization that both preceded and followed the two great world wars of the twentieth century. What emerges from this careful attention is a greater appreciation of how food has served as an analytical category for ranking, organizing, and understanding the stakes, experiences, and impacts of conflicts around the world. *The Provisions of War* documents how food not only "wins the war"—as modern students of total warfare have long proclaimed—but also how food serves as an organizing principle for making sense of the chaos and violence that wracks the world in moments of crisis. The contributors to this book, as well as its editor, Justin Nordstrom, approach these challenging topics with a sensitivity and thoughtfulness that urges reflection and encourages us to think about both food and conflict as inseparable aspects of human existence that demand serious contemplation.

JENNIFER JENSEN WALLACH AND MICHAEL WISE

ACKNOWLEDGMENTS

This book would not be possible without the team of insightful and creative contributors whose chapters appear in the following pages. I have been extremely fortunate to dialogue with, and learn from, the contributors to *The Provisions of War*, who hail from around the world, but who share an interest in global food studies. Thanks to all of you for sharing your work to create this book.

I am grateful for the support of my colleagues at Penn State Hazleton for their encouragement and advice, particularly Lisa Hartz, Erik Angel, Val Lynne, Shannon Riche, and Maggie Froehlich. A special thanks to Liz Wright, for her mentorship and support. I have also benefited from conversations with other scholars in American food history as I edited this anthology—particular thanks goes to Amy Bentley, Katherine Magruder, Kellen Backer, and Andrew Case. At the University of Arkansas Press, I was fortunate to work with an exceptional team, including David Scott Cunningham, Jenny Vos, Janet Foxman, Liz Lester, and Molly Bess Rector, and the series editors of the Food and Foodways Series, Michael Wise and Jennifer Wallach. Thanks also to Steve Ingle and Bill Morrison of WordCo Indexing Services for their work preparing the book's index.

I want to say a special thank you to my parents, Harold and Mary Jo Nordstrom, for inspiring my love of food and history, and to my son, Levi, who is the funniest and most sincere person I have ever met. Most importantly, I want to once again thank Alicia, my wonderful and amazing wife, for showing me perseverance, love, humor, and kindness for so many years. And thanks for never complaining about my cooking.

THE PROVISIONS OF WAR

Geography and Chronology in Food and Warfare

JUSTIN NORDSTROM

This anthology brings together historians employing a diverse range of methodologies and international perspectives to study the relationships between food, warfare, and postwar debates during the past hundred and fifty years. While intentionally broad in scope, the book's unifying theme is how soldiers, civilians, and communities have attempted to use food (and its absence, deprivation and hunger) as both a weapon of war and a unifying force in establishing governmental control and cultural cohesion during times of conflict.

Although they are tremendously varied, the essays in *The Provisions of War* fall into two broad categories. Chapters in part I ("Expanding Geographic Boundaries") examine lesser-known conflicts in the nineteenth and twentieth centuries from the perspective of foodways or discuss how an emphasis on food systems allows for an examination of armed conflict in a more general sense—such as the role of food and starvation in decolonization, passivist resistance, counterinsurgency, civil warfare, and internal uprisings. Other chapters in part I examine familiar conflicts such as World War II or the U.S. Civil War from international perspectives, emphasizing the study of foodways as a means of comparative history.

Chapters in part II ("Expanding Chronological Boundaries") discuss the role of food in shaping prewar political debates and postwar experiences of both soldiers and civilians. As these chapters point out, war-related hunger did not end the moment a battle concluded or a treaty was signed—indeed, malnutrition and hunger often caused hardships far after the war's conclusion. As the chapters in part II demonstrate, the echoes of war continue in successive generations, as dietary adjustments brought on by military campaigns reshaped national and individual foodways and identities long after the cessation of hostilities.

In short, this anthology argues that a focus on foodways problematizes historians' typical periodization of war and prompts a reexamination of which conflicts receive scholarly attention and of how warfare is studied. Examining how communal kitchens and food sellers were targeted by counterinsurgency programs in Malaysia and Peru, for instance (as discussed by Yvonne Tan and Bryce Evans in this volume), or how agricultural reform aimed to subjugate the post–Civil War South and colonial Africa (as argued by Erin Mauldin) broadens the definition of warfare to include a range of conflicts and policies that are often overlooked in conventional textbooks. Several chapters in this volume address the broad issues of colonization and decolonization, arguing that the impact of European colonization (in terms of violence, pacifism, and internal civil conflict) relied on reconceptualizing food (a point made by Karline McLain, Christopher Rose, and Ahmar Alvi). In short, rather than illustrating how a single nation mobilizes its food resources during one of the great cataclysms of the past, the essays in this anthology examine food as a way of drawing comparative perspectives and highlighting understudied aspects of armed conflict.

300 Million Hungry People Are Watching Your Plate

Hanging on my office wall, only a few feet from where I write this, are two historical posters that summarize the contrasts that form the basis of this anthology on food and warfare. Both posters demonstrate the centrality of food to home-front mobilization, government propaganda, and wartime preparedness in World War I—pivotal themes in the efforts of Great War belligerents and an overarching premise of the chapters that make up this book. Yet these two expressions of propaganda from a century ago present diametrically opposing views of food and wartime motivations.

The first poster displays U.S. president Woodrow Wilson's proclamation "Hunger Breeds Madness" to depict a nightmarish image of wartime violence, deprivation, and loss. The foreground shows a woman and boy, slumped with downcast faces. The woman's outstretched hand rests near an empty food plate, and her child rests motionless on her lap (suggesting to the viewer that the child is starving or has starved to death). A man, shown in profile, raises a torch and clenches his fist, staring toward the background, which shows a bold, gleaming city. The city's brilliant white skyline contrasts sharply with the dark hues of the starving family and the smoldering torch. Wilson's statement "Hunger Breeds Madness" appears next to the desperate man, as he prepares to descend on the city. The poster's message is unmistakable, even more than a century after it was printed—wartime starvation has pushed the man to inflict violence and destruction on the distant city, thus securing food for all is a military necessity and a matter of national survival.[1]

Ironically, given the nightmarish imagery in this first poster, nations mobilized for World War I with an enthusiasm and bravado that would later seem shocking on six continents and among a myriad of ethnic, religious, linguistic, and national groups. Eager to embrace what philosopher John Dewey termed "the social possibilities of war," the other propaganda poster describes wartime food in an uplifting, even utopian light.[2] This broadside depicts a ship of immigrants arriving in New York harbor. In the background, the Statue of Liberty, framed by a brilliant rainbow, beckons newcomers to the U.S.—new arrivals in the foreground gesture toward the statue and wave. The first line of text (which was printed in multiple languages to be read by new immigrants) exclaims "FOOD WILL WIN THE WAR," and continues, "You came here seeking Freedom, you must now help to preserve it. Wheat is needed for the allies. Waste nothing."[3]

This visual appeal to viewers (both immigrant and native-born alike) is two-fold. First, newcomers flocked to wartime participation, in both military and civilian life, as a chance to demonstrate to native-born observers that they too were good Americans and deserved recognition for their patriotism.[4] Second, the reference to "the allies" reminds viewers, especially those of French, British, Italian, Romanian, Serbian, or Greek descent, that supporting American food conservation could provide aid to extended family overseas. This international focus promoted U.S. wartime mobilization (evoking the phrase "America's food must save the world") but also positioned these efforts during the Great War alongside allies throughout the world (a topic echoed by Nel de Mûelenaere, Carol Helstosky, and Evan Sullivan later in this anthology).

Following 1917, the U.S. mobilized not only soldiers but also an informal army of volunteer speakers charged with promoting the sale of war bonds, conscription drives, and, importantly, food conservation efforts. Nicknamed the "Four Minute Men" because of the short and pointed addresses, these speechmakers received detailed instructions

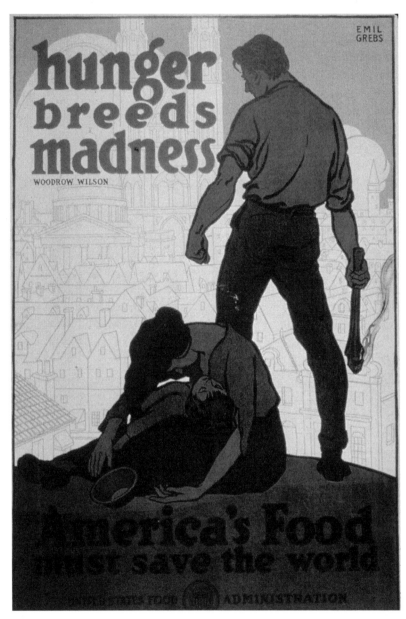

Hunger Breeds Madness. *U.S. Food Administration.*

from the wartime Committee on Public Information (CPI) and U.S. Food Administration (USFA). A prevailing theme in such wartime speeches was the need for allied cooperation—as one instructional bulletin put it, American wartime efforts were "sealed in the mingled blood of the fighting men of so many nations," a sentiment followed by an appeal to citizens, "not [to] rest content with speaking no evil of our friends; rather let us resolve to hear no evil of them and to lose no opportunity to call attention to the splendor of their services and sacrifices in our common cause."[5]

Nowhere was the CPI's message of "services and sacrifices" more significant than in promoting efforts to increase food production on farms and ranches and decrease domestic consumption. Propagandists congratulated themselves and their allies, saying "the roster of heroism is too long to even touch upon" while also warning of ongoing starvation in Europe, especially in Serbia, where for thousands "nothing was left to eat, and old men, women, and children could be seen tramping the roads looking for a morsel of food."[6] Likewise, USFA posters warned viewers "300 Million Hungry People Are Watching Your Plate" hoping U.S. food conservation could enable more food shipments.[7] Propagandists warned of global starvation in a staggering variety of regions—not simply Western Front allies (Britain, France, and Belgium,) but a variety of countries that desperately required food imports, including Syria, Persia, Poland, Armenia, Greece, and Japan. Since most of these regions contained virtually no U.S. military presence, American food shipments and rhetoric had a much broader reach than the American Expeditionary Force itself.

Weeks before the Great War's conclusion, the CPI issued a "Food Program," laying out a vision of food production and conservation that would extend beyond the armistice. Insisting that "the American people appreciate the importance of food in this war, to the winning of which we have dedicated our life as a Nation, our entire resources, and our honor among nations," speakers were tasked with expressing a need for food to maintain armies in the field and thwart civilian starvation. "We have sent our sons and loaned our funds to weave the fabric of force," the CPI directives stated, "so we shall sustain that fabric with whatever may be asked of us at home in the saving and conservation of food. Indeed, none will ask it more earnestly than our own hearts." Yet, as the U.S. Assistant Secretary of Agriculture Clarence Ousley warned, the armistice and peace treaty ending the war would prompt an increase, not a reduction of Europeans' dependence on American food supplies. "Truly," Ousley insisted, "the need for careful conservation will not end with the war."[8] American food

Food Will Win the War. *U.S. Food Administration.*

שפייז וועט געווינען דיא קריעג!

אידר קומט אהער צו געפינען פרייהייט.

יעצט מוזט אידר העלפען זיא צו בעשיצען.

מיר מוזען דיא עלליים פערזארגען מיט ווייץ.

לאזט קיין זאך ניט גיין אין ניוועץ

יוניטעד סטייטס שפייז פערוואלטונג.

Food Will Win the War. *U.S. Food Administration.*

could sustain Europe, both on battlefields and home fronts. Or, as the CPI more triumphantly put it, "We must save food to save civilization."[9]

Of course, this euphoric vision of American magnanimity and paternalism faltered when delegates assembled at Versailles a century ago. When food was mentioned in the Treaty of Versailles it was in the context of German indemnification and the requirement to pay the cost of feeding and maintaining Allied occupiers. Food, in the post-armistice era, became a tool for occupation, and the postwar peace reflected the paradox of optimism and destruction reflected in USFA materials.[10] Yet, I begin with the Great War and Versailles treaty not only because of its present centennial but because the themes mentioned here—international dimensions of wartime food policy and the lingering postwar implications of food and warfare—are the central components of this anthology. The forthcoming chapters explore the role of warfare on six continents and examine wartime and postwar implications of foodways, describing soldiers' and civilians' postbellum traumas and political conflicts surrounding food and deprivation.

Expanding the Boundaries of Food and Warfare

As this brief case study from a century ago demonstrates, food is a crucial lens through which to view military fronts and civilian home fronts. The connections between food and identity are many and varied—beyond the simple phrase "you are what you eat" lies a more complex social identity linked to food that creates a common set of assumptions and attitudes that bind eaters together. The word "companion," as historian Hasia Diner reminds us, literally translates to "someone you share bread with."[11] As Etta Madden and Martha Finch demonstrate, "foodways that regulate what goes into one's body . . . reflect a primary concern with regulating the social boundaries around the community."[12] Nearly all religious communities highlight food's meaning through restrictions, culinary taboos, or fasting rituals. Likewise, the CPI and other wartime messengers elevated this message to a national or international audience. Wartime rationing and food sacrifices therefore are reimagined as a shared national fast experienced by civilians and soldiers alike.

Furthermore, maintaining and mobilizing the nation's food resources extends government control and curtails individualism and personal rights under auspices of wartime exigency. Christopher Capozzola calls the propaganda of wartime food conservation an exercise in "coercive voluntarism." Promoting solidarity through food in wartime served as "significant manifestations of coercive voluntarism" that positioned political obligation ahead of individual choice, Capozzola maintains.[13] Celia Kingsbury echoes this argument. Throughout World War I, she argues, "food became a powerful political force. Because it is a necessary commodity, food served the cause of social control as well as any other source of propaganda."[14] One of the salient issues for this anthology, then, will be to address this essential contradiction in food and warfare—how and why does food serve to both heighten communal solidarity among soldiers and civilians on one hand, while limiting individual food choices on the other?

From Plutarch's comment that "the same intelligence is required to marshal an army in battle and to order a good dinner" to Napoleon's notion that "an army marches on its stomach," politicians, writers, commanders, and philosophers have mused about the overlap between food and war.[15]

Numerous prior studies have examined how one particular army or nation addressed its own food concerns in a specific conflict. But one of the first examinations of how food could be an effective lens though which to study such broad concepts as imperialism, colonization, warfare, civil conflict, and international diplomacy was Lizzie Collingham's exemplary studies *Taste of War: World War II and the Battle for Food* and, in particular, *The Taste of Empire: How Britain's Quest for Food Shaped the Modern World*.[16] Collingham emphasizes how food was the major impetus for British exploration, trade, and colonization for centuries and how foodways reinforced colonial mindsets among natives and foreigners around the world. Similarly, food emerges as the focal point of revolution in Stephane Henaut's *A Bite-Sized History of France: Gastronomic Tales of Revolution, War, and Enlightenment* and Katarzyna Cwiertka's *Cuisine, Colonialism, and Cold War: Food in Twentieth-Century Korea* and *Modern Japanese Cuisine: Food, Power, and National Identity*. These works, and similar historical studies, demonstrate how access to food shaped warfare and revolution from the perspectives both of conquerors and of colonized people.[17]

Yet, other writers focus on the absence of food—how hunger, deprivation, and famine have shaped global conflicts for the past two centuries. In *Silent Violence: Food, Famine, and Peasantry in Northern Nigeria*, Michael Watts outlines the impact of famine through a case study of village life, emphasizing how emerging market capitalism and the impact of colonialism contributed to the disruption of rural life in Nigeria through the 1970s.[18] Likewise, Melanie Tanieliean's examination of the Middle East during World War I demonstrate the role of warfare and the challenges of humanitarian aid in wartime, while Alex De Waal outlines how similar patterns of violence, food disruption, and global inequality persist into the modern era.[19]

These historians provide a foundation on which *The Provisions of War* rests in two important and interconnected ways. First, viewing food as the focal point for studies of warfare, violence, revolution, and empire disrupts previous notions that food should be reserved for a private place of home and family, moving it to the center stage of public life. Second, these studies bring an international dimension to the study of foodways, emphasizing how food and starvation are linked to global conflict. By examining food and food denial campaigns as part of wartime strategy and the efforts to expand (or challenge) imperialism, historians have begun to consider food as essential to broader social, political, and military trends throughout the past two centuries.

In short, as prior studies and the forthcoming chapters in this book clearly demonstrate, food is history and can be viewed alongside such traumatic international events as battlefield maneuvers, violent uprisings, colonial and anti-colonial campaigns, and political clashes. The chapters in *The Provisions of War* are organized chronologically within two sections. In part I of this anthology ("Expanding Geographic Boundaries") authors present global comparisons and international perspectives on food and warfare, beginning with Erin Mauldin's discussion of food and conquest in the U.S. South and colonial Africa in the late nineteenth century. Her chapter on "Yankee Pigs," argues that armies on both sides of the Atlantic forced subjugated people to adapt to new agricultural methods that reflected and benefited the attitudes of conquerors under the guise of improving or developing the land and also outlines how the wartime spread of hog cholera provided justification for postwar debates about food policy in conquered territory. Matthew Richardson's chapter on the Boer War likewise features discussions of colonial Africa, focusing on food as a weapon of war during sieges between British and Dutch colonial forces in South Africa. Richardson examines efforts at long-distance provisioning and links between food, soldier morale, and the impact of food in wartime on civilian populations in Africa.

While these chapters emphasize food as an aspect of colonization efforts in the nineteenth century, Karline McLain's chapter on Gandhi's intentional communities in Africa and India and Ahmar Alvi's discussion of Indian vegetarianism make clear that food can be a powerful symbol in resisting foreign colonial powers. McLain outlines how two foods— sugar and salt—served to shape Gandhi's early opposition to British rule in India and his formation of discrete communities in which to enact his growing commitment to pacifism and protest. Adopting a restrictive diet meant that Gandhi distanced himself from the British plantation agriculture as well as the violent colonial practices that made crops like sugar, coffee, and tea profitable. Alvi also examines food and colonization, outlining a discourse of eighteenth- and nineteenth-century India in which meat-eating symbolized British colonizers' domination, masculinity, and social control while Indian vegetarianism came to represent inferiority, impoverishment, and savagery. His chapter on "The Making of Indian Vegetarian Identity" explains how Indians challenged this mindset and questioned the binary between the meat-eating of allegedly superior foreigners and vegetarian natives. Moreover, his chapter examines warfare in a broad sense, discussing how Indian vegetarianism shaped British military strategy, internal riots, and violence and sparked civil warfare during and after British colonization.

Next, Jing Sun examines several different regions (Japan, Southeast Asia, and East China) to describe a crucial paradox in food policy and military strategy. Japan's elusive quest for self-sufficiency in its food supply prompted its invasion of Manchuria (followed by other regions of East Asia) which, ironically, required greater imports of food than they produced in exports, ultimately making them a drain on Japan's food supply during the Second Sino-Japanese War. International perspective on the World War II are also the focus of Leslie Przbylek's chapter "We Don't Need More Red Tape, We Need More Red Meat." Przbylek examines rationing practices in the U.S., Australia, Canada, and United Kingdom in the 1940s, explaining that wartime propaganda often clashed with the realities of the black-market sale of meat and other commodities.

The following chapter, Yvonne Tan's discussion of the New Villages in Malaysia, describes how food insecurity overlapped with imperialism, Cold War politics, chemical warfare, ethnic conflict, and counterinsurgency during the period of emergency that extended from 1948 through the 1960s. Tan focuses on street hawkers and small-scale food producers, who were demeaned and attacked by governmental authorities but served a vital role in the national food supply, creatively providing food for a population that has itself been the target of imperial aggression and military occupation. Her chapter emphasizes how Cold War counterinsurgency and deployment of chemical weapons used food denial as a weapon of war in the twentieth century.

Taken together, the chapters in part I emphasize how international warfare was both focused on and exacerbated by access to food, and how food served as both a military necessity and a cultural symbol as nations struggled with issues of invasion and autonomy. The chapters in part II focus on shifting the chronological focus of war, particularly by discussing prewar planning and postwar implications of food and hunger. Christopher Menking's chapter on the U.S.–Mexico War, for instance, describe how the conquest of Mexico exposed soldiers to new cultures and cuisines, which sparked the growth of Mexican-American foods in later decades. Foods that are ubiquitous today first became available outside of Mexico as soldiers sought to "calm [their] rebellious stomachs" in the 1840s.

The next four chapters examine the role of food in World War I, especially its postwar implications. Christopher Rose's chapter "Food, Hunger, and Rebellion" examines wartime hunger in Egypt and how the British colony was pressured to provide food for soldiers even as its civilian population suffered skyrocketing food prices and food riots. Hunger and food scarcity, which lasted well after the 1918 armistice, resulted in political turmoil and contributed to postwar revolutions and calls for Egyptian independence in the 1920s. Evan Sullivan likewise examines how access to food influenced postwar debates. He discusses military hospitals and soldiers' recovery from illness in the 1920s, demonstrating that debates surrounding food and hygiene provided soldiers a way to express complaints and demand fair treatment well after the final battles of the Great War were fought. Carol Helstosky's chapter also points out the role of food in postwar debates. Using early twentieth-century cookbooks printed in the U.S. that featured foreign recipes, Helstosky explains how food and recipes provided a sense of community identity between U.S. citizens and immigrants to North America before and during World War I, and anticipated the growth of European fascism in the decades after 1919.

Nel de Mûelenaere's chapter "Still Poor, Still Little, Still Hungry?" examines how food and hunger during World War I continued to shape the diets and bodies of Belgian children throughout the 1920s. Using health records from schools and philanthropic agencies, de Mûelenaere describes wartime food scarcities from 1914 to 1919 as well as limitations in Belgians' postwar diet in successive years. Breanne Robertson focuses on a different facet of food and warfare—her chapter "Planting Pan-Americanism" describes how the United States' Good Neighbor Policy in the 1930s and 1940s employed images of corn to promote a sense of shared identity and culture in North America through the advent of World War II. Studying artistic murals, food advertising, children's books, and other examples of popular culture, Robertson maintains that corn became a symbol of cooperation and interdependence within the hemisphere, establishing cultural and culinary connections between nations. Kwong Chi Man's chapter "Six Taels and Four Maces (*Luk-Leung-Sei*)" describes wartime starvation in Hong Kong from the Pacific War in the 1930s through 1946. Describing British imperialism and Japanese occupation in China, Kwong recounts efforts to mitigate starvation during invasion and occupation and explains how wartime food shortages led to a refugee crisis, ultimately shaping postwar memories throughout the late twentieth century. Lastly, Bryce Evans's discussion of food and counterinsurgency in Peru during the outbreaks of violence in the 1980s and 1990s likewise connects food and internal conflicts. During the late Cold War era, both sides of the Peruvian insurgency singled out community kitchens (and the women that served food there) for punishment and intimidation. Like other chapters in this anthology, that by Evans describes the conflict over food and hunger as examples of counterinsurgency, civil and guerilla warfare, and decolonization—arguing that the conception of warfare exists beyond pitched battles and massed armies, and includes the crucial role of propaganda and civilian population control.

The contributors to this anthology describe a diverse set of geographical regions and chronological periods, yet they share a common belief that an emphasis on foodways is an essential part of the methodology of studying the history of international conflict. For the past hundred and fifty years (and before), food has served as a means of cementing alliances and waging war and of establishing or destabilizing colonial regimes, and as a sign of supporting or deteriorating home-front mobilization, and a way of extending the war into successive generations or shifting the methodology of warfare itself. In short, as the anthropologist Sydney Mintz has noted, "War is probably the single most powerful instrument of dietary change in human experience."[20] Thus, the aim of this anthology is to showcase several dimensions of this overlap between food and warfare and to encourage further research in this crucial area of historical study.

1. *Hunger Breeds Madness . . . America's Food Must Save the World* [Poster]. U.S. Food Administration. Educational Division. Advertising Section. (01/15/1918–01/1919) Still Picture Records Section, Special Media Archives Services Division, College Park, MD [hereafter NARA]. ARC Identifier 512553 / Local Identifier 4-P-114.

2. Kennedy, *Over Here: The First World War and American Society* (New York: Oxford University Press, 2004): 50.

3. *Food Will Win the War* [Poster]. NARA. ARC Identifier 512499 / Local Identifier 4-P-60.

4. On immigrant wartime participation, see: Christopher M. Sterba, *Good Americans: Italian and Jewish Immigrants during the First World War* (New York: Oxford University Press, 2003); On the role of visual media in mobilization and food conservation efforts, see: Pearl James, *Picture This: World War I Posters and Visual Culture* (Lincoln: University of Nebraska Press, 2010).

5. *Four Minute Man Bulletin*, December 24, 1918, 2. On the role of speakers in wartime mobilization, see: Alfred E. Cornebise, *War as Advertised: The Four Minute Men and America's Crusade 1917–1918* (Philadelphia: American Philosophical Society, 1984).

6. *Four Minute Man Bulletin*, December 24, 1918, 20.

7. "300 Million Hungry People are Watching Your Plate," NARA, ARC Identifier 512557 / Local Identifier 4-P-118.

8. *Four Minute Man Bulletin*, October 4, 1918, 2.

9. *Four Minute Man Bulletin*, October 4, 1918, 2.

10. The classic account of the Treaty of Versailles is Margaret MacMillan, *Paris 1919: Six Months that Changed the World* (New York: Random House, 2003); On the specific role of food in the World War I and its aftermath, see: Avner Offer, *The First World War, an Agrarian Interpretation* (New York: Oxford University Press, 1989).

11. Hasia R. Diner, *Hungering for America: Italian, Irish, and Jewish Foodways in the Age of Migration* (Cambridge, Mass.: Harvard University Press, 2001,): 4.

12. Etta M. Madden and Martha L. Finch, eds., *Eating in Eden: Food and American Utopias* (Lincoln: University of Nebraska Press, 2006): 15.

13. Christopher Capozzola, *Uncle Sam Wants You: World War I and the Making of the Modern American Citizen* (New York: Oxford University Press, 2008): 101.

14. Celia Kingsbury, *For Home and Country: World War I Propaganda on the Home Front* (Lincoln: University of Nebraska Press, 2010): 36.

15. Plutarch's full statement continues: "The first must be as formidable as possible, the second as pleasant as possible, to the participant." Qouted in Peter Nowak, *Sex, Bombs, and Burgers: How War, Pornography, and Fast Food have Shaped Modern Technology* (Guilford, Conn.: Lyons Press, 2011): 144.

16. Lizzie Collingham, *The Taste of Empire: How Britain's Quest for Food Shaped the Modern World* (New York: Basic Books, 2017). For another example of Collingham's description of food and Empire, see: *Curry: A Tale of Cooks and Conquerors* (New York: Oxford University Press, 2007).

17. Stephane Henaut, *A Bite-Sized History of France: Gastronomic Tales of Revolution, War and Enlightenment* (New York: New Press, 2018); Katarzyna

Cwiertka, *Cuisine, Colonialism, and Cold War: Food in Twentieth-Century Korea* (London: Reaktion Books, 2012); Cwiertka, *Modern Japanese Cuisine: Food, Power and National Identity* (London: Reaktion Books, 2015). For discussions of the role of food in colonization and warfare, see also: Jeffrey Pilcher, *Food in World History* (New York: Routledge, 2017); Erika Rappaport, *A Thirst for Empire: How Tea Shaped the Modern World* (Princeton, NJ: Princeton University Press, 2017); Helen Zoe Veit, *Modern Food: Moral Food: Self-Control, Science, and the Rise of Modern American Eating in the Early Twentieth Century* (Chapel Hill: University of North Carolina Press, 2013); Amy Bentley, *Eating for Victory: Food Rationing and the Politics of Domesticity* (Urbana: University of Illinois Press, 1998); Anastacia Marx de Salcedo, *Combat-Ready Kitchen: How the U.S. Military Shapes the Way You Eat* (London: Current, 2015).

18. Michael J. Watts, *Silent Violence: Food, Famine, and Peasantry in Northern Nigeria* (Berkeley: University of California Press, 1983).

19. Melanie Tanielian, *The Charity of War: Famine, Humanitarian Aid, and World War I in the Middle East* (Palo Alto: Stanford University Press, 2017); Alex De Waal, *Mass Starvation: The History and Future of Famine* (Cambridge: Polity, 2018). On the overlap between food and warfare, see also: Rachel Laudan, *Cuisine and Empire: Cooking and World History* (Berkeley: University of California Press, 2015).

20. Sydney Mintz, *Tasting Food, Tasting Freedom: Excursions into Eating, Power, and the Past* (Boston: Beacon Press, 1997): 1.

PART I

Expanding Geographic Boundaries

CHAPTER 1

Yankee Pigs and Dying Cattle

Military Logistics, Animal Disease, and Economic Power in the U.S. and Colonial Africa in the Nineteenth Century

ERIN STEWART MAULDIN

Between 1861 and 1865, animals fueled and facilitated the movement of Civil War armies across the United States. Troops extracted calories from cattle and hogs to power human bodies; they used horses and mules to transport soldiers and their goods. Historian Ann Greene calls this process, the herculean task of marshaling the resources of the home front for utilization on the battlefield, war's "ecology of energy."[1] But the increased mobility of animals during the Civil War provided ideal conditions for the transmission of diseases such as hog cholera. Now referred to as "classical swine fever," hog cholera was a highly contagious virus that spread from animal to animal with a mortality rate of up to 70 percent. The disease was first recorded in the United States in the 1830s, but it was generally unknown in the Deep South states until the Civil War, when infected herds in army supply trains and depots carried it through the Confederacy. States across the South reported hundreds of thousands of swine dying from hog cholera, typically in the wake of major troop movements or the arrival of the U.S. Army. Looking back, historian Paul Gates contended, "With the exception of yellow fever, no disease hurt the Confederacy more than hog cholera."[2]

Historians of the U.S. Civil War only mentioned animal diseases in passing until recently, when a wave of scholarship incorporating environmental history began to clarify the role of livestock illness in Civil

War battle outcomes, supply-chain stability, and home-front subsistence in the South.[3] However, this literature currently suffers from two major omissions. Many environmental historians limit their work to the years between 1861 and 1865, not yet connecting the large-scale environmental changes resulting from wartime livestock disease to the years of economic hardship that followed the Confederate surrender in any sustained way. The loss of so many animals did not cease its relevancy to farmers' lives simply because the war was over, and continued or worsening outbreaks of Civil War era–diseases—such as hog cholera, glanders, and cattle tick fever—fueled discussion about the proper care of southern livestock for decades after 1865.[4] Furthermore, the environmental history of the U.S. Civil War has overlooked questions of international comparison and global context. As scholars such as Sven Beckert and Andrew Zimmerman have argued, the U.S. South was not an isolated system, but rather one piece of a globally interconnected industrial capitalist network of commodity-driven agriculture, and the second half of the nineteenth century was remarkable for the number of panzootics spread by trade across North America, Europe, Asia, Africa, and Australia.[5]

This essay uses hog cholera outbreaks to demonstrate the usefulness of studying Civil War animal disease over a longer time frame and within a larger global context. The nineteenth-century debates over the treatment and meaning of hog cholera in the U.S. South often paralleled responses to animal diseases in colonial Africa, where livestock-control policies reflected concerns about race, economic power, and white scientific expertise in agricultural development as much as they did disease. In the wake of the Civil War epizootic, the newly formed United States Department of Agriculture (USDA) promoted "scientific agriculture" to cure the South of hog cholera. In the absence of any understanding of the disease's etiology, USDA agents recommended penning livestock year-round to protect swine from the elements that made them vulnerable to illness—a practice in contradiction to the South's traditional free-range animal husbandry. Local white elites seized upon this advice, not only for its supposed scientific merits, but also because it provided a justification for requiring tenants to pen their stock, rather than allowing them to graze freely (and cheaply) on others' land. Veterinary science became part of a matrix of arguments favoring planters' control over the subsistence of ex-slaves and landless whites who clung to more traditional methods of agriculture. However, postwar southern agricultural reform, as directed by scientific expertise and deployed by white elites, was directly connected to a broader narrative of Western occupation and development of colonial lands. As in the U.S., agricultural commissioners, medical officials, and white politicians used the outbreak of animal disease in colonies across the global South to justify the restructuring of what they saw as chaotic or wasteful traditional practices. Over time, epizootics typically shifted the balance of economic power more firmly into the hands of Europeans and left the subsistence of native societies in doubt outside the white market economy.

Across the nineteenth-century world, then, the seemingly straightforward biomedical issue of animal disease was often used as an opportunity to raise other concerns about racial demarcations and economic development, in addition to worries concerning the more tangible issues of subsistence, military strength, transportation, and supply. From this perspective, the transformation of southern animal husbandry after the Civil War was not so much a parochial attempt at reform, but part of a global conversation about the integration of traditional or indigenous natural economies into more capitalistic, intensive systems that favored white elites. Ultimately, using a comparative lens might help scholars of the U.S. South slough off exceptionalist discussions of postwar agricultural practices and recognize the colonial nature of white power in the Reconstruction-era South.

Hog Cholera in the U.S. South

Hog cholera is a highly contagious hemorrhagic fever caused by an RNA virus of the family *Flaviviridae*. It causes previously healthy swine to stop eating or drinking, to vomit and seize until, increasingly emaciated, they die after lying helpless in their pens for several days. Hog cholera is pantropic, meaning it affects many different types of tissues at once, including the skin, lungs, kidneys, larynx, intestines, and lymph nodes. The incubation period of the virus ranges from days to weeks depending on the age and condition of the animal, making it difficult for owners to separate out an infected hog before it spreads the virus. If a hog survives, they have lifelong immunity, but seldom return to full health. Because hog cholera produces a wide range of symptoms and affects so many parts of the body, a cure or even effective treatment consistently eluded nineteenth-century scientists. In fact, hog cholera was not eradicated in the U.S. until 1978.[6] Hog breeders inadvertently imported hog cholera to the U.S. during the antebellum period, but the lower and coastal South remained relatively untouched by the disease—at least until 1861. The Civil War proved to be a "massive stir of the biotic soup," historian Stephen Berry writes, and as army quartermasters gathered together animals of varying immunity and moved them from one place to another, they created ideal conditions for a region-wide epizootic.[7]

The Civil War hog cholera outbreak began in the border states and followed the Union Army into the Confederate heartland. In 1860, before the war started, farmers reported a cluster of infections in the stock-raising border state of Kentucky. In fact, hog cholera spread so quickly that the state legislature of Kentucky offered a reward of $1,000 (around $30,000 today) to anyone who could cure the disease.[8] Hog cholera failed to spread widely, however, until after Union and Confederate armies began purchasing hogs from stockyards or farmers and then transporting them in railroad cars and wagon trains to depots or camps. However, supply issues and changing military strategies meant that both armies also foraged and confiscated hogs. Any infected hog traveling within an army train, regardless of how it was acquired, spread the infection further afield. In southern Missouri, for instance, rebel supporters rounded up hogs and cattle from local farms in December 1861 and drove them into Arkansas to a Confederate supply depot near Batesville, the origin of a subsequent outbreak of hog cholera that devastated herds throughout that state.[9]

One by one, the states of the Confederacy watched as the mysterious disease ravaged their herds. Although nailing down the timeline of its spread forces historians to rely primarily on Confederate recollections of the invasion by "Yankee pigs," the sporadic reports of hog cholera in military communications following troop movements confirm the relationship between army presence and an outbreak. In northwest Georgia, farmers reported that the disease appeared in 1863, brought in by a shipment of hogs for the support of the Confederate army. Another correspondent from Claiborne County, Tennessee, wrote, "Hog cholera was unknown in this county until about the close of the late civil war . . . it was caused by the hogs eating carcasses of dead horses and mules in the path of the army." In Louisiana, it appeared first in 1863, "carrying off fully three-fourths" of the swine in Franklin Parish.[10] It is particularly ironic that in the Confederacy, the acquisition of hogs actually harmed livestock production over the course of the war, especially when short grain harvests, the loss of hog-raising states such as Tennessee to Union soldiers, and a chronic lack of preservatives meant pork shortages were already intense. In 1863, a Tennessee newspaper reported that if hog cholera continued, Confederate soldiers would have to fight on rations of bread and water. By 1864, a North Carolina newspaper lamented that hogs were scarce in their area, and those left were rapidly dying.[11]

The disease's appearance on farms and in depot enclosures sparked a desperate search for a cure. Newspapers and agricultural publications reported testimonies of allegedly successful eradication methods, most of them horrifying to a twenty-first-century reader. For instance, some farmers swore that mixing strychnine or arsenic into hog feed killed the infection, while others promised that tar and grease in equal measures were a certain antidote. "Catch the infected animal, turn it upon its back, gag it, and drench it with nearly a gill of the [tar and grease] mixture," one editorial states, continuing, "If you can get the tar and grease in him, you count good for bacon." Another experimental cure involved withholding water from hogs for various lengths of time. A Dr. James of Savannah, Georgia claimed that after losing a hundred pigs to the disease, he kept the rest three weeks without water. No additional hogs died (allegedly).[12]

Because of the Civil War, hog cholera became endemic in the South. Devastating outbreaks continued in Deep South states every few years, and the disease attracted the attention of the newly formed USDA and its subagency, the Bureau of Animal Industry. During the 1870s, in monthly USDA reports, agricultural magazines, and the minutes of agricultural society meetings, what had been conflicting, almost random recommendations for the treatment of the disease began to coalesce around a common theme: southern farmers did not care for their livestock properly, exacerbating the spread of the infection.[13] Southern farmers and stock-raisers had practiced free-range animal husbandry since the colonial era, a legacy of conditions in which abundant land and forests kept animals fed cheaply. Instead of residing in enclosures, as hogs did in northern states, southern livestock grazed and foraged for their food for seven months of the year on "common lands"—a term used to denote any uncultivated, unfenced area, regardless of ownership. Forests and fallowing fields provided ample forage for animals, and free-range animal husbandry allowed all classes to raise stock cheaply.[14] The USDA and some southern white planters, however, argued that the South's traditional stock-raising practices were improper, backward, and weakened animals' constitutions.

To halt the disease, the USDA and the editors of southern agricultural publications pushed for an intensive, modernized stock-raising system that centered on penning stock year-round, eliminating free-range animal husbandry, and replacing the South's inferior breeds of swine with heartier, fattier ones. The first decades of hog cholera outbreaks occurred before germ theory or any organized veterinary response to disease through inoculation or dipping. Prescriptions for disease control, then, were a mixture of quarantines, checkpoints, and fencing—i.e., physical control of hogs' movement and care, rather than biological control of the virus.[15] A bulletin published by an agricultural experiment station, for example, maintained that hog cholera did not spread as quickly in districts where livestock were legally required to be fenced, and in some cases, the disease had been "checked or stopped at the border line between stock-law and non-stock law districts." A Bureau of Animal Industry report claimed that only in places where farmers failed to provide proper food or shelter was hog cholera truly a danger.[16] Northerners had previously described southern swine as the "longest, lankiest, boniest animals in creation," "fleetfooted 'piney woods rooters' used to depending on Providence for food."[17] Replacing half-feral breeds that were supposedly less immunologically stable with ostensibly improved ones was seen as another way of preventing additional outbreaks.

Why would southern farmers listen to the USDA? It is not clear that they did, at least in any way historians can measure. However, the timing of debates over the disease coincided with the height of white planters' political interest in the subject of the South's open range, and white planters were the primary audience for and contributors to the agricultural publications that reported USDA advice. White planters were also the ones making local laws about fencing. In reality, USDA recommendations on the prevention of hog cholera resurrected the writings of agricultural reformers of the antebellum South—white enslavers whose exploitation of the labor of others gave them the leisure time to study and publish agricultural science.[18] Before the war, fights over fencing and the free range tended to split along class lines. Wealthier whites in densely populated areas favored penning their stock; poorer whites did not. Slaves did not have a say. The "doctrine of improvement" endorsed by agricultural reformers such as enslaver Edmund Ruffin claimed that the elimination of common spaces would create a more ordered landscape. But as historian Daniel Rood has shown, such advocacy was also to consolidate elites' landholdings and control over natural resources. Early calls for fencing stock fit within this narrative, as well.[19]

After the Civil War and the freeing of the South's four million slaves, however, the issue of free-range animal husbandry became entangled with the region's upended racial hierarchies, and the restriction of common lands acted as a method of racial control in areas with high densities of ex-slaves. Emancipation created a new class of agriculturalists whose autonomy was scratched out from marginalized spaces that white landowners allowed them to buy, rent, or work. Freedpeople, both during and after the war, showed a preference for growing food crops and raising livestock rather than cultivating cash crops, but white planters feared a shortage of labor on cotton farms and the creation of a large, volatile rural peasantry.[20] Thus, longstanding access to common lands threatened the social and racial order southern whites clung to in the wake of the war. If free-range animal husbandry continued, Black tenants and sharecroppers could potentially manage their own subsistence. Getting rid of the practice would increase the dependency of Black southerners on large landowners and merchants for rations or provisions and reduce the ability of ex-slaves to make a living outside of the plantation economy.

Southern farmers had genuine, biological cause for concern regarding the effects of hog cholera on their stock, of course, and fencing them was as close to quarantine as one could get. However, USDA rhetoric also provided a practical, medical reason for overturning subsistence practices. Between 1865 and 1880, states across the Deep South passed laws that either prohibited "animals running at large" or gave individual counties the right to choose whether animals could graze freely.[21] At the same time, it became increasingly common for plantation owners to prohibit their tenants or sharecroppers from keeping livestock for fear of the disease spreading to owners' animals, or to require that livestock "be penned and fed at the workers' expense rather than allowed to forage in woods, swamps, or other uncultivated acreage," as one sharecropping contract read.[22] In short, one of the primary results of the deaths of hogs from hog cholera, in addition to the policies that emerged in their wake, was a reduction in the self-sufficiency of poorer farmers, tenants, and sharecroppers during a decade of violent economic and political change. Being forced to purchase meat for one's family drove up the costs of tenancy, and without animal manure, tenants had to pay for fertilizer as well. Any food or fertilizer obtained from the landlord or the landlord's creditor was taken out of the cropper's share.[23]

Hog cholera did not have a uniform effect on stock raising across the South. In Appalachia, for instance, railroad incursion and logging operations fueled fencing debates more than did animal disease.[24] Furthermore, many Black farmers resisted efforts to restrict stock raising, especially during the first decade following emancipation, when the presence of the U.S. Army and federal agencies supported their calls for freedom and access to subsistence. Tenants might continue to raise stock in violation of property owners' wishes or use access to weapons for hunting swine or cattle. Whites responded by doubling down on fencing livestock to protect them from both hog cholera and "thieving freedmen." A contributor to the *Southern Cultivator* whined that since the war, "each negro [has been] almost crazy for a long range rifle" to hunt others' livestock on the range. The *Carolina Farmer* warned agriculturalists in that state: "Thieves are numerous and ready to pounce upon anything which may be taken and converted into money. The horse in your stable is not safe. Your cattle and hogs in the range are less so!"[25] Planters claimed that freedpeople pilfered livestock to keep from working; Freedmen's Bureau agents largely assumed that such crimes occurred because Black farmers were destitute. In general, however, hog cholera forced farmers to make difficult decisions regarding the South's most popular livestock breed—decisions that, over time, harmed poorer farmers more than wealthy (white) ones. Especially in the lower South, where greater numbers of people of color resided in the wake of the Civil War, animal disease management reflected both biological understandings of the infection and the complicated tapestry of class and race concerns among a deeply divided populace.

The case of hog cholera in the U.S. South was part of a larger, global history of animal disease consolidating, or sometimes subverting, white power, particularly in regions whose economies relied on agricultural or mining exports produced by people of color. The spread of diseases through trade among North America, Africa, Australia, Europe, and Asia during the nineteenth century hampered European-led commercial economic development and threatened native autonomy from the Xhosa tribes of southern Africa to the Navajo of the American West. Attempts to control animal disease in these places were, as historian Richard Waller writes, "never merely a matter of marshalling sufficient scientific understanding." Solutions for infectious outbreaks were often more about controlling livestock owners, rather than the animals themselves: they created boundaries and fences where there had been none, used legislation to assert the authority of colonial science over established native practices, and ensured compliance through violence or police presence.[26] While studies of East Coast Fever, bovine tuberculosis, anthrax, glanders, and other murrains reflect this general pattern, the largest body of literature on stock disease in the nineteenth century is that which considers the African rinderpest epizootic of the 1890s.[27] Not only was this outbreak

utterly devastating to cattle and wildlife on the continent—with 90 percent mortality rates in some areas—it also significantly destabilized powerful African pastoralist societies who relied on livestock for food, transportation, and socioeconomic status. The response to rinderpest varied
across the continent, but in some areas, it mirrored the causes and effects
of hog cholera: spread by military movements and the clash of colonial
powers, solutions to rinderpest became a competition between scientific
knowledge and traditional practices, ultimately harming African independence during a crucial moment of political and economic transition.[28]

Rinderpest across Africa

An acute, highly contagious virus spread by close contact within a
herd, rinderpest was not endemic to most of Africa prior to the 1890s.
Rinderpest is a *Morbillivirus* of the family *Paramyxoviridae* that affects
ruminants such as cattle, water buffalo, African buffalo, yaks, wildebeest,
goats, and sheep to varying degrees. Contagion requires direct contact
between infected animals and a new host, but since the virus is spread
through mucus secretions, saliva, urine, and feces, rinderpest could be
passed through water sources, enclosure soil, pastures, and other forms
of indirect exposure. Infected animals display fever, depression, decreased
appetite, low milk yield, and congestion, followed by oral lesions.[29]
Epidemiologists describe the breath of infected animals as "fetid"; one
historian called it a "loathsome stench." Diarrhea is common, as is severe
abdominal pain and thirst. Like hog cholera, rinderpest sometimes causes
the increasingly emaciated sufferers to die of dehydration. Brought from
Asia to Europe before Charlemagne, rinderpest claimed millions of cattle
across those continents for centuries. A conference of Europeans agreed
on standardized control measures following the rinderpest outbreaks of
the Franco-Prussian War (1871) to protect borders, establish disinfection
procedures, and mandate quarantines. The outbreak response guidelines, however, did little to stop the progress of the disease as Europeans
scrambled for Africa.[30]

Despite a plurality of primary accounts, the exact timeline of rinderpest outbreaks in Africa remains murky, but its relationship to the
movement of European militaries and colonial forces is clear. Rinderpest
arguably first appeared in Africa in 1841, when a ship carrying infected
cattle from Russia docked in Alexandria, Egypt. The virus decimated
stock and wildlife around Egypt for decades, and military competition

in the area among the British, French, and Italians spread the disease into what became French West Africa by the 1860s and 1870s. The great epizootic that later swept the continent was the result of the movement of infected cattle to support the Italian military in present-day Eritrea and Ethiopia between 1885 and 1889. The capture of the port of Massawa by Italian troops and their subsequent incursion into other territory coincided with a horrible drought, which clustered animals at fewer and fewer watering holes. The transport of infected cattle from place to place and the direct and indirect contact of those animals with fresh hosts at watering holes were ideal conditions for the spread of rinderpest. The results were unimaginable—across Ethiopia it was said that only one or two out of every one thousand cattle were spared. The disease then spread west toward Dakar, spurred on by the Mahdist Islamist wars against colonizers, and southward in 1890, presumably carried along the Nile by the Italian armies toward present-day Kenya and Uganda. One account of the destruction in Uganda notes that the dead cattle were "far too numerous for any wild scavenger animals to devour, and no attempt was made by the people of the districts to bury or destroy the decaying carcasses. The smell near any village . . . was beyond description."[31]

As rinderpest continued its grim march amid the concomitant disasters of famine, drought, and locust plagues, Africans widely suspected the introduction of the cattle disease was a conspiracy among Europeans to impoverish native societies.[32] For their part, many Europeans in Africa had not yet connected this particular cattle scourge with rinderpest, a disease with which they had centuries of experience. Historian of German East Africa Thaddeus Sunseri explains that until 1896, when rinderpest reached South Africa, European officials could not confirm that the infection was, in fact, rinderpest. The virus reached colonial Tanzania in 1891, but wildly divergent descriptions of the disease and its symptoms from Africans, veterinary officials, and missionaries made diagnosis difficult. Further complicating identification was the enormous die-off of wildlife that accompanied this mysterious African cattle disease, something that did not, to anyone's knowledge, occur in European rinderpest outbreaks.[33]

Before the disease was positively identified and vaccine development begun, in many territories, officials believed better borders would stop its spread. Europeans commissioned large-scale fencing projects to divide African-held cattle from European cattle, to stop trade between unaffected and infected areas, or to prevent Africans from moving their cattle to new grazing lands. They also set up quarantines, disinfection of stalls and railway cars, and shut down cattle markets, especially near port cities and military camps. Some of these methods of containment, while in line with the European rinderpest control guidelines set in the 1870s, were both expensive and largely ineffective given the nature of the African landscape and cattle economy. The British Commissioner of Agriculture at Durban spent almost £180,000 between 1895 and 1896 on fencing and border guards, but rinderpest continued to wipe out herds. British colonial officials tried to fence off the Orange River, but to no avail. German agents closed the border between present-day Namibia and South Africa, and, when that failed, established a policed border zone in northern and northeastern areas of colonial Namibia that were under African control. Neither project succeeded.[34]

Rinderpest control solutions regularly protected Europeans and the colonial economy over the interests and property of Africans. Once officials positively identified the disease in 1896, a network of international scientific researchers developed an effective means of inoculation against the disease using the infectious bile or blood from animals, and later, a series of vaccine therapies. These treatments reduced rinderpest mortality to around 40 percent, and eventually, were able to eliminate it.[35] However, the political constructions of this scientific knowledge limited its efficacy in the 1890s. Factional rivalries riddled the European veterinary establishment, preventing an aggressive, coordinated application of new inoculation methods, and, in some areas, officials downplayed the spread of the virus in order to keep cattle hide exports high and help offset the economic burden of tenuous colonial rule. The most drastic measure undertaken by colonial officials to halt the spread of rinderpest involved shooting entire herds suspected to contain infected animals—preventative slaughter. In some areas, the owners received compensation for their losses, but compensation never met the market value of the slaughtered animals. Destroying herds outright, especially without compensation, was a practice disproportionately deployed against African cattle. The annual report of the Krantzkop Division in Natal admitted that while officials ensured that European cattle were inoculated, African-owned animals were often shot or left to their fate. This "gave the natives good cause for complaint, of which they will always make the most," the official wrote. The magistrate at Bulawayo mentioned "much dissatisfaction" among natives regarding preventative slaughter. He wondered why "they could not see the necessity for destroying the whole herd of cattle simply because one or two had died of the disease."[36]

European disparagement of African veterinary knowledge and racialized understandings of African agricultural abilities further complicated disease responses. On the southeastern coast of present-day South Africa, colonial veterinary departments established rinderpest camps where Europeans from all over could be trained to recognize the symptoms of rinderpest, to extract the necessary bile, and to perform inoculation. White farmers engaged by Native Affairs were then dispatched to relay the techniques to African pastoralists.[37] Historians Wesley Mwatwara and Sandra Swart contend that programs like these were not only about controlling rinderpest, but also an attempt by the state to "slot Africans into their world view and an effort towards replacing African livestock management techniques." When Africans rejected the instruction, the technique, or both, officials spilled considerable ink blaming the ineffectiveness of disease control measures on African intransigence. Traditional African environmental and pharmacological methods of disease treatment were dismissed as superstition, and any resistance to European interference with African cattle was explained away by the backwardness of the native mind.[38]

Indeed, French and British agents routinely criticized native stock-keeping efforts as being marred by laziness and a lack of industry, claiming these were the reasons for rinderpest's greater virulence among African herds. Across commercially intertwined regions in the U.S. South, Africa, and Europe, elites held similar assumptions about free labor and the ability of peoples of color to produce commodities or livestock without some measure of coercion or force. Ann Whitehead writes that "two pictures of [African] men" emerged from European rhetoric of the era: "first as idle wastrels, pursuing selfish interests" rather than prioritizing productivity, and "second as child-like dependents." *The Times* of London called African stock-raisers "indolent" in an editorial meant to show support for the beleaguered efforts of colonial officials in the fight against rinderpest.[39] Both images resonate with the characterizations of the African American work ethic in the U.S. South. Whereas the slave was "contented," "obedient," and "industrious," the freedman was "wandering" and "insolent." As Andrew Zimmerman argues, even as ideas of personhood, liberty, and citizenship were extended to African Americans by the state in the U.S., and Europeans promised to uphold the banner of Christianity and civilization in Africa, people of color were seen more as a potentially pliable, bound workforce than equals whose property needed to be protected.[40]

Responses to rinderpest revealed a multitude of fissures in the colonial project, especially where large numbers of European cattle raisers clashed with African pastoralists. There, colonial officials argued that more intensive stock-raising practices using cattle from Europe created more civilized, healthier herds. Echoing the breakdown of practices between southern white elites and poorer southerners (especially people of color), African pastoralism in British Kenya, for instance, was extensive and often transhumant—relying on open grazing across common lands or on fallowing agricultural fields—whereas settler stock raising was intensive and fixed. This meant that British policy drew on cultural understandings of proper and improper care of animals, imagining an intensive (British) system as the former and African practices as the latter. Just as white elites and the USDA argued that free-range animal husbandry and its neglect of animal conditions spread hog cholera, assumptions that natives cared for cattle improperly the infused official rhetoric regarding rinderpest. Historian Richard Waller writes that in this view, only Western veterinary methods such as fencing and dipping could create a "clean" pasture; transhumance and the existence of native cattle made a pasture "dirty." Even when Africans adopted Western veterinary methods, officials blamed the "indifferent" results of their treatments on the "bad hygienic conditions" of native pastures and Africans' "want of proper attention" to animal health.[41] The unsuitable breeds of native cattle were also suspected of being more susceptible to the virus. According to Europeans, native breeds were not as productive for milk or meat, and for a commercially oriented stock-raising economy to flourish, African cattle needed to be replaced with European or Indian breeds. In German East Africa, at least, this belief kept colonial officials relatively complacent in the face of the rinderpest outbreak, for the disease's devastation of African cattle meant herds could be started from scratch.[42]

Debates over the reasons for rinderpest's spread, its treatment, and the appropriate method of stock raising unfolded against a backdrop of fear, hunger, and violent resistance to European incursion. Estimates of African cattle losses during this epizootic vary between 70 and 98 percent, and the disease caused widespread impoverishment and starvation among pastoral communities. Transportation and trade broke down because of oxen deaths; tribes that adopted farming by plow could not fully cultivate their land and lost valuable sources of manure. The cost of goods, and particularly food provisions, skyrocketed due to demand and lack of transportation, and the pressure to relieve famine through the distribution of rations pushed German and British colonial regimes to finish large railroad projects, further threatening African natural economies. Of course, cattle were not only food, fuel, and transport—for many African societies, cattle designated social status, represented portable wealth, and were used in dowries.[43]

In some areas, the epizootic sparked rebellion against colonial regimes. The Second Matabele War in British Rhodesia, now Zimbabwe, was arguably a result of the devastation of rinderpest and drought; the Northern Ndebele (historically called the Matabele) were convinced the British were responsible for both disasters, or were at least making them worse. Colonial documents and press reports of the time call rinderpest "merely an excuse" for the uprising, dismissing Africans' urgent, material concerns. The administrator of the British South Africa Company, instead, blamed the rebellion on the "natural incapacity" of the Matabele to give up their nomadic habits and "accept their natural place" in a settled, civilized society.[44] In other areas, however, rinderpest's effects directly and noticeably eroded African economic power. The most famous example is among the Maasai, a powerful nomadic pastoral people who controlled trade in the region in and around present-day Kenya and Tanzania through tolls and raids. Famine in the wake of rinderpest weakened their numbers and economic power, and internal division followed. Scholars often link the loss of Maasai cattle, and the upheaval it caused, to expanding British control of the region. While rinderpest had the ability to harm the colonial project by keeping exports and taxes low (and spending on infrastructure and the police high), most historians argue that the disease's subversion of African autonomy and the economic dislocation that occurred in its wake largely facilitated colonial conquest.[45]

Conclusion

The histories of the U.S. South and colonial Africa in the second half of the nineteenth century were intertwined in a variety of ways. Scholars have ably demonstrated that British, German, American, and Dutch statesmen and scientists were aware of the various development policies of other leading powers during this time, especially as they related to the intensive capitalist exploitation of natural resources. Scientists and researchers working in Africa were often educated in the U.S., and there are specific instances in which Europeans imported American agricultural methods into colonial Africa.[46] For example, transatlantic efforts between Africa and America resulted in German colonies in western Africa adopting U.S. sharecropping arrangements for cotton-growing. Like their American counterparts, German officials believed that Blacks "had a special affinity for growing cotton," and, because of cotton's unyielding hold on world markets, hoped to grow it "by reproducing the oppressive and exploitative conditions of the United States." Historian Andrew Zimmerman has detailed these efforts at length, showing how German officials believed "family farming presented an ideal model of controlling emancipated workers." German officials even invited African Americans from Tuskegee, Alabama to advise their efforts; British and French colonial operations subsequently took notice.[47]

However, the nineteenth-century global trade in goods, ideas, and prejudices among empires produced another, less-studied transnational history, at least as it relates to events in the U.S.: the reaction and response to the frequent outbreaks of animal disease. Rinderpest, bovine pleuro-pneumonia, Texas fever (cattle tick fever), and even hog cholera spread between Europe, the U.S., Asia, and Africa during the nineteenth century. Hog cholera traveled from the U.S. to Europe in the 1880s; classical swine fever is still a major threat to European swine thanks to the reservoir provided by the continent's wild boar population. Similarly, international trade carried rinderpest to the U.S. in the 1860s, although it did not become established.[48] Just as entangled within international currents as the physical spread of infections was the effort to control them and the remarkable effects of such diseases on subsistence and economic power. Competing patterns of knowledge often meant that the proposed cure for or rhetoric about animal disease reflected class, racial, or ideological lines as much as any particular scientific advice. Even when vaccine therapies were available, local conditions, political purposes, and race relations complicated their utilization.[49] Thus, animal disease is a window into the common fault lines that fragmented a variety of colonial projects across the world, from the nascent European regimes of sub-Saharan Africa to the postwar U.S. South.

NOTES

1. Ann Norton Greene, *Horses at Work: Harnessing Power in Industrial America* (Cambridge: Harvard University Press, 2008): 121.
2. Quote from Paul Gates, *Agriculture and the Civil War* (New York: Alfred Knopf, 1965): 90; U.S. Department of Agriculture (USDA), *Hog Cholera: Its*

History, Nature, and Treatment, an investigation of the Bureau of Animal Industry (Washington, DC: GPO, 1889): 9; V. Moennig et al., "Clinical Signs and Epidemiology of Classical Swine Fever: A Review of New Knowledge," *Veterinary Journal* 165 (2003): 11; Douglas Gregg, "Update on Classical Swine Fever," *Journal of Swine Health and Production* 10, no. 1 (2002): 35; C. A. Lueder, *Hog Cholera: Its Prevention and Control* (Washington, DC: Published for the U.S. Department of Agriculture and the West Virginia Experiment Station, 1913): 10.

3. See: Lisa Brady, *War Upon the Land: Military Strategy and the Transformation of Southern Landscapes during the American Civil War* (Athens: University of Georgia Press, 2012); R. Douglas Hurt, *Food and Agriculture during the Civil War* (Westport: Praeger Publishers, 2016); Mark Fiege, *The Republic of Nature: An Environmental History of the United States* (Seattle: University of Washington Press, 2012); Ted Steinberg, *Down to Earth: Nature's Role in American History* (New York: Oxford University Press, 2011); Erin Stewart Mauldin, *Unredeemed Land: An Environmental History of Civil War and Emancipation in the Cotton South* (New York: Oxford University Press, 2018); Judkin Browning and Timothy Silver, *An Environmental History of the Civil War* (Chapel Hill: University of North Carolina Press, 2020).

4. See: Claire Strom, *Making Catfish Bait out of Government Boys: The Fight against Cattle Ticks in the Yeoman South* (Athens: University of Georgia Press, 2009); Erin Stewart Mauldin, "The Stockman's War: Hog Cholera in Nineteenth-Century Alabama," *Alabama Review* 70, no. 2 (April 2017): 126–40; G. Terry Sharrer, "The Great Glanders Epizootic, 1861–1866: A Civil War Legacy," *Agricultural History* 69, no. 1 (Winter 1995): 79–97.

5. Sven Beckert, "From Tuskegee to Togo: The Problem of Freedom in the Empire of Cotton," *Journal of American History* 92, no. 2 (September 2005): 501; Andrew Zimmerman, *Alabama in Africa: Booker T. Washington, the German Empire, and the Globalization of the New South* (Princeton: Princeton University Press, 2012); Karen Brown and Daniel Gilfoyle, eds., *Healing the Herds: Livestock Economies and the Globalization of Veterinary Medicine* (Ohio University Press, 2010): 7.

6. Raymond Russell Birch, *Hog Cholera: Its Nature and Control* (New York: The Macmillan Company, 1922): 1, 36, 38, 40; Anna Rovid Spickler, "Classical Swine Fever: Technical Factsheet," *The Center for Food Security and Public Health at Iowa State University*, 11; USDA, "Contagious Diseases of Domesticated Animals," Special Report No. 34 (Washington, DC: GPO, 1881): 143–44; National Research Council, *Emerging Animal Diseases: Global Markets, Global Safety: Workshop Summary* (Washington, DC: The National Academies Press, 2002): 11.

7. Stephen Berry, "The Future of Civil War Era Studies: Predictions," *Journal of the Civil War Era* 2, no. 1 (March 2012), accessed January 16, 2021, http://journalof thecivilwarera.org/wp-content/uploads/2012/02/Final-Berry.pdf.

8. "Hog Cholera," *Yorkville Enquirer* (Yorkville, SC), July 5, 1860.

9. F. W. Desha to William E. Woodruff, January 5, 1863, in *At Home in Confederate Arkansas: Letters to and from Pulaski Countians, 1861–1865*, ed. Ted Worley, (Little Rock: Pulaski County Historical Society, 1955): 22; USDA, *Hog Cholera: Its History, Nature, and Treatment*, 81; W. Stephen McBride, "More Than a Depot: Camp Nelson, Kentucky," accessed January 16, 2021, http://www.camp

nelson.org/history/historic.htm; Captain Robert O. Zinnen Jr., "City Point: The Tool that Gave General Grant Victory," *Quartermaster's Professional Bulletin* (Spring 1991).

10. USDA, *Fourth and Fifth Annual Reports of the Bureau of Animal Industry* (Washington, DC, 1889): 192, 204, 241, 249–50, 280.

11. Frank Ruffin to Col. Northrup, Report on Subsistence dated January 1862, in United States War Department *The War of the Rebellion: a Compilation of the Official Records of the Union and Confederate Armies* 4, (Washington, DC: Government Printing Office, 1900), 1:873; Gates, *Agriculture and the Civil War*, 83, 90–92; John Solomon Otto, *Southern Agriculture during the Civil War Era* (Westport: Greenwood Press, 1994): 24, 36; R. Douglas Hurt, *Agriculture and the Confederacy: Policy, Productivity, and Power in the Civil War South* (Chapel Hill: University of North Carolina Press, 2015); *Nashville Daily Union* (Nashville, TN), October 22, 1863; *Western Democrat* (Charlotte, NC), August 23, 1864.

12. "Investigations of Swine Diseases," in USDA, *Hog Cholera: Its History, Nature, and Treatment*, 14–17; "Certain Cure for the Hog Cholera," *Abingdon Virginian* (Abingdon, VA), May 1, 1863; quote from *Fayetteville Observer* (Fayetteville, TN), October 10, 1861; "Hog Cholera—Cured," *Southern Cultivator,* July and August 1862, 141.

13. See: Mauldin, "The Stockman's War"; USDA, *Contagious Diseases of Domesticated Animals*, Special Report No. 34, 304; USDA, *Fourth and Fifth Annual Reports,* 202, 241, 191.

14. Mauldin, "Deferring Crisis," in ch. 1 in *Unredeemed Land*; Joseph Reidy, "Obligation and Right: Patterns of Labor, Subsistence, and Exchange in the Cotton Belt in Georgia, 1790–1860," in *Cultivation and Culture: Labor and the Shaping of Slave Life in the Americas* ed. Ira Berlin and Philip Morgan (Charlottesville: University Press of Virginia, 1993): 143–44.

15. Birch, *Hog Cholera*, 17–19; USDA, *Rules and Regulations Governing the Operations of the Bureau of Animal Industry* (Washington, DC: GPO, 1895): 59.

16. Appendix, Bulletin No. 22, Agricultural Experiment Station of the Agricultural and Mechanical College, Auburn, AL (Montgomery: Smith, Allred, & Co., 1891): 78–79; USDA, *Contagious Diseases of Domesticated Animals*, Special Report No. 34, 304.

17. Gates, *Agriculture during the Civil War*, 6–7.

18. For examples of prewar writings on the subject by white planters, see: "Fences," *Alabama Baptist* (Birmingham, AL), April 5, 1845; "The Enclosure System of Virginia," *Southern Planter,* August 1852, 233; "Plantation Work for July," *American Cotton Planter*, July 1858, 204–5; "On the Cotton Plantation or the Stock Farm," *American Cotton Planter*, June 1858, 196.

19. For more on antebellum efforts to eliminate common spaces or subsistence practices in the south, see: Daniel Rood, "Bogs of Death: Slavery, the Brazilian Flour Trade, and the Mystery of Vanishing Millponds in Antebellum Virginia," *Journal of Southern History* (June 2014): 20–21; Jack Temple Kirby, *Poquosin: A Study of Landscape and Society* (Chapel Hill: University of North Carolina Press, 1995): 130–40, 174.

20. For the larger history of the class divide on this issue, see: Drew Addison Swanson, "Fighting over Fencing: Agricultural Reform and Antebellum Efforts to Close the Virginia Open Range," *Virginia Magazine of History and Biography*

117, no. 2 (2009): 105–6. For the entanglement of race and stock raising, see: Mauldin, "Accelerating Change," *Unredeemed Land*,; J. Crawford King Jr., "The Closing of the Southern Range: An Exploratory Study," *Journal of Southern History* 48, no. 1 (February 1982): 54–57; Steven Hahn, "Hunting, Fishing, and Foraging: Common Rights and Class Relations in the Postbellum South," *Radical History Review* 26 (1982): 47. For reports of white concerns over Black labor, see: Testimony of John Covode dated March 3, 1866, *Report of the Joint Committee on Reconstruction at the First Session Thirty-Ninth Congress* (Washington, DC: GPO, 1866): 116–17; Reports dated June 1, 1865 and August 1865 by C. W. Buckley, Reports of Operations from the Subdistricts, Records of the Assistant Commissioner for the State of Alabama, M809, Reel 18, BRFAL, NARA I.

21. For local or state laws passed regarding penning stock during this period, see: Act no. 258, *Acts of the Session of 1866-7 of the General Assembly of Alabama* (Montgomery: Reid and Screws, 1867): 256; *Acts of the General Assembly of the State of Virginia, Passed at the Session 1869–70* (Richmond: James E. Goode, 1870): 544; Resolution number 437, *Acts and Resolutions of the General Assembly of the State of Georgia, Passed at its session in July and August 1872* (Atlanta: W. A. Hemphill and Co., 1872), 1:529; *Laws of the State of Mississippi, 1865–1866* (Jackson: printed for the state of Mississippi, 1866): 199–200, 289–90.

22. Steven Hahn et al., *Freedom: A Documentary History of Emancipation, 1861–1867* 3, Vol. 2. *Land and Labor 1866-7* (Chapel Hill: University of North Carolina Press, 2013): 372–373.

23. "Advance in Corn and Bacon," *Macon Telegraph* (Macon, GA), April 28, 1870. See also: Mauldin, "Facing Limits," ch. 5 in *Unredeemed Land*.

24. Ronald L. Lewis, *Transforming the Appalachian Countryside: Railroads, Deforestation, and Social Change in West Virginia, 1880–1920* (Chapel Hill: University of North Carolina Press, 1998): 8–10, quote on 47; Wetherington, *Plain Folk's Fight*, 304.

25. "Loss of Livestock," *Carolina Farmer*, August 1869; "Immigration," *Carolina Farmer*, April 1869, 196.

26. Richard Waller, "'Clean' and 'Dirty': Cattle Disease and Control Policy in Colonial Kenya, 1900–1940," *Journal of African History* 45, no. 1 (2004): 46–47; Brown and Gilfoyle, eds., introduction to *Healing the Herds*.

27. For more on these diseases, see: Saurabh Mishra, "Beasts, Murrains, and the British Raj: Reassessing Colonial Medicine in India from the Veterinary Perspective, 1860–1900," *Bulletin of the History of Medicine* (Winter 2011): 587–619; John Fisher "A Pandemic (Panzootic) of Pleuropneumonia, 1840–1860," *Historia Medicinae Veterinariae* 11, no. 1 (1986): 26–32; Paul F. Cranefield, *Science and Empire: East Coast Fever in Rhodesia and the Transvaal* (Cambridge: Cambridge University Press, 1991); Karen Brown, "Tropical Medicine and Animal Diseases: Onderstepoort and the Development of Veterinary Science in South Africa, 1908–1950," *Journal of Southern African Studies* 31, no. 3 (2005): 413–529; John McCracken, "Experts and Amateurs: Tsetse, Nagana and Sleeping Sickness in East and Central Africa," in *Imperialism and the Natural World*, ed. John MacKenzie (Manchester: Manchester University Press, 1990): 187–212; Helge Kjekshus, *Ecology Control and Economic Development in East African History: The Case of Tanganyika, 1850–1950* (London: James Currey, 1996).

28. The rinderpest literature is vast. See: Clive A. Spinage, "Rinderpest the Great

Panzootic and its After Effects," ch. 22 in *African Ecology: Benchmarks and Historical Perspectives* (New York: Springer, 2012); Charles van Onselen, "Reactions to Rinderpest in Southern Africa, 1896–97," *Journal of African History* 13, no. 3 (1972): 473–88; Pule Phoofolo, "Epidemics and Revolutions: The Rinderpest Epizootic in Late Nineteenth-Century Southern Africa," *Past and Present* no. 138 (February 1993): 112–43; Daniel Gilfoyle, "Veterinary Research and the African Rinderpest Epizootic: The Cape Colony, 1896–98," *Journal of Southern African Studies* 29, no. 1 (2003): 133–54; Holger Weiss, "'Dying Cattle': Some Remarks on the Impact of Cattle Epizootics in the Central Sudan during the Nineteenth Century," *African Economic History* 26 (1998): 173–99.

29. Jeremiah T. Saliki, "Rinderpest (Cattle Plague)," *Merck Veterinary Manual* (2020), accessed January 16, 2021, https://www.merckvetmanual.com /generalized-conditions/rinderpest/rinderpest; Center for Food Security and Public Health, "Rinderpest: Cattle Plague," in cooperation with Iowa State University and the USDA (2016), accessed January 16, 2021, http://www .cfsph.iastate.edu/Factsheets/pdfs/rinderpest.pdf; Amanda Kay McVety, *The Rinderpest Campaigns: A Virus, its Vaccines, and Global Development in the Twentieth Century* (Cambridge: Cambridge University Press, 2018): 4–6.

30. Comments about "stench" and the ancient history of rinderpest from Clive A. Spinage, introduction to *Cattle Plague: A History* (Springer, 2003), especially 5. See also: Paul-Pierre Pastoret et al., "Rinderpest—An Old and Worldwide Story: History to c. 1902," in *Rinderpest and Peste des Petits Ruminants*, ed. Thomas Barrett, Paul-Pierre Pastoret, William Taylor, and Gordon Scott (Elsevier, 2006): 87–91. International guidelines in Thaddeus Sunseri, "International Collaboration and Rivalry in the Early Fight Against Rinderpest," *EuropeNow Journal* 15 (March 2018), https://www.europenowjournal.org/issues/issue -15-march-2018/.; Mark Harrison, "Disease, Diplomacy and International Commerce: The Origins of International Sanitary Regulation in the Nineteenth Century," *Journal of Global History* 1, 2 (2006): 197–217.

31. Spinage, *Cattle Plague*, 501–15, quote about Uganda on 512; Sunseri, "International Cooperation"; Pasturet et al., "Rinderpest—An Old and Worldwide Story," 100–102.

32. "Report on the Matabeleland Rebellion, by Earl Grey, the Administrator of the Company," *British South Africa Company's Territories*, Great Britain Colonial Office (London: H. M. Stationery Office, 1898): 69.

33. Thaddeus Sunseri, "The Entangled History of *Sadoka* (Rinderpest) and Veterinary Science in Tanzania and the Wider World, 1891–1901," *Bulletin of the History of Medicine* 89, no. 1 (2015): 99–100.

34. Commissioner of Agriculture Report, Durban, February 16, 1898, and Engineer-in-Chief's Report for the year 1897, both in *Colony of Natal: Department Reports* (Pietermaritzburg: P. Davis and Sons, 1898); "Rinderpest in South Africa," *The Times* (London), November 19, 1896; D. Hutcheon, Colonial Veterinary Surgeon, "Memorandum on Measures to be Adopted for the Suppression of the Disease known as Rinderpest or Zambesi Fever in Cattle," reprinted in *Miscellaneous Pamphlets on South Africa*, (London: Colonial Office, 1898) 2: 14–15; Lorena Rizzo, *Gender and Colonialism: A History of Kaoko in North-Western Namibia, 1870s-1950s* (Basel: Basler Afrika Bibliographien, 2012): 55–56.

35. Sunseri, "International Cooperation." Francis Dube makes a very similar argument in reference to East Coast fever outbreaks. See: Dube, "'In the Border Regions of the Territory of Rhodesia, There Is the Greatest Scourge': The Border and East Coast Fever Control in Central Mozambique and Eastern Zimbabwe, 1901–1942," *Journal of Southern African Studies* 41, no. 2 (2015): 219–35.

36. First quote from Annual Report by Magistrate of Upper Tugela Division for Year Ended 31st December 1897, *Colony of Natal: Department Reports, 1897;* second quote from Resident Magistrate at Bulawayo, *British South Africa Company's Territories,* Great Britain Colonial Office (London: H. M. Stationery Office, 1898): 19. For policy on destroying cattle, see: "Rinderpest Regulations," Proclamation No. 435, 1897, *Government Gazette* (UK), October 19, 1897. For British astonishment that natives resented their cattle being shot, see: Cape of Good Hope, *Debates in the House of Assembly,* Third Session of the Ninth Parliament, 1st May to 29th July 1896 (Cape Town: Cape Times Printing Works, 1896): 500. Disciplinary rivalries among veterinarians and cattle exports' effects on rinderpest response in Sunseri, "The Entangled History of *Sadoka*," 112–16.

37. Annual Report of the Magistrate in the Klip River Division for the Year Ended 31st December 1897, *Colony of Natal: Department Reports, 1897.*

38. Wesley Mwatwara and Sandra Swart, "'If Our Cattle Die, We Eat Them but These White People Bury Them and Burn Them!': African Livestock Regimes, Veterinary Knowledge and the Emergence of a Colonial Order in Southern Rhodesia, 1860–1902," *Kronos* 41 (November 2005): 128–29, quote on 113.

39. Ann Whitehead, "'Lazy Men,' Time-Use and Rural Development in Zambia," *Gender and Development* 7, no. 3 (November 1999): 49–51, quote on 53; Zimmerman, *Alabama in Africa,* 11–12; "Bechuanaland," *The Times* (London), June 16, 1896. See also: Klas Rönnbäck, "The Idle and the Industrious— European Ideas about the African Work Ethic in Precolonial West Africa," *History of Africa: A Journal of Method* 41 (2014): 117–45.

40. Entry dated August 1865, Farm Journals, John Horry Dent Collection, Box 1, Folder 7, SCA, Auburn University; Andrew Zimmerman, "Booker T. Washington, Tuskegee Institute, and the German Empire: Race and Cotton in the Black Atlantic," Lecture at the GHI, April 24, 2008, *GHI Bulletin* 43 (Fall 2008): 18.

41. Quotes from officials come from Commissioner of Agriculture Report, Durban, February 16, 1898, *Colony of Natal: Department Reports, 1897.* See: Waller, "'Clean' and 'Dirty'," 45–80; Gary Marquardt, "Building a Perfect Pest: Environment, People, Conflict, and the Creation of a Rinderpest Epizootic in Southern Africa," *Journal of Southern African Studies* 43, no. 2 (2017): 349–63. Contemporary accounts using the "clean" and "dirty" designation include *Agricultural Journal* 11, July–December 1897, published by the Department of Agriculture, Cape of Good Hope (Cape Town: Townshend, Taylor and Snashall, 1897): 586.

42. Remarks about German East Africa from Sunseri, "Entangled History of *Sadoka*," 121. See also: Wesley Mwatwara and Sandra Swart, "'Better Breeds?' The Colonial State, Africans and the Cattle Quality Clause in Southern Rhodesia, 1912–1930," *Journal of Southern African Studies* 42, no. 2 (2016): 333–50; Saverio Krätli, "Animal Science and the Representation of Local Breeds," in *Healing the Herds*, ed. Brown and Gilfoyle, 232–49. Remarks about German East Africa from Sunseri, "Entangled History of *Sadoka*," 121.

43. *The Times* (London), May 18 and June 16, 1896; R. S. S. Baden-Powell, *The Matabele Campaign, 1896: Being a Narrative of the Campaign in Suppressing the Native Rising in Matabeleland and Mashonaland* (London: Methuen and Co., 1897): 44; Phoofolo, "Epidemics and Revolutions," 115–16; Rizzo, *Gender and Colonialism*, 55–58.

44. See: "Report on the Matabeleland Rebellion, by Earl Grey," 68–70; "Mr. Selous on Rhodesia" and "An Incident of the Matabele War," *The Times* (London), November 5, 1896; "South Africa," *The Annual Register 1896* (London: Longmans, Green, and Co., 1897): 370.

45. "Report by Sir A. Hardinge on the Condition and Progress of the East African Protectorate from its Establishment to the 20th July 1897, presented to both Houses of Parliament by Command of her Majesty," *Colonial Office* (London: Harrison and Sons, 1897): 25–28. See also: Richard Waller, "Emutai: Crisis and Response in Maasailand 1883–1902," in *The Ecology of Survival: Case Studies from Northeast African History*, ed. Douglas H. Johnson and David M. Anderson (Boulder, Colo.: Westview, 1988): 73–112; Charles Ambler, *Kenyan Communities in the Age of Imperialism* (New Haven: Yale University Press, 1988).

46. There is a large literature that exists outside of discussions of animal diseases regarding the role of scientific knowledge and colonial agricultural schemes in Africa during this period, some of which acknowledges the transnational nature of colonial practices and ideas. See: Frederick Cooper, "Modernizing Bureaucrats, Backward Africans, and the Development Concept," in *International Development and the Social Sciences: Essays on the History and Politics of Knowledge*, ed. Frederick Cooper and Randall Packard (Berkeley: University of California Press, 1997); Andrew Bowman, "Ecology to Technocracy: Scientists, Surveys, and Powers in the Agricultural Development of Late-Colonial Zambia," *Journal of Southern African Studies* 37, no. 1 (March 2011): 135–53; Joseph Morgan Hodge, *Triumph of the Expert: Agrarian Doctrines of Development and the Legacies of British Colonialism* (Athens, OH: Ohio State University Press, 2007); Erik Green, "A Lasting Story: Conservation and Agricultural Extension Services in Colonial Malawi," *Journal of African History* 50, no. 2 (2009): 247–67.

47. Zimmerman, *Alabama in Africa*, 15.

48. Daniel Beltran-Alcrudo et al., "Transboundary Spread of Pig Diseases: The Role of International Trade and Travel," *BMC Veterinary Research* 15 (2019): 2; M. Artois et al., "Classical Swine Fever in Wild Board Europe," *Scientific and Technical Review of the Office International des Epizooties* 21, no. 2 (2002): 287–303; David Morens, et al., "Global Rinderpest Eradication: Lessons Learned and Why Humans Should Celebrate Too," *Journal of Infectious Diseases* 204, no. 4 (2011): 502–5.

49. William Beinart, Karen Brown, and Daniel Gilfoyle, "Experts and Expertise in Colonial Africa Reconsidered: Science and the Interpenetration Knowledge," *African Affairs* 108, no. 432 (2009): 413–33; Karen Brown, "From Ubombo to Mkhuzi: Disease, Colonial Science, and the Control *Nagana* (Livestock Trypanosomosis) in Zululand, South Africa, 1894–1953," *Journal of the History of Medicine and Allied Sciences* 63, no. 3 (2008): 285–322.

CHAPTER 2

The Decisive Weapon?

*Rations and Food Supply
in the Boer War of 1899–1902*

MATTHEW RICHARDSON

This chapter examines the role that food and food supply played in the South African (or Boer) War of 1899–1902. This was the costliest of Britain's nineteenth-century colonial adventures and pitted the might of her empire against two Boer republics, the Transvaal and the Orange Free State. Belying their small size, these republics proved to be formidable adversaries, and for the first time in modern war, several British forces were besieged by the enemy. The ability of these garrisons to control food supply internally became a critical factor in their survival.[1] Supplying the largest British field force assembled up to that time presented new challenges. In another first, morale, foodstuffs, and propaganda became linked as special patriotic Christmas products were sent from civilians in Britain to the troops in the field. On the home front, food products and producers eagerly sought to associate themselves with the war, particularly through advertising, in a way that many people today might find surprising or distasteful.[2] Finally, food (or food control) was used by the British as a weapon against the Boer civilian population, an aspect of this war that was controversial at the time (with conditions in concentration camps coming under special scrutiny, particularly in the report prepared by Emily Hobhouse) and remains so to this day.

  Much British historiography concerning the Boer War has focused on military and political aspects of the campaign, though it is apparent that the proliferation of literature produced during the war (and in its aftermath) has not been matched in volume by subsequent scholarly work. The Boer War has largely been overshadowed in this respect by the two world wars. Perhaps the definitive account is that by Thomas Pakenham, first published in 1979 and reissued in 1993. Exhaustive though it is, and commendable as the first major work to address the impact of the war on Boer civilians and the Black population, it could be argued that even this does not go far enough in analyzing the impact of food supply on the war.[3]

Space does not permit a detailed discussion here of why imperial Britain came into conflict with the two republics that occupied part of the southern tip of Africa in the late nineteenth century. Suffice to say that conflicting ambitions between the Boers (largely of Dutch descent) and British colonial administrators in that part of the continent resulted in Boer forces invading Britain's colonies of the Cape and Natal in October of 1899. Lack of strategic awareness by the largely amateur Boer forces at this early juncture led them to become focused on besieging three major railway junctions—the towns of Ladysmith, Kimberley, and Mafeking—rather than sweeping the ill-prepared British out of southern Africa entirely.[4] Within these towns, food supply became of critical importance as it would take several months for British reinforcements to even arrive in South Africa, let alone fight their way through to relieve the troops already present.

The Boer War, and in particular the early setbacks the army experienced, produced a great outpouring of patriotic fervor in Britain. While there was undoubtedly some opposition to the war, this was largely confined to the intelligentsia and the radical wing of the Liberal Party.[5] Among ordinary working people, particularly in urban areas with high enlistment rates, there was a good deal of support.[6] Awareness was high because this was arguably the first media war, given that newsreel footage of the conflict was some of the earliest shown in theaters and that during the conflict, newspaper war correspondents (including a young Winston Churchill) proliferated.[7] Additionally, literacy among the working classes was at a peak, and so families at home were left in no doubt about the blandness and unpalatable nature of much army food.[8] All of this, together with the fact that many formations (for example the City Imperial Volunteers) were "citizens in uniform," meant that food parcels from home became a new aspect of the British military experience.[9]

In Ladysmith, Sir George White was in command, while Mafeking was under the control of Robert Baden-Powell. Kimberley, meanwhile, was under the orders of Colonel Robert Kekewich. Kimberley was at the center of diamond mining operations, and control of food supplies for the inhabitants was crucial to its survival in the face of the siege.[10] Early on, the Boers cut the fresh water supply to the town from the Vaal River. Thereafter, the fresh water that existed in the mines became of vital importance. Cattle grazing on the outskirts of the town presented an early conundrum for the defenders. If left alive, they represented a gift to the advancing Boers. If slaughtered, there was apparently no way to preserve the meat for a long siege. However, the presence of the mines again squared the circle for the British because one of the mine engineers was able to build an industrial refrigeration unit underground in which to store the meat.[11] The defenders attempted to send the native workforce of the mines out of the town, but twice the Boers drove them back in, aiming to increase pressure on food and water supplies. One civilian diarist in Kimberley recorded the tensions between townspeople and military authorities, which existed even early on:

> We are now just going to begin to feel the nip of the siege. . . . we had a proclamation that various necessaries, such as flour, meal, bread, rice, sugar, etc., would in future only be issued in stated quantities, and that only to the holders of permits. . . . to get a little, say, sugar, you would have to give the military a list of everything you had, and I have no doubt they would keep a list of those things which you had rather a large quantity of, and commandeer them later on. . . . having myself been one of the provident ones, I don't at all appreciate the idea of being looted for the benefit of the improvident ones.[12]

More recent historians have drawn attention to the discrimination in rationing that took place in Kimberley, with the military garrison receiving the most, followed by white civilians and then Black civilians. This was reflected in the much higher death rate for Africans.[13]

Ladysmith had a larger military garrison than Kimberley and Mafeking, totaling 12,500 officers and soldiers, compared to 5,400 white civilians and 2,400 Black and Indian civilians.[14] Again divisions were evident between the two factions. Rumors abounded that the civilian population of the town had prepared for an expected siege by stockpiling provisions, which they had kept for themselves while still drawing their allotted ration of siege biscuits, which, it was alleged, they had given to their dogs. Soldiers' disdain for the civilians was further strengthened when it was reported that civilian orderlies had stolen cakes and other luxuries donated by officers for their sick comrades. Growing numbers of dysentery and enteric fever cases continually depleted the strength of the garrison; this steady drain of manpower was caused by drinking untreated water and did not begin to improve until January 1900, when a condenser was set up at the town railway station to provide clean water. On January 31 of that year, horseflesh was issued for the first time as a ration item, since fodder was no longer available for any animal other than artillery horses, which were vital to the defense.[15] One officer recorded:

> Chevril was issued to the men. . . . It was nourishing and the men liked it, which was a good thing. There was nothing else by which to recommend it. The men were also allowed to go down to the chevril factory, which was close to the station, and buy the flesh of the horse after it had passed through the boiling process. This did not appear appetizing, but again the men liked it, and when cooked up with wild spinach which grew about the lines it was considered very tasty.[16]

The close links between food supply and morale among the besieged garrison are well illustrated by a remark made in late February of 1900, indicating that rations were further reduced to a single biscuit and one pound of "chevril" per soldier, which constituted "perhaps the most distressing circumstance connected with the siege" and had "a most depressing effect."[17]

For those British soldiers fighting their way through to the besieged towns, food supply was also erratic at times, and afterward the general lack of acknowledgment of this fact became a cause of irritation. One of those who took part in the relief of Ladysmith, Private Frederick Tucker, wrote in his diary of an exchange between men of the field force and the defenders, following the lifting of the siege:

> They were kept on short rations, without potatoes or bread for some time. Reduced to eating biscuits and horse flesh they had been forced to drink river water. We let them talk on in this strain. They thought nothing of what we had gone through for months in the field. Had we never gone without food or water?[18]

As the war moved on it evolved from one of set piece battles to a game of cat and mouse as mobile columns tried to pin down elusive Boer commandos. Food supply for the average British soldier was still erratic, and Tucker, again writing in his diary, commented a month on biscuits of the army type is enough for any man—even if his teeth were like steel.[19]

It is worth noting that in this era, one of the most frequent causes of rejection for potential army recruits was bad teeth; being able to chew hardtack biscuits was as essential to military efficiency as the ability to march or hold a rifle. These biscuits, baked from a simple mixture of flour and water, were attractive to the army authorities because if kept dry, they would last indefinitely.[20] Although officials noted the dental shortcomings of the British army as a concern during the Boer War, these biscuits remained as part of the soldier's diet until World War I. Only then, in the light of previous experience, were artificial dentures supplied by the army in an effort to mitigate the problem.[21] One other result of British experience in the Boer War was that the iron or emergency rations issued to the soldiers in the field were discovered simply not to be nutritious enough to enable men to exist for several days at a time in a situation where regular food supplies could not reach them. The standard British emergency ration at this time was manufactured by Bovril and consisted of a metal cylinder divided into two compartments. One end contained beef extract (paste), the other contained chocolate. Other superior tinned products (containing stew for example) were commercially available, and individual soldiers or commanders generally preferred these when they had access to them. As a result of these discoveries, by the time World War I broke out in 1914, British iron rations had undergone significant improvement.[22]

The patriotism of the age also frequently found expression through the multitude of special food products sent to the troops. In 1899 Queen Victoria herself sent a present of a tin of chocolate to each of her soldiers in the field.[23] Well-meaning civilians also sent tinned plum puddings. On the home front, British producers frequently tried to associate their products with the war; British generals Kitchener and Roberts appeared on tins of tea, while lancers appeared on tins of biscuits. Stock manufacturer Bovril used their association with the troops as a marketing device, with the slogan "At the Front & in the Front" appearing in their advertising alongside a depiction of British soldiers using the product to make a hot drink.[24] Another Bovril advertisement made use of a quote from an official report by Sir William MacCormack, stating:

> Awaiting their turn the wounded were lying outside in rows which were being continually augmented by the civilian bearers coming in from the field. As each wounded man reached the hospital he was served with a hot cup of Bovril, large cans of which were boiling outside the tents.[25]

Bovril issued its owned bulletins on headed paper, giving news of the war, and even produced a print depicting a heroic vision of the relief of Ladysmith, which customers could obtain by collecting tokens.[26] The company became intimately associated with the war as a result. Keen's Mustard similarly advertised itself as "the Empire builder."[27] Other products that sought association with the war were Usher's whisky, which used a depiction of a heroic wounded soldier with bandaged head, and Borwick's baking powder, which used an illustration of a British camp scene. Interestingly, some of the biggest names on the British high street— Rowntree's, Fry's, and Cadbury—did not use imagery from the war or association with it in their advertising. All were family firms founded by Quakers, though it remains to be shown conclusively that opposition to war was deliberately manifested in advertising policy.[28]

Despite the fact that the British possessed the world's largest merchant fleet, the war (located six thousand miles from Britain) put its shipping under great strain. At the start of the war, the bulk of the supplies for the army were shipped from Woolwich, but overreliance on sea transport would prove to be a recipe for chaos, partly because the cape lacked the port infrastructure necessary to overcome backlogs at the dockside.[29] These difficulties were overcome largely through Kitchener's efforts to simplify supply arrangements, but more so because the army commissariat instead attempted to obtain as much as possible from within the region, with much food bought locally. The supply of meat to the troops at the cape was contracted out to the South African Cold Storage Company. The British colonists also grew and raised their own food. During the guerrilla phase of the war, they took control of seventy vacant Boer farms for this purpose. Even land around blockhouses and lines of communication were cultivated. The other major advantage the British possessed in terms of food supply was the railway network. In particular the Natal Government Railway system was invaluable in ensuring that supplies reached the front lines quickly, and that the British soldier was rarely short of food (even if the flavors were monotonous).[30] The Boer forces, by contrast, lacked an equivalent means of keeping large bodies of troops supplied.

Without Salt We Would Not Be Able to Live

For the British army, if food supplies had been erratic at the start of the war, as the conflict progressed, they gradually improved. For the Boer forces, the opposite was the case. As the tide of war turned against them, the chain of supply increasingly broke down, and they were forced to subsist on what they could find. Boer commander Ben Viljoen recalled:

> As early as March, 1901, we experienced the difficulty of adequately providing our commandos with the necessities of life . . . the task of feeding the Boers was one of the most serious, and I may say disquieting, questions with which we had to deal. We were cut off from the world, and there was no means of importing stores . . . By this time a large portion of the Republic had been occupied by the British, all food-stuffs had been removed or destroyed, and most of the cattle had been captured. salt supplies were especially low, and we feared that without salt we would not be able to live, or . . . we might bring upon ourselves an epidemic of disease.[31]

Despite the eventual defeat of the Boers on the battlefield and the capture of the two Boer capitals, armed resistance continued as the war entered what came to be known as the guerrilla phase. British policy (devised by Field Marshal Lord Roberts but administered with ruthless effect by his understudy Kitchener) evolved as a consequence into one of scorched earth. The Boer commandos were to be deprived of food by the destruction of farms, and the removal of their support network among the civilian communities. Britain's policy of containing the Boer population in concentration camps can be traced to September 1900, when the first two refugee camps were established at Pretoria and Bloemfontein. Initially the aim in instituting these facilities was to protect the burghers who had surrendered voluntarily. As the fighting and lack of resources drove the families of combatant burghers into these and other similar establishments, they ceased to be refugee camps and became concentration camps. A whole raft of other camps would soon follow.[32] The families typically had only a short time to pack and limited space on wagons, so they were rarely able to carry anything more than a day's supply of food (if that), and thereafter became totally dependent on the largess of their British captors. Initially, camp administrators enforced food discrimination, with the families of those Boers who had surrendered allowed full rations, while the families of those still on commando received only half rations. However, this had largely been rescinded by the spring of 1901, following questions in the Westminster parliament.[33] By her own initiative, the British social campaigner Emily Hobhouse made a tour of these camps (or at least those that the military authorities allowed her to visit) and returned to Britain to raise awareness about the shocking conditions she found. In her pamphlet *Report of a Visit to the Camps of Women and Children in the Cape and Orange River Colonies,* she summarized the reasons for the high fatality rate, including sparse rations dealt out raw, lack of fuel to cook them with, and shortage of water both for drinking and for cooking with.

The Hobhouse report laid bare what the author saw as incompetence in planning to provide suitable nutrition for the inhabitants of the camps—a problem that continued to cause unnecessary deaths even after the deliberate policy of food deprivation had ended. She highlighted the difficulties of providing something as basic as safe, clean drinking water, even though the hazards of drinking untreated river water were well known to the medical establishment. She wrote:

> We have much typhoid, and are dreading an outbreak, so I am directing my energies to getting the water of the Modder River boiled. [Might] as well swallow typhoid germs whole as drink that water—so say doctors. Yet they cannot boil it all, for—first, fuel is very scarce; that which is supplied weekly would not cook a meal a day, and they have to search the already bare kopjes for a supply. There is hardly a bit to be had. Secondly, they have no extra utensil to hold the water when boiled. I propose, therefore, to give each tent another pail or crock . . . I suggested a big railway boiler to boil every drop of water before it is served out. This would economise fuel, and be cheaper in the long run . . . [however] none could be had, so the Government built furnaces and tanks.[34]

Considering the quantity and quality of food issued to the Boer civilians, and in spite of the fact that all were now supposedly on full rations, Hobhouse concluded that:

> Unfortunately the weight often falls short, and at times the supply does not go round. The meat is sometimes maggoty, and the coffee much adulterated.[35]

In an attempt to save face shortly after Hobhouse published her damning report, the British government commissioned its own report: *Report on the Concentration Camps in South Africa.* Perhaps not surprisingly, this inquiry sought to downplay the shortcomings in camp food and administration Hobhouse had identified. One typical paragraph, while acknowledging that there were problems, sought to place blame on the Boer civilians for exacerbating the situation out of bloody-mindedness:

> The meat which we saw served out on the four days we were in this camp was extremely poor and thin. A whole sheep often

weighed only 18 lbs. We were told that no better meat was to be had . . . people showed their discontent with the meat by throwing large portions . . . into the wide roadway of the camp. It would have made very good broth or stew. We supposed that this wicked waste was a sort of bravado for the purpose of showing us how discontented they were; but we took it as proof that, at any rate, the people in the camp were not short of food. Almost any poor family in England would have been thankful for such meat, and would have made excellent meals from it.[36]

Despite attempts by the press to discredit Hobhouse as "Pro-Boer," the government's own report in fact confirmed much of what she had claimed, and the matter became a national scandal. At the same time, Hobhouse lobbied anyone at Westminster who would listen. She had the ear of many in the radical wing of the Liberal Party, but her greatest success was in swinging the party leader Henry Campbell Bannerman against the war, leading to his famous "methods of barbarism" statement.

A little-known aspect of the concentration camp system is the fact that a parallel network was created to hold Black captives. These were mainly the laborers from Boer farms that had been overrun, but again the prejudices of late-nineteenth-century imperialism found expression through food supply. The inhabitants of these camps were routinely supplied with rations inferior to those available to their white counterparts, and to add insult to injury, while the enemy Boers were fed for free, these Black prisoners (who were effectively neutrals in a white man's war) were expected to pay for their fare. Their captors put them to work (usually on railway construction) to earn wages in order to pay for their food, so these might be better described as forced labor camps. Not surprisingly, the leaders of the imprisoned Black workers protested their treatment (which Hobhouse overlooked) and by the latter part of the war conditions did improve.[37]

For the Boers who remained out on commando, the food resources available became scarcer and scarcer, as British columns made great sweeps across the veldt, commandeering such livestock and crops as they could carry with them and destroying what they could not. Only in the British-ruled Cape Colony was the situation different, and here a Boer column under General Jan Smuts found easy pickings.[38] Deneys Reitz, a young Boer fighter who was with Smuts, recalled encountering a small hamlet where "there were plenty of beer and spirits at the inn, and although few of the men had tasted liquor for a year or more, there was no drunkenness."[39]

At other times they lived, literally, off the land. One soldier noted "a strange growth known as 'Hottentot's bread' (*Encephelartos altensteinii*), a wild fruit not unlike a large pine-apple," which was so unripe that men eating it reacted by violently "groaning and retching on the ground in agony, some apparently at their last gasp."[40]

Yet Smuts's column was lucky. For the Boers still fighting in the Orange Free State and Transvaal, it was a different story, as Reitz discovered when he met some at a council of war a short while later:

> Nothing could have proved more clearly how nearly the Boer cause was spent than these starving, ragged men, clad in skins or sacking, their bodies covered with sores, from lack of salt and food, and their appearance was a great shock to us, who came from the better-conditioned forces in the Cape. Their spirit was undaunted, but they had reached the limit of physical endurance, and we realized that, if these haggard, emaciated men were the pick of the Transvaal Commandos, then the war must be irretrievably lost. Food was so scarce that General Botha himself had only a few strips of leathery biltong to offer us, and he said that, but for the lucky chance of having raided a small herd of cattle from the British a fortnight before, he would have been unable to hold the meeting at all.[41]

The situation for the Boers was so desperate that, in some cases, they began to raid the cattle of neighboring Zulu tribes. There had been ongoing tensions over food supplies since 1900, when a Boer force had first entered the province of Zululand. Initially the Boers had tried to win the trust of the Zulu population (which was largely pro-British) through generous access to food supplies. The Zulus themselves were in dire straits, having suffered two years in the 1890s of poor harvests due to red locust attacks, and cattle disease that had wiped out considerable numbers of stock.[42] Many of their young men had, as a result, sought work in the mines, but with the disruption of the war, these youths were now back in the kraals, further adding to the pressure on resources. Cattle that the commandos had initially seized was returned to the Zulu chiefs by commandant Louis Botha as a gesture of good will. The British, however, armed the Zulus and encouraged them to act as scouts, even to the extent of seizing Boer livestock and grain supplies.[43] The Boers responded in kind, and skirmishing and small-scale conflict began to escalate. The most serious engagement followed the confiscation of Zulu cattle by a Boer commando, for which the former launched reprisals. In May 1902, at

Holkrantz, near Vryheid, Zulus attacked a Boer laager, killing a number of men. Thus far, the Zulus had not attacked Boer women and children (who were ironically by that time in greater danger because they were back on the farms, following the abandonment of the British concentration camp policy). As such, pressure on food resources indirectly affected the morale of those "bitter enders" still on commando, for they feared for the safety of their unprotected families in the face of growing Zulu and other Black native hostility.[44]

Ultimately, the British largely won the Boer War through control and manipulation of the food supply in South Africa. They not only overcame their own difficulties in procurement and supply of food but also managed to successfully drive the Boer forces away from their supplies. By herding the enemy civilian population into new and controversial concentration camps (where inadequate food and medical resources would leave an indelible stain on Britain's reputation), and by destroying supplies in the field, the British arguably weaponized food control for the first time in modern history. The pressure this weaponization brought to bear on the Boer forces was the decisive factor in bringing them to the negotiating table in 1902.

NOTES

1. For an overview of the political and military dimensions of the Boer War, see: Ronald Hyam and Peter Henshaw, *The Lion and the Springbok: Britain and South Africa since the Boer War* (Cambridge: Cambridge University Press, 2003); Keith Wilson, *The International Impact of the Boer War* (New York: Palgrave, 2001); David Omissi and Andrew S. Thompson, eds., *The Impact of the South African War* (New York: Palgrave, 2002).
2. On propaganda in the Boer War, see: Amy Shaw, "Fathers and Sons of Empire: Domesticity, Empire, and Canadian Participation in the Anglo-Boer War," in *Fighting with the Empire: Canada, Britain, and Global Conflict, 1867–1947*, ed. William Pratt (Vancouver: University of British Columbia Press, 2019); Frans-Johan Pretoriu, "Justifying the South African War: Boer Propaganda, 1899–1902," in *Justifying War: Propaganda, Politics and the Modern Age*, ed. David Welch and Jo Fox (New York: Palgrave, 2012).
3. For a recent academic discussion of food in the Boer War, see: Matthew Doherty, "The Boer War and Malayan Emergency: Examples of British Counterinsurgency Pre- and Post-'Minimum Force,'" *Small Wars Journal*, accessed January 14, 2021, https://smallwarsjournal.com/jrnl/art/boer-war -and-malayan-emergency-examples-british-counterinsurgency-pre-and -post-minimum. See also: Peter Donaldson, *Remembering the South African*

War: Britain and the Memory of the Anglo-Boer War, from 1899 to the Present (Liverpool: Liverpool University Press, 2013).

4. Charles N. Robinson, *With Roberts to the Transvaal* (Preston: James Askew, sd): 58.

5. John W. Auld, "The Liberal Pro Boers," *Journal of British Studies* 14, no. 2 (May 1975): 78–101. On the literary and intellectual response to propaganda surrounding the war, see also: Steve Attridge, "Character, Sacrifice, and Scapegoats: Boer War Fiction," in *Sacrifice and Modern War Literature: The Battle of Waterloo to the War on Terror*, ed. Alex Houen and Jan-Melissa Schramm (Oxford: Oxford University Press, 2018).

6. Guy Hinton, "Newcastle & the Boer War: Regional Reactions to an Imperial War," *Northern History* 52, no. 2 (2015): 272–94.

7. Winston S. Churchill, *My Early Life* (London: Thornton Butterworth, 1930). For more recent discussion of Churchill's journalistic career in the Boer War, see: Candice Millard, *Hero of the Empire: The Boer War, a Daring Escape and the Making of Winston Churchill* (New York: Doubleday, 2016). On the causes of the Boer War and British imperialism in Africa, see: John Stephens, *Fueling the Empire: South Africa's Gold and the Road to War* (Hoboken, NJ: Wiley, 2003).

8. Amy J. Lloyd, *Education, Literacy and the Reading Public* (Detroit: Gale, 2007).

9. Anon., *The CIV: Being the Story of the City Imperial Volunteers* (London: Newnes, 1900).

10. Arthur Conan Doyle, *The Great Boer War* (London: Smith, Elder, 1900): 303. Doyle states "The question of food was recognised as being of more importance than the enemy's fire."

11. T. Phelan, *The Siege of Kimberley* (Dublin: M. H. Gill, 1913).

12. Evelyn Oliver Ashe, *Besieged by the Boers: A Diary of Life and Events in Kimberly during the Siege* (Hutchinson: London, 1900): 92.

13. Thomas Pakenham, *The Boer War* (Orion: London, 1993): 169.

14. Lewis Childs, *Ladysmith: The Siege* (Barnsley: Pen & Sword, 1999): 75.

15. M. Jackson, *The Record of a Regiment of the Line* (London: Hutchinson, 1908): 86. On the siege, see also: Giles Foden, *Ladysmith*. New York: Knopf, 2000.

16. Jackson, *Record of a Regiment*, 88. On attempts to supply British troops with beef, imported from Argentina, see: Lizzie Collingham, *The Taste of Empire: How Britain's Quest for Food Shaped the Modern World* (New York: Basic, 2017): 232.

17. Jackson, *Record of a Regiment*, 96.

18. Pamela Todd and David Fordham, *Private Tucker's Boer War Diary* (London: Elm Tree, 1980): 89.

19. Todd and Fordham, *Boer War Diary*, 94.

20. On army biscuits, see: Collingham, *Taste of Empire* and Anna Zeide, *Canned: The Rise and Fall of Consumer Confidence in the American Food Industry* (Berkeley and Los Angeles: University of California Press, 2018).

21. "History of the Royal Army Dental Corps," Museum of Military History, accessed January 14, 2021, https://museumofmilitarymedicine.org.uk/about/corps-history/history-of-the-royal-army-dental-corps/.

22. For a general discussion of the evolution of British army emergency rations, see: "From Beef and Chocolate to Daily Ration: British Rations in Transition 1870-1918," Knacker Squaddies, accessed 16 January 2021, http://17thdivision.tripod.com/rationsoftheageofempire/id5.html.

23. Canadian Anglo-Boer War Museum, "Boer War Discovery 90v," accessed January 16, 2021, http://www.goldiproductions.com/angloboerwarmuseum /Boer90v_pastdis_tinchoc.html.
24. Bovril, advertisement, *Sphere* (London), February 17, 1900.
25. Bovril, advertisement, *Sphere* (London), February 3, 1900.
26. Giles Foden, "Bringing it All Back Home," *Guardian* (London), September 4, 1999, This article is available online at https://www.theguardian.com/books /1999/sep/04/books.guardianreview.
27. *Black and White Budget* 3, no. 39 (London: W. J. P. Monckton, July 7, 1900): 9.
28. "Queen Victoria Chocolate Bar Gifted to Soldiers in Boer War Emerges for Sale," *Express* (London), July 5, 2018, UK, https://www.express.co.uk/news /uk/984377/Queen-Victoria-chocolate-bar-british-soldiers-Boer-War-sale -auction-south-africa.
29. For a detailed discussion of British transport arrangements, see: Alfred T. Mahan, *The Story of the War in South Africa* (London: Sampson, Low, Marston, 1900).
30. Lady Briggs, *The Staff Work of the Anglo Boer War 1899–1901* (London: Richards, 1901): 108.
31. Ben Viljoen, *My Reminiscences of the Anglo-Boer War* (London: Hood, Douglas, & Howard, 1902): 496.
32. "Women and Children in White Concentration Camps during the Anglo-Boer War, 1900–1902," South African History Online, accessed January 16, 2021, https://www.sahistory.org.za/article/women-and-children-white-concentration -camps-during-anglo-boer-war-1900-1902.
33. "Women and Children in White Concentration Camps."
34. Emily Hobhouse, *Report of a Visit to the Camps of Women and Children in the Cape and Orange River Colonies* (London: Friars Printing Association, 1901): 5.
35. Hobhouse, *Report*, 36.
36. Concentration Camps Commission, *Report on the Concentration Camps in South Africa* (London: HMSO, 1902): 40.
37. On her coverage of the concentration camps, see: Emily Hobhouse, *The Brunt of the War and Where it Fell* (London: Methuen, 1902). On Black African imprisonment in camps, see: Peter Warwick, *Black People and the South African War* (New York: Cambridge University Press, 1983): 151.
38. Conan Doyle, *Great Boer War*, 436.
39. Deneys Reitz, *Commando—A Boer Journal of the Boer War* (New York: Charles Boni, 1930): 230.
40. Reitz, *Commando,* 234.
41. Reitz, *Commando,* 309.
42. Kathleen Pribyl et al., "The Role of Drought in Agrarian Crisis and Social Change: The Famine of the 1890s in South Eastern Africa," *Regional Environmental Change* 19, no. 8 (2019): 2683–95.
43. For a detailed discussion of the role of the Zulu people in the Boer War, see: Simon Jabulani Maphalala, "The Participation of The Zulus in the Anglo-Boer War 1899–1902," (PhD diss., University of Zululand, 1978), http://uzspace .unizulu.ac.za:8080/xmlui/bitstream/handle/10530/925/The%20participation %20of%20the%20zulus%20in%20the%20Anglo-boer%20war%201899-1902 .%20SJ%20Maphalala.pdf?sequence=1.
44. Packenham, *The Boer War*, 281.

CHAPTER 3

Food and Anticolonialism at Gandhi's Intentional Communities in South Africa and India

KARLINE McLAIN

Mohandas K. "Mahatma" Gandhi is well known for his advocacy of nonviolent methods of political resistance against British colonial rule. Lesser known are the intentional communities Gandhi established as social expressions of his commitment to nonviolence, vegetarianism, and equality in South Africa and India. He founded Phoenix Settlement in 1904 outside of Durban, South Africa; Tolstoy Farm in 1910 outside of Johannesburg, South Africa; Sabarmati Ashram in 1915 near Ahmedabad, India; and Sevagram Ashram in 1936 near Wardha, India. These intentional communities were back-to-the-land farms wherein all residents (Indian and European, regardless of gender) lived and labored together, growing produce, building houses, educating children, and working to confront colonial injustices. They were residential efforts to create a counterworld to the colonialist and capitalist status quo, one built on a foundation of simplicity, self-sufficiency, and equal labor. Experiments with food were central to life at these communities, and these experiments had significant implications for how Gandhi would politically engage the British colonial government to fight for Indian civil rights and, ultimately, India's independence.[1]

This chapter takes sugar and salt as its two case studies. In South Africa, Gandhi focused on sugar: its consumption, which he sought to minimize in his personal diet and in the meals served at his intentional communities; its production through Indian indentured labor, which he deemed unethical and akin to slavery; and its global trade as part of the economics of imperialism, which he eventually protested through acts of civil disobedience. In India, Gandhi turned his attention to salt. Once again, he began by minimizing the consumption of this substance in his own diet and in the meals served at his intentional communities. Eventually, Gandhi waged a nonviolent anticolonial battle that revolved around salt in the form of the famous Salt March of 1930. Gandhi's nonviolent methods have received much attention in scholarly analyses of his politics, and more recent scholarship has also begun to investigate the relationship between Gandhi's diet and his nonviolent politics.[2] This chapter seeks to contribute to growing conversations about Gandhi's diet and his politics by focusing on the communal-relational context, arguing that the food experimentation that took place at Gandhi's intentional communities in South Africa and India was central to his anticolonial struggle.

Sugar and Empire in South Africa

Gandhi arrived in South Africa in 1893, and quickly became aware of the plight of Indian laborers on the sugar plantations there.[3] At that time, South Africa consisted of four colonies that were ruled by Europeans: the Transvaal and the Orange Free State under Dutch rule, and Natal and the Cape under British rule. The British colonies began in 1860 to bring in Indians as indentured laborers to work in the agriculture industry, particularly sugar fields and tea plantations. In Natal Colony alone, a total of 152,641 Indian indentured workers arrived between 1860 and 1911.[4] These laborers were typically contracted for a period of five years; after this term ended they could either return to India (with their boat passage paid as part of their indenture contract), renew their contract of indenture for an additional term, or remain in the colony as a free citizen on a small plot of land (allotted by the government as the equivalent in value to the cost of return passage to India). Free Indians also began to migrate to South Africa as traders shortly after indentured labor began.

Gandhi was initially hired as a business lawyer by a group of free Indian merchants but became aware in his first year in South Africa of the racial discrimination targeting Indians throughout the colonies (Gandhi was himself physically thrown out of the first class carriage of a train at Pietermaritzburg Station in May 1893 and told that only whites could ride in that carriage). Gandhi also quickly became aware of the difficulties faced by Indian indentured laborers working at the plantations. He describes his encounter with an indentured worker named Balasundaram in his *Autobiography*, writing that he had scarcely been practicing law for three to four months "when a Tamil man in tattered clothes, head-gear in hand, two front teeth broken and his mouth bleeding, stood before me trembling and weeping."[5] Balasundaram, who served his indenture under a "well-known European resident of Durban," complained that his master had beaten him. Gandhi began to study the indenture laws to determine how to transfer Balasundaram to another employer. After accomplishing this, Gandhi notes that "a regular stream of indentured labourers began to pour into my office, and I got the best opportunity of learning their joys and sorrows."[6]

In December 1894, after getting to know more indentured laborers, Gandhi wrote a long letter to the Legislative Assembly of Natal Colony. He first states that his "one and only object is to serve India . . . and to bring about better understanding between the European section of the community and the Indian in this Colony." After commenting on how despised the Indians are by the Europeans, he then reminds the legislators that they are in a position of power over the Indians, and they have the choice to either "govern them despotically or sympathetically." Gandhi then sets forth an argument explaining why the Indians ought to be considered valuable citizens in the colony, presenting a utilitarian argument about their contributions as indentured laborers:

> The indentured Indians are indispensable for the welfare of the Colony; whether as menials or waiters, whether as railway servants or gardeners, they are a useful addition to the Colony. The work that a Native cannot or would not do is cheerfully and well done by the indentured Indian. It would seem that the Indian has helped to make this the Garden Colony of South Africa. Withdraw the Indian from the sugar estate, and where would the main industry of the Colony be?

Ramachandra Guha has summed up the sugar production statistics, writing that the average annual production of sugar in Natal Colony was less than five hundred tons in the 1850s, rose to nearly ten thousand tons in the 1870s, and was in excess of twenty thousand tons by the 1890s as a result of indentured Indian labor.[7] These indentured plantation laborers were to be given housing on the plantation, rations, a monthly wage of ten shillings, and basic medical assistance when needed. In spite of this, Gandhi noted that while all Indians were discriminated against, indentured Indians were treated very poorly in practice: "If I am to depend upon one-tenth of the reports that I have received with regard to the treatment of the indentured Indians on the various estates, it would form a terrible indictment against the humanity of the masters on the estates."[8] At this time Gandhi was not actively campaigning for Indian independence from British rule as he would later in life. Rather, at this stage Gandhi sought equal rights for Indians with Europeans in the colony. And significantly, he sought to model this in micro at his intentional communities.

It was in South Africa, as Gandhi worked for the rights of the Indian community—not just the free Indians he was initially hired to represent, but also the indentured laborers working on the sugar estates and elsewhere—that he began to transform himself into a farmer and endeavored to model what it could look like to live and labor together in a community of equals. In October 1904, Gandhi's friend Henry Polak gave him a copy of John Ruskin's *Unto This Last.*[9] Gandhi read it on the overnight train from Johannesburg to Durban, and immediately decided to change his life in accordance with its ideals, which he summed up in three points:

1. The good of the individual is contained in the good of all.
2. A lawyer's work has the same value as the barber's inasmuch as all have the same right of earning their livelihood from their work.
3. A life of labour, i.e. the life of the tiller of the soil and the handicraftsman is the life worth living.[10]

Following that fateful train ride, Gandhi sprang into action and founded his first intentional community, Phoenix Settlement, in 1904. Purchasing farmland outside of Durban, Gandhi and a cohort of likeminded friends from Indian and European heritages sought to build, in Phoenix Settlement, a simple, self-sufficient, and equitable life together: growing their own produce, building their own houses, educating their children, and printing the weekly activist newspaper *Indian Opinion.*[11] In living and laboring together as equals, Gandhi and his coresidents sought to enact a counterworld to the colonialist and capitalist status quo. They endeavored to establish a just society on their farm, one that would advance the economic well-being of all residents—Indians and Europeans—through shared labor, while simultaneously advancing their equity with and affection for one another.[12]

Gandhi was strict in specifying the dietary rules of Phoenix Settlement. Although Gandhi was raised in a vegetarian Hindu family, as a teenager in India he had secretly experimented with meat-eating in an effort to gain the same strength as his British rulers. But as a law student in London, Gandhi renewed his commitment to vegetarianism, emphasizing not only the health effects of a vegetarian diet (he then claimed that vegetarians could have equivalent strength as meat eaters) but also the moral superiority of a vegetarian diet over a flesh-based diet in its compassion for all beings.[13] In keeping with Gandhi's practice of nonviolence, all of the Phoenix settlers committed to a vegetarian diet. However, Gandhi also insisted that all residents consume only a minimal amount of sugar and no coffee, tea, or cocoa. He explains that this is not only for health reasons, noting that "things such as tea are harmful even to adults, and much more so to children" but also for ethical reasons:

> Moreover, tea, coffee and cocoa are produced through the labour of men who work more or less in conditions of slavery. In Natal, for instance, it is the indentured labourers who work on tea and coffee plantations. Cocoa is produced in the Congo, where indentured Kaffirs are made to work beyond all limits of endurance. We think that slave labour is used even in the production of sugar. Though it is not possible to look too deeply into these matters, we are firmly of the view that these things should be used as sparingly as possible.[14]

Gandhi's firsthand access to the sugar plantations was limited, but the reports from individual indentured laborers about their working conditions and maltreatment caused him to begin to condemn sugar, coffee, tea, and cocoa as agricultural products that were tied to colonialist and capitalist systems of injustice that relied upon immoral labor practices. Gandhi first made these changes in his own diet, minimizing his consumption of sugar and eliminating tea, cocoa, and coffee. He next enforced these dietary restrictions at Phoenix Settlement; rather than drinking tea, residents steeped wheat in boiling water, and Gandhi encouraged residents to eat fruit grown on the farm's orchard in place of cultivated sugar. Gandhi emphasized the need for dietary self-discipline, insisting that such restraint was crucial for both individual and communal well-being.

In his recent book on Gandhi's diet, Nico Slate examines in depth Gandhi's evolving dietary experimentation, including vegetarianism, fasting, and limiting his intake of sweets, salt, and milk. Slate's work is laudable in its focus on the interconnectedness between dietary choices, moral discipline, and political activism in Gandhi's thought. In his chapter focusing on sweets, Slate points out that Gandhi's rejection of sugar and cocoa was a form of dietary asceticism that "was driven by a utopian vision that reframed self-denial as the freedom not just of the individual but of the nation."[15] Indeed, this connection between Gandhi's dietary restrictions and his political vision is significant. However, what Slate's otherwise astute analysis largely overlooks is the central role of Gandhi's intentional communities as the necessary communal-relational ground for enacting his utopian vision. By growing their own produce and by refusing to consume sugar and other agricultural products grown through indentured labor, the residents of Phoenix Settlement sought to cultivate equality with one another and to collectively opt out of colonial injustices.

Gandhi founded his second intentional community, Tolstoy Farm, in 1910. Tolstoy Farm was a thousand-acre farm located approximately twenty-one miles outside of Johannesburg on land that was donated by Hermann Kallenbach.[16] On August 22, 1906, the Asiatic Law Amendment Ordinance became law, requiring all Asians to register with the Transvaal government, including fingerprinting and body stripping to identify birthmarks. Gandhi viewed this law as discriminatory and humiliating, and he began mobilizing his coresidents at Phoenix Settlement to protest through *satyagraha*, nonviolent civil disobedience. As their campaign against this law mounted and more residents of Phoenix Settlement were sent to prison for refusing to register, Gandhi created this second intentional community nearer to Johannesburg so that the families of those imprisoned *satyagrahis* could be within a day's commute of the courthouse and prison. Gandhi named this community Tolstoy Farm in honor of Leo Tolstoy, with whom he had exchanged correspondence in 1909 and 1910 about their mutual interest in nonviolent civil resistance and communal living. In addition to caring for these families, now bereft of their primary breadwinners due to mounting imprisonments, the goal of this community was to promote simplicity, self-sufficiency, and equity. All residents agreed to earn their living by handicraft or agriculture and agreed not to use any indentured labor or servants for household or farming work.[17]

During this period of radical communal experimentation, Gandhi formulated his most famous political treatise, *Hind Swaraj* (or *Indian Home Rule*, 1909). At this time, many nationalist Indian politicians were advocating for *swaraj*, a Sanskrit term that translates as "self-rule," and commonly referred to the goal of Indian Home Rule as opposed to British colonial rule. But in *Hind Swaraj*, Gandhi emphasized the need to first understand swaraj as self-rule on an individual level, writing, "If we become free, India is free. And in this thought you have a definition of Swaraj. It is Swaraj when we learn to rule ourselves. It is, therefore, in the palm of our hands. . . . But such Swaraj has to be experienced, by each one for himself."[18] Gandhi believed that self-rule was central first and foremost at the individual level, as part of everyday communal life, for only when each individual practiced self-rule could the community as a whole flourish. On his farms, Gandhi hoped to cultivate self-rule within himself, and encouraged his coresidents to cultivate it as well. Together, by leading a disciplined and equitable life wherein everyone works and equally shares the fruits of their communal labor, the residents could forge a model for the ideal India that Gandhi hoped to help bring about.

After this initial period of dietary and agricultural experimentation at Phoenix and Tolstoy farms, Gandhi began, through public speeches and essays, to encourage Indians throughout South Africa to refrain from consuming sugar, tea, coffee, and cocoa. He also began to publicly call for an end to indentured labor. Gandhi was expressly critical of the Protector of Indian Immigrants, whose duty it was to ensure that indentured workers were not abused. Gandhi responds to the Protector's annual report in 1910 by asserting "The 'Protector' seems to have assumed the role of 'Exploiter'," and then calling out the treatment of children on the sugar estates in particular:

> Last year, 2,487 indentured labourers arrived from Madras, including 176 boys and 195 girls of all ages. . . . What has been the fate of all these boys and girls? The Government has shown no interest in this matter. The Protector has not a single word to say about them. The employers of indentured labourers do nothing for them. . . . From early morning when the parents go to toil like beasts, these delicate children are left to themselves and those of them who are strong enough for a little work are employed on payment of a paltry 5s. Thus, it is sugar made with the blood of indentured labourers that we use for gratifying our palate.[19]

The government of India prohibited Indian indenture to Natal, effective July 1, 1911. Although this was a political victory, Gandhi urged his fellow Indians to continue their struggle for civil rights for all Indians in South Africa.

In 1913, Gandhi organized another *satyagraha* campaign, seeking redress for the three-pound tax imposed on all Indians who had completed their term of indenture and desired to stay in South Africa as free Indians, and other discriminatory measures such as restrictions on the movement of Indians across the South African colonies. Residents from Phoenix and Tolstoy farms were the key leaders of this civil disobedience campaign, which began on September 15 when a party of twelve men and four women led by Gandhi's wife, Kasturba, set out from Phoenix Settlement. They crossed into Transvaal, courting arrest for crossing the border without a permit. They were arrested the next day and Kasturba was sentenced to three months in prison with hard labor. The next phase of the campaign entailed a strike of Indian laborers beginning in October, which culminated in the Great March of November. During this march, Gandhi led a group of striking workers in protest against the three-pound tax. In all, seven to eight thousand Indian workers went on strike from the sugar fields and refineries, as well as the mines, railways, and docks. Gandhi was arrested on November 11 and sentenced to nine months in prison with hard labor. On his way to prison, Gandhi praised the indentured laborers for their suffering and urged them not to cease the strike until the three-pound tax was repealed. He also called upon the entire Indian community in South Africa to aid the strikers. Those who were not willing to court a prison sentence should supply the strikers with food: "Hundreds of men, who are not ready for jail, can play their part. They have only to resolve that they themselves will go without meals but feed the strikers. . . . Every Indian may take a pledge. He can cut out a meal every day, and with the money so saved provide food to the hungry."[20]

During his years in South Africa, Gandhi connected the dots between food and empire. He witnessed the maltreatment of indentured laborers working in the sugar plantations. In response, he began to eliminate sugar from his diet, along with other agricultural products that relied upon indentured labor. Then Gandhi became a farmer, seeking to model in micro at his intentional communities what it could look like to live and labor together in a community of equals. Finally, Gandhi initiated nonviolent civil disobedience campaigns to combat colonial injustices. In 1914, after years of civil resistance, the Smuts–Gandhi agreement was reached and the Indian Relief Act was passed, providing an amelioration of laws that discriminated against Indians in South Africa. Reflecting on this triumph, Gandhi wrote:

Tolstoy Farm proved to be a centre of spiritual purification and penance for the final campaign. I have serious doubts as to whether the struggle could have been prosecuted for eight years, whether we could have secured larger funds, and whether the thousands of men who participated in the last phase of the struggle would have borne their share in it, if there had been no Tolstoy Farm. . . . The Indians saw that the Tolstoy Farmers were doing what they themselves were not prepared to do and what they looked upon in the light of hardship.[21]

As he returned to India, Gandhi would carry with him this belief that it took a community of people who were collectively disciplined in physical labor, ethically committed to nonviolence, and willing to voluntarily undergo personal hardship for the greater good in order to achieve political victory against colonial injustice. In India, Gandhi would turn his attention to salt as he worked to connect with the masses in his growing battle against empire.

Salt and Empire in India

In the summer of 1914, as Gandhi was sailing to London to visit friends and colleagues before returning to India, World War I broke out. Gandhi decided that it was his duty as a citizen of the British Empire (and particularly as one who was demanding equal rights as a British citizen), to help in Britain's hour of need. He would not enlist as a soldier in the war due to his commitment to nonviolence, but he did organize a volunteer ambulance corps made up of eighty Indians living in London who completed a six-week course in first aid. Gandhi had previously organized an ambulance corps in South Africa during the 1899 Boer War and the 1906 Zulu Rebellion. For this work, Gandhi was awarded the Kaiser-i-Hind Medal for Public Service in 1915 by the viceroy of India.[22]

At the start of 1915, Gandhi returned to India. He spent his first six months traveling to reacquaint himself with the condition of his home country. Then he settled down, founding his third intentional community, Sabarmati Ashram, on May 25, 1915, on the banks of the Sabarmati River outside Ahmedabad. At the founding of this community, Gandhi articulated a mission statement: "The object of this Ashram is that its members should qualify themselves for, and make a consistent endeavor towards, the service of the country, not inconsistent with universal welfare [*sarvodaya*]."[23] He enumerated eleven observances as essential for fulfilling this mission. The first and foremost of these was truth: "Truth is God, the one and only Reality. All other observances take their rise from the quest for, and the worship of, Truth." The remaining observances included: 1) nonviolence, 2) celibacy, 3) control of the palate, 4) non-stealing, 5) non-possession, 6) physical labor, 7) economic independence, 8) fearlessness, 9) removal of untouchability, and 10) tolerance.[24]

Control of the palate is a traditional self-discipline arising from the Hindu tradition of ascetic renunciation that is meant to minimize worldly attachments, as are celibacy, non-stealing, and non-possession. Gandhi had begun to experiment with such control of the palate during his years living at Phoenix and Tolstoy farms, and now continued this experiment at Sabarmati Ashram. In a speech given in 1916 about the ashram vows, which was printed in the *Indian Review*, Gandhi explained that the emphasis on condiments in kitchens and restaurants is "slavery to the palate, rather than mastery over it," and he emphasized the need for control of the palate in order to live a simple, disciplined, and nonviolent life:

> Unless we take our minds off from this habit, and unless we shut our eyes to the tea shops and coffee shops and all these kitchens, and unless we are satisfied with foods that are necessary for the proper maintenance of our physical health, and unless we are prepared to rid ourselves of stimulating, heating and exciting condiments that we mix with our food, we will certainly not be able to control the overabundant, unnecessary, exciting stimulation that we may have. If we do not do that, the result naturally is, that we abuse ourselves and we abuse even the sacred trust given to us, and we become less than animals and brutes.[25]

In the Indian context, Gandhi began to focus increasingly on salt. In South Africa, Gandhi had begun to limit his salt intake for health reasons.[26] In India, he continued to experiment with minimizing his salt intake and advised his fellow ashram residents to do so as well to improve their health and control their passions. But in India, Gandhi also became aware of the politics of salt. In speech after speech, Gandhi emphasized that the poor masses of India often can eat only one meal of bread and salt per day. Indeed, in the above speech about the ashram vows, Gandhi continues by turning from control of the palate to the observance of non-stealing, and claims that as long as such inequality exists, then eating more than a simple meal is a form of stealing: "In India we have got

FOOD AND ANTICOLONIALISM

three millions of people having to be satisfied with one meal a day, and that meal consisting of a *chapati* [unleavened flatbread] containing no fat in it, and a pinch of salt. You and I have no right to anything that we really have until these three million are clothed and fed better."[27]

Given the poverty and hunger of the masses in India, Gandhi was especially angered by the salt tax. The India Salt Act of 1882 made the collection and manufacture of salt a monopoly of the colonial British government in India, and provided that salt could only be manufactured at government salt depots, with a tax levied per maund (eighty-two pounds) of salt. As World War I drew to a close in 1918, some British politicians advocated for doubling the Indian salt tax to pay for the expenses of war. Gandhi wrote to such politicians, urging them to reconsider and emphasizing the toll that the salt tax places upon the poor: "The monopoly has artificially raised the price of salt and today the poor find it most difficult to procure salt at a reasonable price. To them salt is as necessary as water and air."[28] Salt, Gandhi argued, was a basic need. To monopolize and tax it was an unjust law that served colonialism and capitalism at the expense of India's poor.

Throughout the 1920s, Gandhi spoke out publicly about the unjustness of the salt tax and its impact upon the poor, while simultaneously advising his coresidents to minimize salt in their diets. He also continued to think about swaraj, both in its personal meaning as self-discipline and in its political meaning as self-rule or home rule. Following the Jallianwala Bagh massacre of 1919, wherein a crowd of peaceful Indian protestors in Amritsar was fired upon under the command of Brigadier-General Reginald Dyer, Gandhi and the Indian National Congress publicly committed to the goal of obtaining swaraj, political home rule for India. Gandhi inaugurated this campaign for swaraj by writing a letter to the viceroy wherein he returned his Kaiser-i-Hind medal along with the other medals he had received for his humanitarian services in wartime, stating that he could no longer keep them for he no longer retained "respect nor affection" for the British government.[29] Yet, whereas some Indian politicians in the Congress Party advocated for dominion status within the British Empire, and others advocated for total independence, Gandhi was ambivalent at this time, waiting to see whether the British would agree to a meaningful dominion agreement for India.

Throughout the 1920s, Indian politicians lobbied for political reforms and rights, but to little avail. Ultimately, in December of 1929, Gandhi agreed that it was time to call for *purna swaraj*, complete independence from Britain. On January 26, 1930, the Indian National Congress released their declaration of independence, publicly asserting the goal of purna swaraj and committing to attaining it through nonviolent means. Gandhi wrote to the viceroy, Lord Irwin, stating that if the British Cabinet would agree to eleven reforms, then they would hear no further talk of civil disobedience and would meet together to determine how to move forward. The fourth of the eleven reforms was the abolition of the salt tax.[30] The British did not agree to these terms, and thus Gandhi began planning a satyagraha campaign.

On March 12, 1930, Gandhi began a march to the coast of Gujarat. On April 6, Gandhi and his fellow marchers arrived at the coast, where they broke the Salt Act simply by collecting natural salt. Known as the Salt March, this was the start of a nationwide anticolonial civil resistance campaign, and it has received much attention in analyses of Gandhi's politics.[31] Yet such analyses tend to neglect both the centrality of food and the centrality of the ashram community to the Salt March. In his book on Gandhi's diet, Nico Slate has sought to redress the gap of the centrality of food to the march, writing that Gandhi "may never have imagined the march had he not grappled so incessantly with salt in his daily diet."[32] To this important observation I would add that Gandhi may never have successfully completed the march had it not been for his fellow ashram residents. When Gandhi first set out on the Salt March, he was accompanied by seventy-eight coresidents from Sabarmati Ashram. Gandhi chose these coresidents because he wanted his fellow marchers to be disciplined—disciplined in palate control, and equally disciplined in nonviolence and committed to it not as a (temporary) political strategy but as a (lifelong) moral practice.

During the twenty-four-day march, Gandhi took his intentional community on the road. He continued to emphasize the economic injustice of the Salt Act, proclaiming that it made the already destitute masses pay a tax on a primary need. In solidarity with these masses, Gandhi demanded that his coresidents-turned-comarchers maintain simple standards of living throughout the march. They were instructed to accept only the simplest of food from the villages they passed through, and to inform Gandhi personally if they needed any extra items. Gandhi also published essays requesting that residents of the villages they would pass through should "be miserly rather than lavish" in their hospitality and should only provide bread, vegetables, or goat's milk if it does not deprive the women or children in their families.[33] Gandhi allowed representatives of the press to travel alongside them on the march, but only on the condition that they agree to live on the same simple alms for the duration of the march. Gandhi emphasized that "hundreds of thousands will follow this batch of seventy-eight in whatever they do," thus they must cultivate nonviolence and self-sacrifice.[34]

In addition to such dietary self-control, Gandhi also demanded that his fellow marchers be willing to make the sacrifice of serving time in jail for breaking the law, and even of sacrificing their lives if needed. In a speech delivered to his fellow ashram inmates the night before the march began, Gandhi characterized the Salt March as a "life-and-death struggle," and emphasized that the only ashram residents who could join him on the march were those who did not have dependents to care for, who had taken vows of celibacy and poverty, and who could commit to dying in this nonviolent struggle. Using strong rhetoric, Gandhi declared that they would not return to the ashram until they had either attained swaraj or died trying:

> This fight is no public show; it is the final struggle—a life-and-death struggle. . . . I do ask you to return here only as dead men or as winners of swaraj. . . . Even if the Ashram is on fire, we will not return. . . . We are entering upon a life-and-death struggle, a holy war; we are performing an all-embracing sacrifice in which we wish to offer ourselves as oblation.[35]

After collecting natural salt from the ocean and gaining national attention through the Salt March, Gandhi set his sights on his next target: the government-run Dharasana Salt Works in Gujarat. Gandhi began to make speeches about this intended raid, inviting the Indian people to join him if they would wear *khadi* (homespun cloth, not imported fabric), be sober, and commit to nonviolence. In one such speech at Chharwada on April 26, 1930, Gandhi proudly proclaimed: "People have conferred upon me the title of salt-thief as a substitute for Mahatma. I like it." But then he went on to state: "You may call me a salt-thief but only when we take possession of the salt-beds of Dharasana. What is there in picking up a seer or two of salt from here and there? Even the Government must be wondering what a childish game we are playing. If you mean to play the real game, come out and loot the salt-beds of Dharasana, or Bhayander, or Kharaghoda."[36]

After writing to the viceroy to explain his intention to raid the Dharasana Salt Works, Gandhi was arrested on May 5, 1930, and sent to

Yeravda Central Prison. The raid of Dharasana went forth as planned, led initially by Abbas Tyabji, who began the march with Gandhi's wife, Kasturba, at his side. At this raid, hundreds of nonviolent protestors were brutally beaten down by British forces before being arrested. In total, over eighty thousand Indians were arrested throughout the country during the Salt Satyagraha. The raid on Dharasana Salt Works was covered by the international press, resulting in an outpouring of global sympathy for the cause of Indian independence; as Dennis Dalton points out, direct comparisons of Gandhi with Christ had become common in popular commentary on the Salt Satyagraha in Britain and the United States.[37]

Gandhi was released from prison on January 26, 1931 and sailed for London to try to negotiate with the British Government for the terms of India's independence at the Second Round Table Conference. However, this conference ended in failure to make progress, and the struggle for independence would last another fifteen years, until 1947. Thus, in fulfillment of his vow not to return to Sabarmati Ashram unless they had won swaraj, Gandhi disbanded the ashram on July 22, 1933. In a letter to the home secretary, Gandhi offered the ashram to the colonial government and described its closing as a sacrifice for independence, promising that the satyagraha struggle would continue.[38] After closing Sabarmati Ashram, Gandhi spent the next two years moving throughout rural India. In spring of 1936, he settled down near Wardha, in eastern Maharashtra, where he founded his final intentional community: Sevagram Ashram, which means "village of service." Here Gandhi lived in a hand-built hut and ate a simple vegetarian diet of food grown on the ashram land. And it was here, far from the capital of New Delhi, that Gandhi planned the famous Quit India movement, which he launched on August 9, 1942, engaging in a final nonviolent civil disobedience campaign against the British to demand complete independence.

Concluding Remarks:
Fighting an Empire with Sugar and Salt

In a 1919 essay in his Gujarati-language newspaper *Navajivan*, Gandhi wrote: "India lives in farmers' huts. The weavers' skill is a reminder of India's glory, and so I feel proud in describing myself as a farmer and a weaver. . . . If the farmers continue to live in fear, buried under heavy debt, if they are diseased in body, I see nothing but ruin in store for India."[39] Gandhi is most famously remembered as a politician and a lawyer. But as we have seen Gandhi was also a tiller of the soil, a proud salt-thief, and a founder of multiple back-to-the-land utopian communities. Arguably, these characteristics were as central to his identity as his formal professions. But they were also central to his method for fighting against colonialism. Gandhi experimented with his diet throughout his lifetime, and these experiments led him to think about the conditions under which his food was grown, to embrace the farmers who grew it, and to question the economics of imperialism that put the farmers at such dire risk to their personal well-being. These experiments with diet also led Gandhi to become a farmer himself, founding four intentional communities as model alternatives to the colonialist and capitalist status quo, wherein Indian and European residents could live and labor together as equals. Finally, these experiments with diet and community led Gandhi to refine his definition of swaraj, beginning with his own personal cultivation of self-rule through dietary restrictions, and evolving into an ultimate battle for purna swaraj, complete independence for India from British colonial rule.

NOTES

1. Research for this essay was supported by an Enhancing Life grant through The University of Chicago in collaboration with Ruhr-University Bochum and the John Templeton Foundation. Writing time for this essay was supported by a fellowship from the National Endowment for the Humanities and a sabbatical leave from Bucknell University. I am grateful for the feedback received from the cohort of Enhancing Life grant recipients, and from Justin Nordstrom and the anonymous reviewers on earlier drafts of this essay.
2. Some of the significant scholarly analyses of Gandhi's politics of nonviolence include Dennis Dalton, *Mahatma Gandhi: Nonviolent Power in Action* (New York: Columbia University Press, 2012); Veena Howard, *Gandhi's Ascetic Activism: Renunciation and Social Action* (Albany: State University of New York Press, 2013); Karuna Mantena, "Another Realism: The Politics of Gandhian Nonviolence," *American Political Science Review* 106, no. 2 (2012): 455–70; and Ajay Skaria, *Unconditional Equality: Gandhi's Religion of Resistance* (Minneapolis: University of Minnesota Press, 2016). For substantial scholarly analyses of the relationship between Gandhi's diet and his politics, see: Joseph S. Alter, *Gandhi's Body: Sex, Diet, and the Politics of Nationalism* (Philadelphia: University of Pennsylvania Press, 2000); and Nico Slate, *Gandhi's Search for the Perfect Diet: Eating with the World in Mind* (Seattle: University of Washington Press, 2019).
3. For scholarly analyses of Gandhi's years in South Africa, see: Ashwin Desai and Goolam Vahed, *The South African Gandhi: Stretcher-Bearer of Empire* (Stanford: Stanford University Press, 2016); and Ramachandra Guha, *Gandhi Before India* (New York: Alfred A. Knopf, 2014).

4. Goolam Vahed, "The Protector, Plantocracy, and Indentured Labour in Natal, 1860–1911," *Pacific Historical Review* 87, no. 1 (2018): 101–27.

5. M. K. Gandhi, *Autobiography: The Story of My Experiments with Truth* (Boston: Beacon Press, 1993): 153.

6. Gandhi, *Autobiography*, 154.

7. Guha, *Gandhi Before India*, 65.

8. M. K. Gandhi, *Collected Works of Mahatma Gandhi* (New Delhi: Publications Division, Government of India, 2015 electronic edition in 100 volumes), 1:170–88.

9. On Gandhi's relationship with Henry Polak, see: Henry S. L. Polak, "Some South African Reminiscences," in *Incidents of Gandhiji's Life*, ed. Chandrashanker Shukla (Bombay: M. K. Vora & Co. Publishers Ltd., 1949): 238–39; and Thomas Weber, *Gandhi as Disciple and Mentor* (Cambridge: Cambridge University Press, 2004): 54–68.

10. Gandhi, *Autobiography*, 298–99. Also see: M. K. Gandhi, *Ruskin: Unto This Last: A Paraphrase* (Ahmedabad: Navajivan Publishing House, 1956).

11. For more on *Indian Opinion* and other activist publications printed at Gandhi's intentional communities, see: Isabel Hofmeyr, *Gandhi's Printing Press: Experiments in Slow Reading* (Cambridge, MA: Harvard University Press, 2013); and Uma Shashikant Mesthrie, "From Advocacy to Mobilization: *Indian Opinion*, 1903–1914" in Les Switzer, ed., *South Africa's Alternative Press: Voices of Protest and Resistance, 1880s–1960s* (Cambridge: Cambridge University Press, 1997): 99–126.

12. But for an important critique of Gandhi's vision of Phoenix as "conspicuous in its exclusion of Africans," see: Desai and Vahed, *The South African Gandhi*, 46.

13. On Gandhi's experiments with meat-eating and his renewed commitment to vegetarianism, see: Gandhi, *Autobiography*, 19–25; and Slate, *Gandhi's Search for the Perfect Diet*, 46–73. On Gandhi's early arguments about the physical and moral benefits of the vegetarian diet, see the series of five essays published in 1891 in the London-based periodical the *Vegetarian Messenger*, in *Collected Works of Mahatma Gandhi*, 1:20–29.

14. Gandhi, *Indian Opinion* essay, in *Collected Works of Mahatma Gandhi*, 9:136. In this quote Gandhi uses the term "Kaffir" to refer to native Africans, a term that was then a racial slur and is now legally considered hate speech in South Africa. For further discussion of Gandhi's usage of this term, see: Arundhati Roy, "The Doctor and the Saint," *Caravan Magazine*, February 28, 2014, https://caravanmagazine.in/essay/doctor-and-saint. For a more sympathetic take on Gandhi's evolving attitude toward native Africans, see: Slate, *Gandhi's Search for the Perfect Diet*, 24–45.

15. Slate, *Gandhi's Search for the Perfect Diet*, 42.

16. On Gandhi's relationship with Hermann Kallenbach, see: James D. Hunt and Surendra Bhana, "Spiritual Rope-Walkers: Gandhi, Kallenbach, and the Tolstoy Farm, 1910–13," *South African Historical Journal* 58 (2007): 174–202; Isa Sarid and Christian Bartolf, *Hermann Kallenbach: Mahatma Gandhi's Friend in South Africa* (Berlin: Gandhi Informations Zentrum, 1997); and Thomas Weber, *Gandhi as Disciple and Mentor* (Cambridge: Cambridge University Press, 2004): 69–83.

17. M. K. Gandhi, *Satyagraha in South Africa* (Ahmedabad: Navajivan Publishing House, 1928): 215.

18. M. K. Gandhi with Anthony Parel, *Hind Swaraj and Other Writings* (Cambridge: Cambridge University Press, 1997): 73.

19. Gandhi, *Indian Opinion* essay, in *Collected Works of Mahatma Gandhi*, 10:309–10. For more on the role of the Protector of Indian Immigrants in Natal Colony, see: Vahed, "The Protector."

20. Gandhi, *Indian Opinion* essay, in *Collected Works of Mahatma Gandhi*, 12:262.

21. Gandhi, *Satyagraha in South Africa*, 235–36.

22. On Gandhi's justification for his volunteer work during World War I in light of his commitment to nonviolence, see: Gandhi, *Autobiography*, 346–50; on his volunteer work during the Boer War, see: *Autobiography*, 214–16.

23. M. K. Gandhi, *Ashram Observances in Action* (Ahmedabad: Navajivan Publishing House, 1955): 65. For more on the evolution of Gandhi's concept of *sarvodaya*, or universal well-being, in the context of his intentional communities, see: Karline McLain, "Gandhi's Ashrams: Residential Experiments for Universal Wellbeing in South Africa and India," *Journal of Utopian Studies* 30, no. 3 (2019): 462–85.

24. Gandhi, *Ashram Observances in Action*, 65–69.

25. Gandhi, *Collected Works of Mahatma Gandhi*, 13:230.

26. See, for instance, Gandhi's 1918 letter to Dr. Kulkarni describing the experiments he had undertaken beginning in 1911 with restricting salt in his and Kasturba's diet in *Collected Works of Mahatma Gandhi*, 14:170–72.

27. Gandhi, *Collected Works of Mahatma Gandhi*, 13:231.

28. Gandhi, *Collected Works of Mahatma Gandhi*, 15:16.

29. Gandhi, *Collected Works of Mahatma Gandhi*, 18:104.

30. See: Gandhi, *Young India* essay, in *Collected Works of Mahatma Gandhi*, 42:432–35.

31. For thorough overviews and analyses of the Salt March, see: Dalton, *Mahatma Gandhi*, 91–138 and Thomas Weber, *On the Salt March: The Historiography of Gandhi's March to Dandi* (New Delhi: HarperCollins India, 1997).

32. Slate, *Gandhi's Search for the Perfect Diet*, 11.

33. Gandhi, *Young India* essay, in *Collected Works of Mahatma Gandhi*, 43:146–149.

34. Gandhi, *Collected Works of Mahatma Gandhi*, 43:72–73.

35. Gandhi, *Collected Works of Mahatma Gandhi*, 43:59–60.

36. Gandhi, speech reprinted in *Navajivan*, in Collected *Works of Mahatma Gandhi*, 43:331–34.

37. Dalton, *Mahatma Gandhi*, 131.

38. Gandhi, *Collected Works of Mahatma Gandhi*, 55:303.

39. Gandhi, *Navajivan* essay, in *Collected Works of Mahatma Gandhi*, 16:94.

CHAPTER 4

The Making of Indian Vegetarian Identity

MOHD AHMAR ALVI

British colonization of India, in addition to disrupting the subcontinent's economic and political fabric, transformed the culinary paradigm of the nation. Colonization was predicated on warfare and military dominance. But justifying warfare and conquest required dietary distinctions between British foreigners, who believed their meat-eating habits reflected and reinforced their muscular and moral superiority, and natives, whose vegetarian diets demonstrated to British observers Indians' frailty and effeminacy. These dietary delineations also exacerbated India's internal distinctions, leading to communal riots, legal restrictions on the slaughter of cattle, and religious pronouncements that inflamed tensions between Hindus and Muslims as well as among rival social castes. While not all Indians embraced vegetarianism, the making of India's vegetarian identity was based on a strategy of influential Hindus to promote cattle veneration and vegetarian diets as indicators of genuine Indian identity, thereby distancing themselves from internal rivals and external colonizers alike. Ultimately, both British colonizers and Indian Hindus embraced a mindset that equated food with political identity and individual morality. Differentiating Indians on the basis of diet set the culinary scene for India for several generations, linking vegetarianism to Indian national identity into the modern era.

British colonizers frequently projected their culinary beliefs in the superiority of eating meat, beginning a discourse on vegetarian and non-vegetarian diets that persisted for decades. The dichotomy between meat-eating colonizers and plant-eating natives simultaneously informed

Britain's wars of empire in the subcontinent and India's ideologically fueled civil warfare in important respects. First, celebrating meat-eating validated British mindsets, illustrating their potential for disciplining and conquering the colonized.[1] Furthermore, the British theory of vegetarian inferiority influenced colonial military ideology and recruitment strategies in India, making Punjabis, Pathans, and Dalits (who consumed meat on a daily basis) desirable for military purposes, shaping regimental recruitment strategies in the subcontinent. Finally, and most significantly for the purposes of this chapter, conflict over vegetarianism and meat-eating sparked violence within India, as ideological wars culminated in violence between Hindus and Muslims that fostered a crisis of Indian identity and internal violence.

One example of Britain's colonial strategy of evaluating Indian natives based on food comes from surveys of jail diets and colonial medical texts in the early nineteenth century. In 1807, Scottish physician Francis Buchanan-Hamilton, tasked by the British East India Company with describing the natural resources, agriculture, foodways, living conditions, and diseases of eastern India, reported on the natives' diets in different parts of India, as well as variations in diets between caste, and the importance of food as an index of social standing and respectability.[2] Another important source in studying British attitudes toward Indian foodways is the inquiry conducted by Dr. A. H. Leith in 1846 into the health of Indian prisoners at Bombay's House of Correction, which documented alarming levels of sickness and mortality. Leith noted that prisoners' diet, consisting of dal and rice with little salt and ghee, fell short of the required amount of protein, making them prone to scurvy and other deficiency diseases.[3] In 1912, prison data made unfounded proclamations outlining dietary and physiological distinctions between Britons and the Indians, as well as between the inhabitants of different parts of India. Professor D. R. McCay of Calcutta's Medical College contrasted jail diets in Bengal with those in the United Provinces (UP; formerly the North-Western Provinces), then used the results to distinguish the apparent frail, stunted, and effeminate vegetarian Bengalis from the robustness, fighting spirit, and martial manliness of the Punjabis, Pathans, and other peoples of northern and northwestern India, whose diet consisted of dairy products, wheat, and meat. According to McCay, dietary differences explained why prisoners in UP (and hence the agrarian classes from which they came) were on a "distinctly higher plane of physical development" than those of Bengal:

THE MAKING OF INDIAN VEGETARIAN IDENTITY

The general muscularity of the body is decidedly better and their capabilities of labour are greater. They are smarter on their feet, more brisk and more alive to the incidents of everyday life, and they do not present such slackness and toneless-ness as one is accustomed to observe in the people of Lower Bengal.[4]

British observers offered different explanations for the Indian preference for a vegetarian diet. James Johnson, one of the influential medical writers of nineteenth century, pointed to historical reasons, while others offered an environmental or racial explanation.[5] British officials equated plant-eating with savagery, poverty, and degradation—which to them differentiated Indians from the British—while meat-eating was showcased as a sign of power and masculinity.[6] However, a meat-eating diet also marked British colonizers as outsiders and "aligned them not with the high castes and 'respectable' classes of Hindus and some Muslims but with the lowest social strata."[7] Hindus were horrified at colonizers' habit of eating pork and beef, which as Buchanan-Hamilton remarked, reduced the colonizers to the status of "lowest drag of Hindu impurity," making them able to find their cooks and table servants only among the low-status community, Doms—a tribe considered vile by upper-caste Hindus.[8] Therefore, the binary between vegetarian and non-vegetarian, introduced by the British, became part of Hindu social imagination. Since Hindus formed a majority of the Indian population, the view that meat-eaters (Muslims, Dalits, and other lower-caste groups) were accomplices of the colonizers—sharing their food habits and serving their militaries—dominated Indian social identity and linked food to Indian nationalism.[9]

Thus, in the late nineteenth and early twentieth centuries, the discourse on vegetarianism versus non-vegetarianism became a question of culture and nationalism.[10] A more liberal group of the colonized Indians accepted the established superiority of meat-eating and suggested Indians include animal protein in their meals, believing that meat-eating would allow them to oppose British rule. According to Chunilal Bose, a chemistry professor at the Calcutta Medical College and one-time Chemical Examiner to the Government of Bengal, a vegetarian diet was rich enough in carbohydrates but acutely deficit in protein, "the muscle forming element." Such a lopsided diet, he argued, slowed growth, limited physical exercise and resistance against infectious diseases, and ultimately produced premature old age and mortality.[11] In order to make up for the deficiency in protein, he prescribed "a more liberal allowance of protein-foods of animal origin [e.g. milk, fish, meat, and eggs] in the present-day diet of the people."[12] The culmination of this discourse emerged in the writings of Swami Vivekananda, who brought the question of Indian vegetarianism within the orbit of contemporary nationalist concerns about masculinity and physical culture. According to Vivekananda, non-vegetarianism, especially meat-eating, was a requirement for Indians to withstand the material and physical realities of modern life. He ultimately argued that meat-eating created the difference between the power to rule others and the abject surrender to more physically robust peoples. His famous and oft-quoted phrase, "beef, biceps, and Bhagavad Gita," demonstrates his view that meat-eating was linked to "strength, manhood, kshaytavirya," or the virility of a warrior. Adopting the dietary habits of the colonizers, in short, would allow Indians to wage war against the British on equal terms.

> As long as men have to practise *rajas*, as required by the modern age, there is no other alternative than meat-eating. It is true that king Asoka saved the lives of a couple of millions of animals by his sword, but is not a thousand years' slavery even more terrible than this? Which is a greater sin—to kill a few goats, or to fail to protect the honour of my wife and daughter, and to fail to prevent others from plundering the food meant for my children? Let those who belong to the elite, and do not have to win their bread by physical labour, shun meat. But as for those who have to provide for their subsistence by means of continuous physical toil, forcing them to be vegetarians is one of the reasons for the eclipse of our national independence. Japan is an illustration of what good, nutritious food can achieve.[13]

Therefore, for Vivekananda and Bose, meat eating signified robust health for the individual and honor, productivity, and progress for the nation as a whole. Conversely, vegetarianism was an emasculating habit that put an impassable hurdle in the path of nation making.

In contrast, upper-caste Hindus viewed meat-eating in opposition to traditional aspects of Indian social life—particularly religious, spiritual, or ascetic practices that equated certain foods with purity, freshness, radiance, and calmness. Bhudeb Mokhopadhyay, a renowned nineteenth-century educator and journalist, protested against linking a vegetarian diet with weakness of the Indian body, and challenged the view that meat-eating was mandatory for Indians eager to wage war against the colonizers. Looking back on ancient history, he argued that the Spartans, the best Greek warriors, never consumed meat.[14] Moreover, Hindu elites believed that *satvik* (pure) Indians should completely remove meat from their diets, promoting vegetarianism as an Indian identity that was under severe attack from colonialism and modern civilization.[15] In Hinduism, food served an important role in the march of the individual soul on its upward path as it seeks union with universal spirit. Foods could emanate negative or positive energy, either impeding or facilitating this unison with the universal spirit. Thus, even vegetables could contain negative force, particularly garlic, onions, turnips, leeks, and leftover or rotten food, as well as meat and food cooked or served by untouchables (the most oppressed and the lowest people in the Hindu caste hierarchy).

However, several renowned Indian historians, such as Romila Thapar and D. N. Jha, have carefully demonstrated that the Sanskrit scriptures on which the modern structure of Hinduism grounds its theology mention killing cattle both for sacrifice and eating purposes. In fact, Hindu taboos surrounding killing cattle first emerged from the fear of losing followers to emergent Buddhism, a reformation movement within Hinduism that condemned the killing of animals in the name of religious and eating practices. As a result, Hindus promoted the discourse of sacred cows and started associating cattle with deities and referencing the "cow mother" or life giver in a desperate and organized attempt to lure Buddhists back to Hinduism.[16] Furthermore, vegetarianism in general (and refusal to eat beef in particular) served more to homogenize Indians politically than to address issues of religious doctrine. This proved especially true in the nineteenth and twentieth centuries as dietary questions inflamed tensions between rival Hindu and Muslim communities.

Nevertheless, by the twentieth century, this discourse on meat-eating and vegetarianism took on new dimensions. First, the cow came to symbolize the "mother of all Hindus" and served to promote Hindu identity and nationality, requiring protection from non-Hindus—both Muslims and the Christian colonizers. To ensure no violence or brutality was inflicted on their "mother," various *gaurakshini sabhas* (cow protection societies), *gauraksha andolans* (cow protection movements), and *gaushalas* (cow shelters) started to emerge across the country. By the end of the century, there was scarcely any town without such a sabha. These sabhas, emulating the structure of the British governance, employed, in C. A. Bayly's phrase, "service and professional people" who provided money and expertise, held inflammatory lectures and talks, and instilled a consciousness for cow protection within the general population.[17] These leaders viewed gau-shalas as an opportunity for Hindus to claim a permanent place in heaven: "The protectors of the cows (who) will remain in heaven . . . will be called gods. . . . All should know that there can be no virtue without taking proper care of cows" was a chant with which every Hindu congregation began and ended.[18] Fundraising for cow protection also served as a means to participate in the noble cause. To this end, tin boxes stamped with the image of the cow were stationed in bazaars, post offices and shops. Attempts were also made to collect subscriptions from all Hindus. A common entreaty of the sabhas was:

> For the protection of gaomata [Mother Cow] each household shall everyday contribute for its food supply . . . 1 *paisa*, per member. From the chituki fund a cow refuge [*gaoshala*] shall be built, and the expenses of its maintenance shall be met. And if any one is compelled to sell a cow at a fair, the cow shall be bought up and interned in the cow-refuge; and if anywhere money be needed for the protection of cows, it shall be paid at once. *The eating of food without setting apart the chituki shall be an offence equal to that of eating cow's flesh.*[19]

Traders were expected to donate one percent of their earnings to the sabhas and no marriage, feast, or successful lawsuit was possible without making a donation.

Under the violent and aggressive demonstrations held by the gauraksha sabhas, the governments of Hindu-ruled states extended protection to cows by imposing legal restrictions on the slaughtering of cattle, even for food purposes. In some states where the majority was Hindu, laws restricted the slaughter of all domestic animals, not only bovines. Licenses for meat markets were limited, and those who received permits were required to slaughter animals in enclosures, away from principal bazaars. Slaughterers were further required to take animals to abattoirs using roundabout routes, so as not to attract public attention.[20] A set of stiffer restrictions was applicable on holy days. Sirohi, a city in southern Rajasthan, issued an order prohibiting the slaughter of goats during the Jain festival of Pachusan. In Jodhpur, Muslims were not allowed "to take out a goat in Bazaar during any period of religious celebration."[21] As a result of these legal restrictions, of the number of butchers per capita in the Hindu-ruled states was significantly lower than those in the British provinces, as demonstrated by the statistical comparison of Alwar and Punjab by Edward Haynes.[22] The cattle restrictions of the late nineteenth and twentieth centuries brought some positive changes to Indian society—previously, those killing cows were "wantonly beaten," buried alive, or flogged to their deaths by elephants. Under the new legislation, offenders had to pay hefty fines or serve lengthy prison sentences.

The organization that came to embody Indian cattle veneration in the 1920s was Rashtriya Swayamsevak Sangh (RSS), a radical group led by the upper caste Hindus, pressing "Hindutva" ideology which promoted Hinduism as the only indigenous Indian religion, Hindu the only indigenous race, and Hindi as the only culture ever found in India. The RSS fostered anti-Islamic sentiments, attempting to establish a Hindu Rashtra (Hindu Nation), and opposed the lower-caste Dalits who, in turn, mobilized resentment and agitation against Brahmans. Therefore, the RSS used cattle veneration as an upper-caste attempt to dissipate and redirect lower-caste assertiveness away from themselves and toward a new set of enemies, Muslims. One of the RSS's major achievements was the inclusion of cow protection in the Indian Constitution's list of "Directive Principles of State Policy" under the principle that deals with animal husbandry. Article 48 binds the Indian state not only to make laws for the benefit of the country by improving cattle breeding, but also to work towards the goal of "prohibiting the slaughter of cows and calves and other milch and draft cattle." Although couched in the language of science and modernity, these bans on cow slaughter and beef-eating were directly linked to Brahmanical religious sentiments, which elevate the sanctity of cattle through India's courts, educational institutions, and governmental bodies, which are in turn dominated by upper-caste Hindus.

These Hindu leaders and public officials used visual media to promote the veneration of cattle throughout the nation, using on telegraphs, messengers, *patias* (chain letters), and broadside images to spread the narrative of cow protection by cow protectors. Visual images circulated among the general public attempted to strengthen the symbolic value of the cow and to instill anti-Muslim sentiments among Hindus. The following is a translation of two patias found in the police report of the Bihar cow riots of 1917:

> Ram: Further you must know that there are strained feelings between the Hindus and the Mohammedans on account of *Qurbani* (sacrifice associated with a Muslim festival called *Id-ul-Adha*). If one is a Hindu he must save the cow. You are, therefore, warned to kill the Mohammedans wherever you find them and plunder their villages. Write 25 copies of this leaflet and send them on to villages. Those who will not write and will not send them should cohabit with their daughters, drink their wife's urine, suck their sister's milk and marry their mothers with Mohammedans. We have nothing to fear. The German Emperor is helping us a good deal. Bear in mind

no Mohammedan breed should be left alive. If you find a collection of Mohammedans inform the Maharaja of Dumaraon and you will immediately have armed forces with guns.[23]

According to Christopher Pinney, locally produced mass visual images played a crucial role in the organization and ideology of the agitation against cow slaughter. In these popular images, the cow became a proto-nation infusing Hindu Indian identity with a divine mission and purpose—one that was willing to generate violence and even civil warfare to differentiate Hindu identity from the culture of colonizers on one hand and internal dissenters (particularly Muslims) on the other. Viewing the cow as a symbolic representation of Hindu cosmology, these popular broadside images literally inscribed divine images on the cow's body.[24] Gauraksha sabhas not only used violence and protest to project cows as a form of protonationalism, but also published posters, distributed handbills and print poems, sang *bhajans* (religious hymns), and performed plays in the praise of "mother cow." Cow veneration provided the sabhas a focal point and helped influence preachers and missionaries. A drama in Hindi depicting India as destitute because of cattle slaughter, *Bharat-dimdima Natak,* was published in Lucknow and copies were sold at railway book stalls.[25] To arouse public sympathy for mother cow, Hindu artists circulated pictures of cattle to incite violence against Muslims for eating beef. One depicted a cow as lying slaughtered by three Muslim butchers under the headline "The Present State." Another presented a cow with Hindu deities and holy persons inscribed on every part of her body. A calf was under her udder and a woman with an empty bowl waiting for her turn to milk it. Fittingly, the woman was labeled "The Hindu." The back and front of the handbill displayed images of Krishna (labeled "Dharmraj" or "king of religion") and a monster intending to kill the cow with a sword (called "Kaliyug," but typifying Muslims and Dalits). A Hindu explained the meaning of the picture as:

> The Hindu must only take the cow's milk after the calf has been satisfied. In the "Dharmraj" of the Satyug no Hindu would kill a cow, but the Kaliyug is bent upon killing the cow and exterminating the kine. As every man drinks cow's milk just as he as an infant has drawn milk from his mother, the cow must be regarded as the universal mother, and so is called "Gau Mata." It is matricide to kill a cow. Nay more, as all the gods dwell in the cow, to kill a cow is to insult every Hindu.[26]

The unmistakable message of this image was that cattle slaughter produced weakness and death among Hindus, as well as the collapse of the nation in this age of "Kalyug." Krishna Mishra, general secretary of *Hindu Sabha* and of *Garhwal Radha-Krishna Gaushala*, remarked:

> Today our mother cow is being slain by the infidels [British colonizers, Indian Muslims, and low social castes] in innumerable numbers. . . . Our helplessness, mental weakness and physical impotency is explicitly telling us that among the many reasons for such changes [today], the main one is the decline of cow wealth.[27]

Here, the cow was clearly linked to Hindu nationalism, where she, like a benevolent mother, is a symbol of life and vitality as she feeds her child. Like a mother, she nourishes her sons with milk and ghee, and eventually makes them stronger.

These images and literature against cow slaughter portrayed Muslims as enemies of the cow and set the stage for an internal civil war in the early twentieth century. For the Hindus, to kill Muslims and free cows from their clutches became an ethical responsibility.[28] According to G. R. Thursby, a writer on British–Indian relations, collective violence between Hindus and Muslims was part and parcel of everyday life, with most conflicts focused on questions of cattle and vegetarianism. Thursby reported fifteen serious episodes of violence in British-administered north India between 1883 and 1891. As the years wore on, these riots became more intense and ubiquitous. "Cow riots" broke out in Fyzabad in 1912, Patna in 1916, and the Shahabad district of Bihar in 1917. During these riots in Bihar alone, which lasted from September 28 to October 10, Muslim houses in 170 villages were looted, 26 mosques were damaged, and 30 persons were killed, with 132 others wounded. Thursby's report called the riot a "general uprising" worse than 1857 Indian mutiny, noting that the riot was planned a month advance.[29]

These riots were executed under the leadership of Maharajas and zamindars as well as the educated elite of the Home Rule movement, gau-rakshaks and gau-sabhas. Another procession of cattle intended for slaughter through Saran district resulted in a series of communal disturbances, culminating in the Basantpur riots. Initially, a group of Hindus barred Muslim butchers entering the district. Two days later, another group of twenty-five Hindus clashed with Muslims taking another route into the district. Over time, the number of Hindu rioters increased to two hundred. Muslim butchers keep switching their routes until they reached a nearby police station in Basantpur to seek assistance. Ultimately, police moved the cattle to their station compound, then tried to disperse the crowd which had gathered nearby. According to the inspector, the crowd responded to his request for dispersal by chanting the names of Hindu gods and goddess "*Pohari Baba ki jai, Mohabir jee ka jai, Kali jee ka jai, gye dey do* ("long live Pohari Baba, long live Mohabir, long live Kali, give us the cows") and left the compound only after buckshot killed two rioters and wounding several others. The angry crowd jeered, "To-day you have escaped, but to-morrow we will see how you will fare," suggesting further outbreaks of violence.[30]

Cattle veneration separated Hindus from both Muslims Indians and British colonizers. In 1889, in one gaurakshini rally, in Amritsar, a *sadhu* (a Brahman Hindu hermit) proposed warfare against the colonizers citing that they, like Muslims, mistreat cows.[31] Similarly, anti-British overtones were conspicuous among Hindu crowds during cattle riots particularly when the Basantpur Commissariat came to the rescue of the Muslim butchers. According to the police inspector at the scene of the riot, the crowd warned him if the cattle was not released "it would be worse for the Saheb lob [British]." Several days before the riot broke out, Hindu leaders proclaimed, "a wind has come from the west, and Ram been [*sic*] born, and the Hindu Raj is at hand."[32] Therefore, political debates and cow riots demonstrated that Indian vegetarianism not only reinforced distinctions between natives and British colonizers but exacerbated longstanding tensions between Indian religious and social groups, celebrating high-caste Hindus as the arbiters of genuine Indian identity and nationalism.

For British administrators, therefore, riots represented not only a threat to public order but to the very existence of their rule in India. Veteran British administrators approached these agitations with extreme caution. British critics charged that the newly constituted Indian National Congress, which mainly consisted of Western-educated, "middle class" Hindus, was using religion to generate popular support for Indian independence. According to other British observers, these agitations were also partly the product of various Hindu orthodox and reformist organizations such as the Sanatan Dharma (an orthodox form of Hinduism) and Arya Sama (a monotheistic Indian Hindu reform movement promoting values and principles of the Vedas). Still others held upwardly mobile trading castes, especially Marwaris, responsible. These groups, having reaped the benefits of *Pax Britannica*, were believed to be bankrolling the cause of Hindu orthodoxy to enhance their social status.[33] Whatever the reason, cow riots solidified Indian nationalism by challenging British colonial rule while simultaneously identifying Muslims as outsiders who collaborated with India's enemies, thereby reinforcing Hinduism and Indian identity as one and the same.

British colonizers, warry of losing control of India and anxious in the aftermath of religious clashes, moved to give more autonomy to India's local religious bodies in resolving internal disputes.[34] Act XX of 1863 established a policy in which British officials withdrew from any involvement with religious communities, and these principles were strengthened by subsequent legislation. In 1880, Ashley Eden proposed that a Board of Revenue, with the help of native committees, would address all disputes— keeping the British away from the charges of partiality and mismanagement.[35] This resulted in an uneven restriction on cow slaughter and meat-eating. Provinces and towns under the strict rule of Hindu princes imposed the strictest rules on cow slaughter, with violations resulted in cruel punishments, while Muslim rulers had milder attitudes towards cow slaughter and meat-eating.

However, following the 1857 Indian mutiny, British attitudes changed dramatically. According to C. J. Lyall, the "turbulent disposition of the Mohammadens to the British power" during the mutiny shifted British sympathy to the Hindus, as demonstrated by an order to forbid sacrifice except in the public slaughterhouses by the Collector of Bareilly.[36]

As several scholars have demonstrated, it was not until Gandhi's protests and advocacy that Indians developed a consensus equating Indian identity with vegetarianism.[37] For Gandhi, morals were closely linked with health, since he believed that only a perfectly moral person could achieve perfect health. The moral person, Gandhi believed, was the one who eschewed impurity and searched for the purity in all aspects of living. Here, Gandhi echoes the Hindu belief that the ultimate goal of an individual soul is the union with the universal spirit. And anything that hampers the union should be avoided. Even Gandhi's ideologies and concerns like *Satyagraha* (military non-violence), *Ahimsa* (respect for all living things), and *Swaraj* (self-governance) were extensions of this belief, as were his preoccupation with diet, sex, and hygiene. For Gandhi, resistance to British colonizers did not require Indians to eat meat like their enemies.[38] Instead, Indians should be spiritually pure and intellectually engaged. These two attributes were impossible if one was polluted, and since meat was described as inherently polluting in the Vedas, Gandhi insisted that all forms of meat-eating should be abandoned.

While addressing the members of the *Rashtriya Yuvak Sangh* (National Association of Youth) in 1942, he half-jokingly boosted the morale of the young boys with bodies like his, that is, "completely devoid of muscles":

> Try to follow my ideals as far as you can. For that we should have a good physique. We have to build our muscles by regular exercise. But that should not be done to indulge in violence. To become a Shadow is not our ideal. . . . Our ideal is to become tough labourers, and our exercises should be towards that end.[39]

Similarly, the act of inflicting any pain on any living creature could corrupt one's soul and served as a reflection of morality. The killing of animals, therefore, demeaned one's morals and soul. Swaraj, for Gandhi, was not limited to material politics. Self-governance meant following dietary habits native to one's land and culture. For Gandhi, eating meat, a western practice, was a means of colonizing the indigenous Indian culture. Indians, therefore, should abstain from a meat-eating diet in order to physically throw the colonizers out of India. Gandhi (an ardent adherent of purity) and his followers interpreted meat-eating as detrimental to transcendental aspects of Indian social life—especially religious, spiritual, or ascetic practices associated with foods that possessed qualities of purity, freshness, radiance, and calmness. According to Gandhi and his followers, satvik (pure) Indians should seek these qualities in themselves, therefore they encouraged Indians to completely abstain from meat-eating as a mode of progress towards an Indian identity that was usurped by the colonizers.[40]

Ultimately, India's anti-colonial resistance not only resulted in geographical bifurcation of the country but in the splitting of religious, caste, and culinary beliefs. The making of Indian vegetarian identity elevated Brahmanical religious sentiments and Hindu religion in its most orthodox form while marginalizing the culture of Muslims in particular and diversity of the country in general.

1. This pattern of colonizers transforming the culture and diets of colonial subjects can be seen prior and subsequent to the British colonization of India. For other examples, see: Jeffrey M. Pilcher, *Food in World History* (New York, London: Routledge, 2006): 71; Warren Belasco, *Meals to Come: A History of the Future of Food* (Berkeley, Los Angles, London: University of California Press, 2006): 8–9; John W. Dower, *War without Mercy: Race and Power in the Pacific War* (New York: Pantheon Books, 1986).

2. Buchanon-Hamilton, "Appendix of Statistical Tables," in *Eastern India,* ed. Martin Montgomery (London: W. M. Allen and Co., 1838): 699–708.

3. A. H. Leith, "A Contribution to Dietetics," *Transactions of the Medical and Physical Society of Bombay* 1 (1851–52): 114–27.

4. D. R. McCay, *Investigations into the Jail Dietaries of the United Provinces with Some Observations on the Influence of Dietary on the Physical Development and Well-Being of the People of the United Provinces* (Calcutta: Superintendent of Government Printing, 1912): 188.

5. Lord Roberts, *Forty-One Years in India: From Subaltern to Commander-in-Chief* (London, 1897): 1:383, 441–43; P. D. Bonarjee, *A Handbook of the Fighting Races of India* (New Delhi, 1975); George McMunn, *The Martial Races of India* (London, 1933).

6. Lizzie Collingham, *Curry: A Tale of Cooks and Conquerors* (New York: Oxford University Press, 2006): 177; Kiranmayi Bhushi ed., introduction to *Farm to Fingers: The Culture and Politics of Food in Contemporary India* (New York: Cambridge University Press, 2018): 11.

7. James Johnson, *The Influence of Tropical Climates, More Especially the Climate of India, on European Constitutions* (London, 1813): 434.

8. Johnson, *Tropical Climates,* 434; Buchanan-Hamilton, *Eastern India,* 1:181, 2:110, 163.

9. Utsa Ray, *Culinary Culture in Colonial India: A Cosmopolitan Platter and the Middle-Class* (New Delhi: Cambridge University Press, 2015): 155, 176–77, 183.

10. Jayanta Sengupta, "Nation on a Platter: The Culture and Politics of Food and Cuisine in Colonial Bengal," *Modern Asian Studies* 44, no. 1 (January 2010): 95.

11. Chunilal Bose, *Food* (Calcutta: University of Calcutta, 1930): 93–94.

12. Bose, *Food,* 95.

13. Swami Vivekananda, letter to the editor of *Bharati,* dated Darjeeling, 24 April 1897, in Swami Vivekananda, *Patrabali* (Letters), 5th ed. (Calcutta: Udbodhan, 1987): 537.

14. Bhudeb Mukhopadhyay, *Samajik prabandha,* with an introduction and exegesis by Jahnavikumar Chakrabarty, ed. (Kolikata: Paschimbanga Rajya Pustak Parshad, 1981): 43–45.

15. Sengupta, "Nation on a Platter," 95; Ray, *Culinary Culture,* 19, 156; Bhushi, introduction to *Farm to Fingers,* 11–12.

16. Romila Thapar, "The History Debate and School Textbooks in India: A Personal Memoir," *History Workshop Journal* 67, no. 1 (Spring, 2009): 87–98; D. N. Jha, *The Myth of the Holy Cow* (New Delhi: Narayana, 2002): 95.

17. C. A. Bayly, *The Local Roots of Indian Politics: Allahabad, 1880–1920* (New Delhi: Oxford University Press, 1975): 57.

18. Translation of *Gari Benair* (prayer of the cow), Madhubani Gaurakshini Sabha, Darbhanga, Forbes Report, Appendix E.

19. C. J. Lyall, "Case for the Consideration of the Honorable Advocate General," Secretary, GOI, Home Dept., in L/P&J/6/367. end. 3.

20. Note by Gurdial Singh, Home Member, Nabha, dated February 22, 1929, Punjab State Archives, Patiala (PSA), Nabha, PM's office, 4133/4224E; "Bye Laws for the Control and Regulation of the Slaughter-House, Nabha," issued on August 14, 1926, *ibid.*, 5703/5768E; and note on press conference at Mahakma Khas, Kotah, dated November 16, 1944, Rajasthan State Archives, Bikaner (RSA), Kotah, confidential. File 27A. In Jodhpur, too, there were complex regulations about what animals could be taken where. She-goats, for example, could be taken through Jodhpur Sireh Bazaar only along two designated roads, during which time it was deemed lawful for Hindus to rescue goats they suspected were being taken for slaughter. Notification by Maharaja of Jodhpur dated April 29, 1929, RSA, Jodhpur, Social, C 2/6A of 1929–41.

21. Fort. report on Rajputana for period ending September 15, 1945, OIOC, L/P&S/13/1442; and office note dated January 5, 1941, RSA, Jodhpur, Social, C 2/6A of 1929–41.

22. Edward S. Haynes, "Comparative Industrial Development in 19th and 20th Century India: Alwar State and Gurgaon District," *South Asia* 3, no. 2 (1980): 31.

23. Government of India (GOI), *Proceedings of the Home Department* (Secret), 52, no. 162 (1919). Appendix 1–3, India Office Library, London.

24. Christopher Pinney, "The Nation (Un)Pictured? Chromolithography and 'Popular' Politics in India, 1878–1995," *Critical Inquiry* 23 (Summer 1997): 841–47; Christopher Pinney, "Indian Magical Realism: Notes on Popular Visual Culture," *Subaltern Studies X,* ed. Gautum Bhadra, Gyan Prakash and Susie Tharu (Delhi: Oxford University Press, 1999): 221–24, 230–33; 210–213 and 2 KW/December 1893, Public, A, Home Dept (NAI).

25. [5.] 210–213 and 2 KW/December 1893, Public, A, Home Deptt (NAI). Also mentioned in 309–414/January 1894, Public, B, Home Deptt (NAI).

26. Kriparam Mishra, "Manhar," *Gauraksha Prakas,* (Moradabad, 1925).

27. Mishra, "Manhar."

28. Anthony Parel, "The political symbolism of the cow in India," *Journal of Commonwealth Political Studies* (2008): 184, 192. Charu Gupta, "The Icon of Mother in Late Colonial North India: 'Bharat Mata,' 'Matri Bhasha' and 'Gau Mata,'" *Economic and Political Weekly* 36, no. 45 (2001): 4297.

29. G. R. Thursby, *Hindu–Muslim Relations in British India: A Study of Controversy, Conflict and Communal Movements in Northern India 1923–1928* (Leiden: E. J. Brill, 1975): 80–82.

30. Anand A. Yang, "Sacred Symbol and Sacred Space in Rural India: Community Mobilization in the "Anti-Cow Killing" Riot of 1893," *Society for the Comparative Study of Society and History* 22, no. 4 (October, 1980): 576–96.

31. Peter Robb, "The Challenge of Gau Mata: British Policy and Religious Change in India, 1880–1916," *Modern Asian Studies* 20, no. 2 (1986): 297.

32. Testimony of Inspector Parmeshwar in *Basantpur Trial,* 36.

33. For different official interpretations, see: "Measure to be taken to control the agitation for the Protection of Kine" and enclosures, in India, Public and

Judicial Papers, L/P&J/6/ 367, no. 257 of 1894. This file consists of the major reports from the various provinces that were affected by the anti-cow-killing agitation.

34. Ian Copland, "What to Do about Cows? Princely versus British Approaches to a South Asian Dilemma," *Bulletin of the School of Oriental and African Studies* 68, no. 1 (2005): 61–63.

35. H. Public A 163–71, February, 1881.

36. C. J. Lyall, 8 June, 1894, H. Public A 134–43, June 1894.

37. Rosinka Chaudhuri, *Freedom and Beef Steaks: Colonial Calcutta Culture* (New Delhi: Orient Blackswan, 2012): 25–26; Tristram Stuart, *The Bloddless Revolution: Radical Vegetarians and the Discovery of India* (New York: Harper Press, 2008): 425–26; Leela Gandhi, *Affective Communication: Anticolonial Thought and the Politics of Friendship* (New Delhi: Permanent Black, 2006): 114.

38. Stuart, *Bloodless Revolution*, 425–26; Leela, *Affective Communication*, 113–14.

39. Mohandas Karamchand Gandhi, *The Collected Works of Mahatma Gandhi* (Delhi: The Publications Division, Ministry of Information and Broadcasting, Government of India), 76:158.

40. Parama Roy, *Alimentary Tracts: Appetites, Aversions, and the Postcolonial* (Durham, NC: Duke University Press, 2010): 83.

CHAPTER 5

Hungry Empire

Manchuria and the Failed Food Autarky in Imperial Japan, 1931–41

JING SUN

"Hideo, do you know where this snack is made?"
"The factory of snacks?"
"Of course, that is right. But the ingredient, wheat, mostly comes from foreign countries. So, half of this snack is made abroad."
"Then we cannot eat it carelessly. . . ."
"Well, snacks like this one are still fine. There are much more that Japan lacks nowadays."

— "Where do snacks come from?" 1932[1]

In the 1932 *Juvenile Reader on Nation* (*Shōnen kokka tokuhon*), young Hideo had the above dialogue with his father before eating a snack. The snack triggered Hideo's appetite for further knowledge of what his "most powerful nation" could possibly be short of.[2] Reading from a news journal, his educated mother, Fujiko, offered Hideo one answer:

> In the past, our country was called Mizuho no kuni . . . It is a wonderful place to grow rice. However, due to the increasing population, there is annually a shortage of nine hundred million koku rice now in our homeland . . . Buying food from a foreign country would disadvantage us. In case of exigency when we cannot buy foreign

food, people would be starved to death. Japanese soldiers would never win a war while only drinking water, however tough they are. The country should attempt to supply to the people most of their food. Nothing is more important than this.[3]

Edited by the Ministry of Education and published by The Social Education Society (*Shakai kyōikukai*), the *Reader* represents only parts of the Japanese government's efforts to call attention to the importance of food autarky in the Japanese Empire. Following the end of World War I, anxiety increased in the Japanese mainland surrounding the need to ensure sufficient food supply for the swelling population. "Food autarky" (*shokuryō jikyū*) dominated the discussion about Japan's food policy and many regarded it as the solution to Japan's "food problem" (*Shokuryō mondai*).[4] Gradually, this led to a broadening social support of the idea and its implementation to turn Manchuria into Japan's new imperial granary. However, such obsession with food autarky and Manchuria's agricultural potential turned out to be fatal to the Japanese Empire, which was engaged in an escalating war with China after 1937.

This chapter examines how Japan's fixation with food autarky influenced its political and military actions between 1931 and 1941. It engages in the discourse that recognizes food issues, particularly food supply, as crucial factors in shaping the history of human societies. As historians have demonstrated, the fear for or the reality of hunger can impact a state's political and military decisions.[5] Japan was no exception. Building upon the recent scholarship on food circulation and its social and political implications in the Japanese Empire, this study reveals the irony of Japan's empire-building in Manchuria and later its war planning.[6] Doing so, it hopes to contribute to a more inclusive understanding of the role of food in warfare, colonialism, and empire-building in world history.[7]

To Manchuria: The Land of Hope

I tried to read the newspapers, where miserable news about fights, murders and suicides appears every day, expressing struggle for life. A better next year is hardly imaginable.

—Ōtani Hayato (Ishikawa Shingo), December 1931.[8]

At the end of 1931, under the pseudonym Hayato Ōtani, the Imperial Japanese Navy officer Shingo Ishikawa published a book entitled *Japan's*

Crisis (*Nihon no kiki*), wherein he spoke frankly about his low expectations for the coming new year.[9] His prediction was partially correct. Caught in the middle of the global economic depression, Japan had experienced a bizarre predicament in 1930, when millions of peasants suffered a "bumper crop famine" (*hōsaku kikin*)—a problem wherein the market forces surrounding high yields of a good harvest caused prices to collapse, subsequently undermining the ability of farmers to cover their costs.[10] Two years later, large parts of rural Japan were still suffering. The cause, however, was different. The low temperatures in the summer of 1931 shocked northeast Japan, causing an extremely poor harvest.[11] In Hokkaido and Aomori, rice production decreased the most, respectively by 59.3 percent and 46 percent.[12] Despite the government's relief measures and donations nationwide, the rural population in these areas remained in distress for food and money. Over the next two years, news coverage of "starving children" (*kesshoku jidō*) and "daughter trafficking" (*musume no miuri*) was overwhelming in national media. Eating only roots of trees and grasses, thousands of school children starved and suffered malnutrition. Many quit schools due to illness and some died from hunger.[13] In order to make money and avoid starvation, some families turned to selling daughters into prostitution or forcing them to work in factories as cheap laborers, and overall the scale of trafficking young girls expanded.[14]

These domestic economic difficulties were not the only cause of public unrest in the early 1930s; political turmoil also contributed. On September 18, 1931, the Kwantung Army engineered an explosion on the South Manchuria Railway and soon began overrunning Manchuria. In December 1931, after failing to reach consensus on how to keep the Kwantung Army and the Manchuria situation under control, the Wakatsuki Cabinet was forced to resign after less than a year in power. The Inukai Cabinet that followed did not last long either. On May 15, 1932, Prime Minister Tsuyoshi Inukai was assassinated at his official residence in a failed coup d'état attempt. Admiral Makoto Saitō was appointed as the new prime minister. The era of the party cabinet system that had lasted since the 1920s ended, making it more difficult to balance the civilian and military powers in Japanese politics.[15]

Japan also faced diplomatic challenges. Following its occupation of Manchuria and the subsequent invasion of Shanghai, international criticism of Japan started to grow. In January 1932, Chinese Foreign Minister Eugene Chen (Chen Youren) requested that Yan Qinghui, the Chinese representative at the League of Nations, call for an economic blockade of

Japan by member countries.[16] In the United States, ten influential intellectuals petitioned the government for American cooperation with the League of Nations on economically blockading Japan.[17] In Britain, the League of Nations supporters took a similar position. Even though the blockade never happened, the attempt caused many people in Japan to fear the possibility of suffering, as German citizens did in World War I, from starvation, malnutrition, and eventually death.[18]

Manchuria, the new territory and anticipated lifeline of the Japanese Empire, eased people's anxieties. Long portrayed as a place with boundless fertile soil, unlimited agricultural resources, and opportunities to experiment with new agricultural technologies, Manchuria was never more appealing to the Japanese people than in the early 1930s. Ishikawa (and the Japanese public at large) believed the fundamental cause of famines was Japan's reliance on food importation. Thus, he insisted, to revitalize the rural economy (and thereby the national economy), Japan must achieve food autarky.[19] To attain this goal and "the survival of Japanese nation" in the ongoing global crisis, Ishikawa believed Manchuria was crucial.[20] When travelling in Manchuria, Ishikawa saw millions of Chinese emigrants settling down and believed more were to come. These emigrants would form a large labor force that could produce food for Japan and potentially consume any surplus rice.[21] Some leading financial figures believed that Manchuria dispelled people's fear of economic blockade since it would supply Japan with wheat and beans, which together amounted to 75 percent of Japanese food importation. With new technology and the cultivation of paddy fields, it would become a helpful rice supplier. In a word, Manchuria appeared to provide the answer to Japan's food problems. Manchuria would "assure food autarky" in Japan and food shortage would be "out of the question."[22]

For more ordinary people, particularly the desperate peasants in northeast Japan and Hokkaido, Manchuria was a new world of hope to find "bread and land."[23] They desired a new life there, away from the overpopulated mainland, where they could only starve.[24] Such enthusiasm urged the Ministry of Colonial Affairs, immigration companies, the South Manchuria Railway Company, and the Ministry of Agriculture and Forestry to decide on a policy.[25] In August 1932, the Ministry of Colonial Affairs requested a 300,000-yen budget to help the first "guided emigrants" settle in Manchuria.[26] At the cabinet meeting on August 16, with the support from the Minister of War and the Minister of Agriculture and Forestry, the Minister of Colonial Affairs, Nagai Ryūtarō, proposed a plan for state-sponsored emigration to Manchuria. According to these ministers, encouraging mainland peasants to emigrate to Manchuria was the path to Manchuria–Japan coprosperity and a solution to Japan's food problems.[27] Despite the dissent from the Minister of Finance, Takahashi Korekiyo, the budget was approved at the National Diet. In October, under the support of the Ministry of Colonial Affairs, the first 493 settler-farmer families departed Japan for Jiamusi in eastern Manchuria.[28]

The arrival of these emigrants marked the beginning of a fourteen-year state project of Japanese agricultural emigration to Manchuria. In 1933, the Saitō Cabinet listed Manchurian agricultural migration as the most urgent project to implement, so as to assure "the gains from the Manchuria Incident."[29] Between 1932 and 1936, the Japanese government sponsored the agricultural emigration annually, sending a total of 2,369 settler-farmer families to Manchuria during the period.[30] By the end of 1936, the total number of Japanese settler-farmers in Manchuria was over ten thousand.[31] After the assassination of Takahashi, who most strongly opposed the project, opposition to the emigration project decisively weakened in 1936. In August of that year, the new Hiroda Cabinet announced the large-scale agricultural emigration to Manchuria as Japan's national policy, ending the previous "experimental stage".[32] In June 1937, sending another 980 settler-farmer families to Manchuria, the Japanese government began to implement its plan for the first five years of a twenty-year emigration project.[33] According to the plan, Japan was to send a hundred thousand families to Manchuria from 1937 to 1941; and in twenty years, the number was to reach one million.[34]

The Broken Promise

In the early 1930s, agriculture in Manchuria seemed promising. Nagai Sōhei, an employee in the agricultural division of the South Manchuria Railway Company, wrote that "land in Manchuria is fertile and boundless; it can produce almost all agriculture products that we import . . . like rice, wheat, soybeans, red beans, and potatoes."[35] Mainland people found out they could make bread, snacks, and even coffee from Manchurian soybeans, eat sorghum shells like chocolates, and have cheap Manchurian buckwheat-meal instead of expensive foreign oatmeal.[36] Confidence in successful rice cultivation in Manchuria also swelled. Manchuria, once thought of as a frozen and barbarous place, was later proven suitable for growing rice thanks to the efforts of the Koreans and Japanese, who had been experimenting on rice cultivation for decades.[37] By 1930, rice farmland spread from south to north Manchuria and produced 1.2 million *koku*. It was still a small amount, but Japanese officials hoped that, as rice farmland expanded, the number would reach ten million.[38]

Japanese officials expected emigration to help develop agriculture in Manchuria and guarantee the food autarky of Japan, thereby solving any possible food problem with food supply. For the people who supported the project, the logic was simple. Japanese settler-farmers would achieve self-sufficiency in food in Manchuria. Their involvement in the local agricultural production could help Japan control the trading rights of Manchurian food products, transforming Manchuria into Japan's granary.[39] To achieve this goal, planners of the emigration project in the Ministry of Colonial Affairs and the South Manchuria Railway Company suggested prioritizing rice cultivation. It was "most profitable" to grow, it would enable the settler-farmers to be self-sufficient in their staple and "contribute to solving the problem of rice shortage" in mainland Japan.[40] From 1932 to 1936, following this guideline, the "experimental emigrants" set foot in the uncultivated lands in northern Manchuria and turned them into rice fields.[41] By 1937, acreage of rice fields in Manchuria reached about 3,143.8 square kilometers (776,850 acres or 1,213.8 square miles); the rice production increased to 3.135 million koku, nearly tripling the 1930 numbers.[42]

Despite the seemingly hopeful results from rice cultivation in Manchuria, Japan did not acquire what it had desired. The positive numbers created an illusion of abundance that kept people's hope high for the potential of Manchurian agriculture and lured more mainland peasants into the uncultivated northern lands. But this was only part of the story of food and agriculture in Manchuria. In reality, Manchuria was also an importer of rice and wheat flour and, beginning in the early 1930s, depended increasingly on mainland Japan for its food supply. Mainland peasants brought their rice-growing knowledge as well as rice-eating habit to the continent.[43] As the number of Japanese immigrants in Manchuria climbed, demand for rice also grew. Annual rice importation in Manchuria rose from eighty thousand koku in 1932 to over seven hundred thousand koku in 1936—a quarter of its total consumption. French Indochina provided most of the rice, followed by China, India, Hong Kong, colonial Korea, and mainland Japan.[44] Japan was also the primary supplier of wheat flour for Manchuria, of which the territory faced an annual shortage of at least 1.8 million koku.[45] Australia followed Japan as the second largest exporter. Production of beans, sorghum, and wheat decreased, and production of millet and corn grew little (see chart below). Accordingly, the overall grain production in Manchuria dropped from 18.4 million to 15.1 million tons, close to an 18 percent loss.[46]

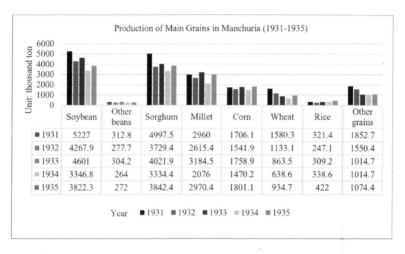

Production of Main Grains in Manchuria (1931-1935)

Year	Soybean	Other beans	Sorghum	Millet	Corn	Wheat	Rice	Other grains
1931	5227	312.8	4997.5	2960	1706.1	1580.3	321.4	1852.7
1932	4267.9	277.7	3729.4	2615.4	1541.9	1133.1	247.1	1550.4
1933	4601	304.2	4021.9	3184.5	1758.9	863.5	309.2	1014.7
1934	3346.8	264	3334.4	2076	1470.2	638.6	338.6	1014.7
1935	3822.3	272	3842.4	2970.4	1801.1	934.7	422	1074.4

Year   ■ 1931   ■ 1932   ■ 1933   ▧ 1934   ▩ 1935

Production of main grains in Manchuria, 1931–35. *Figure created by author.*[47]

Pessimism about Japan's Manchuria policies existed from the start, and these voices strengthened in the mid-1930s. As early as 1932, Ozaki Yukio commented that "no research could support the idea" that emigration to Manchuria would help solve Japan's food problems.[48] In his words, the idea "was not worthy of discussion":

> Our people of Yamato did not even like moving to Korea, Taiwan and Hokkaido. It is impossible that they would emigrate in large scale to Manchuria. From experiences in Taiwan and Kwangtung area, living standard there is low. Immigrants will have to compete with the diligent local people. Even with Manchuria as our sphere of interest, we cannot obtain food there for free. . . . Opinions of Manchuria being our lifeline are merely emotional conjectures lacking honest consideration of facts and national interests.[49]

As emigration to Manchuria continued, social reflections on the project began to rise. People demanded a reexamination of the accomplishments of the emigration, rather than an empty rhetoric of hope. In particular, the difficulty of growing rice in the cold weather of northern

Manchuria caught people's attention.[50] Enthusiasm for agriculture in Manchuria evaporated into disillusionment. One of these critics was Kōzui Ōtani, a Buddhist who later became the advisor to the Konoe Cabinet during the war. In 1936, he spoke about the failure straightforwardly:

> Agricultural development in Manchuria failed. I cannot lie.... People who moved to Manchuria are not used to eating sorghum, millet and corn. These grains are exported to the mainland as animal fodder. How laughable! For what do our people abandon the civilized life for a barbarian one? Such stupidity exists because we cannot renounce the old belief that Manchuria is the land of abundance.[51]

Being dependent on food supplies from mainland Japan and foreign countries, Manchuria failed to bring the anticipated amount of rice supply to the Japanese empire. Nevertheless, it did become one of the imperial granaries that enabled a smooth inner-empire circulation of food between 1932 and 1936. Manchurian millet was transported to colonial Korea as the staple on the peninsula so that Korean rice could feed the mainland Japanese people. Sorghum, corn, and soybeans were shipped to mainland Japan as well as other parts of the empire.[52] However, in 1937, when the Japanese government and the Kwantung Army leadership endeavored to create a self-sufficient Manchuria, the system of food supply began to collapse.[53]

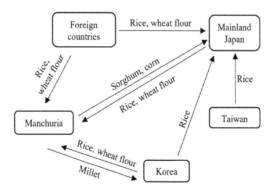

Food supply system of pre-1937 Japanese Empire. *Figure created by author.*

The Hungry Wartime Empire

On January 25, 1937, in the new five-year plan to develop Manchuria, the Kwantung Army Headquarters redefined the role of Manchuria in the economy of the Japanese empire. According to the plan, Manchuria was to become self-sufficient and, in case of emergency, "to provide resources that Japan might lack."[54] Rice produced in Manchuria was listed as a war material and the task of increasing its production was assigned to the local Japanese settler-farmers. Following the guideline, the Manchukuo government planned to invest heavily in fostering local agricultural development, particularly the increase of rice production.[55] Also as a part of the plan, in June of 1937 the government legalized a monopoly over the production, sale, and trade of rice, wheat, and other agricultural products.

With robust financial support planned, the grand design of a self-sufficient Manchuria seemed encouraging. However, this design soon became an empty promise. Soon after the Second Sino-Japanese War broke out in July 1937, the food supply system of the Japanese Empire began to collapse. In 1937, wheat flour importation from the United States, Canada, and Australia to Manchuria was suspended.[56] Meanwhile, the supply from China decreased in large amount.[57] Losing most foreign supplies, Manchuria became more dependent on the inner-empire wheat flour supply, which could no longer reach previous levels.[58] Control over trade in the wartime empire shut the door for nearly all foreign wheat flour. Accordingly, wheat flour importation to mainland Japan dropped dramatically from around 2.27 million koku in 1936 to 1.37 million koku in 1937; and by 1939, the number dropped to 0.23 million koku.[59] Due to such shortages in wheat flour supply, the price of wheat flour rose and remained high during wartime, making the once-affordable staple a rare commodity.[60] Consuming less wheat flour, non-Japanese residents in Manchuria turned to rice, the price of which was lower and more stable. As a result, the total amount of rice eaten in Manchuria increased.

Manchurian residents were not alone in developing a stronger appetite for rice during the war. After occupying large areas in northern China, mainland Japan started to export rice there, to support local troops in their occupation and management of the new territory. Promising to feed the "little brothers" like Manchuria and northern China, mainland Japan became the main rice supplier for its imperial subjects on the continent.[61] Rice production in the empire, however, could not satisfy the increasing appetite. As the war with China persisted, rice shortages became pressing and eventually needed to be addressed. From 1939 to 1940, colonial Korea and west Japan experienced an unprecedented drought that heavily damaged rice cultivation.[62] Rice production in mainland Japan decreased by two percent, from 67.3 million koku in 1938 to 65.9 million koku in 1939.[63] In colonial Korea, rice production dropped more dramatically from 24.1 million koku in 1938 to 14.4 million koku, amounting to a loss of 40 percent. As the other vital rice supplier in the empire, colonial Taiwan also saw a decrease of seven percent in rice production, from 15.1 million koku in 1938 to 13.9 million koku in 1939.[64] In total during that period, colonial Korea and Taiwan supplied mainland Japan with 9.6 million koku.[65] Even after importing foreign rice from Thailand and India, the mainland Japanese home front still faced a rice shortage of 3.74 million koku.[66]

In this hungrier empire, the burden on the Japanese settler-farmers in Manchuria became heavier. Following the droughts, a Japan–Manchuria–Korea "triangle barter system" took shape.[67] While rice from colonial Korea would feed the mainland Japanese population, coarse grains from Manchuria were transported to colonial Korea in large amount to feed the people there.[68] Demand for Manchurian coarse grains thus grew and led to an urgent requirement for increases in the agricultural production. This, in turn, required the Japanese government to send more settler-farmers to Manchuria. In 1939, the number of new Japanese settler-farmer families who migrated to Manchuria reached 12,270, doubling the number in 1938.[69] This number kept increasing in 1940 and 1941. During the course of 1941, 72,600 Japanese settler-farmer families settled in wartime Manchuria; and the total number of Japanese settler-farmers there reached 180,000.[70] Like those who had already settled down, these settler-farmers also preferred rice to other grains. As a result, the total number of rice-consumers in wartime Manchuria rose and was expected to keep growing.[71]

At all home fronts of the empire, words like "thrifty" (*setsuyaku*) and "substitutes" (*daiyōhin*) dominated the discussions about measures to resolve the problem of the rice shortage. In early 1940, the colonial government in Taiwan rationed the population a maximum of three hundred grams of rice per person per day.[72] In colonial Korea, residents endured food shortages by limiting themselves to eating two meals per day, sometimes even one.[73] In Manchuria, Japanese immigrants were urged to mix rice with local grains like sorghum, corn, millet, and soybeans.[74] Cooking specialists also brought recipes for Manchurian mixed rice back to the mainland home front, where saving rice became a new law after October 1939. The Japanese government banned fine-milled white rice, reduced the consumption and production of rice alcohol, and encouraged people to eat other coarse grains.[75]

While attempting to limit rice consumption in the empire, the wartime Japanese government also searched for more supply. As the protracted war with China continued, the Japanese government bought more rice from Southeast Asia to feed the swelling hungry empire. In February 1940, about 108,000 koku of "Rangoon rice" from French Indochina (*Rangun-mai*) was shipped to colonial Korea.[76] In March, the "stiff rice" from Thailand and French Indochina reappeared on mainland Japanese people's dinner tables after twenty-two years.[77] Cooking experts started to teach people new methods to cook it as deliciously as Japanese rice.[78] Having foreign rice became the "new normal" in the wartime empire.

Just when the rice from Southeast Asia seemingly eased the food shortage in the Japanese empire, global turmoil began to destabilize the situation again. After the outbreak of war in Europe in September 1939, news of the invasion of France and Great Britain reached their colonies in Southeast Asia. In June 1940, keeping a close watch on the local situation in British Burma, Consul Kuga suggested that the Japanese government purchase rice quickly, in order to avoid future difficulties the conflicts in Europe might cause.[79] In early 1941, Japanese diplomats discussed a possible Burmese ban on rice exportation.[80] Similarly, in Thailand, an officer in the Japanese Consulate called on the Japanese government to deal with the increasing purchase of rice by Great Britain, as well as the efforts of local ethnic Chinese to support China's war against Japan.[81]

To fundamentally solve the problem of rice shortage and achieve the long-awaited food autarky in the empire, Japanese war planners believed that Japan ought to "go south" to secure rice supply for the empire. In March 1941, when making a plan to invade Southeast Asia, the Ministry of War listed "obtaining the 9 million koku of rice from French Indochina and Thailand" as one of the goals for the coming war.[82] On November 12, 1941, Yukawa Mototake, head of the Office of Food Administration (*shokuryō kanrikyoku*), made a night-time broadcast to the Japanese people that clarified the next move to feed the hungry empire. Japan was to expand to Southeast Asia, "the Ukraine of the Greater East Asian Co-Prosperity Sphere," or in other words, the new imperial rice granary:

As the situation in China continues, I feel more keenly that rice from the south is needed . . . As the leader of the Co-Prosperity Sphere, Japan must secure rice from south for the sake of the people on the Chinese continent. If the ABCD blockade [imposed on Japan from British, Dutch, American, and Chinese enemies] obstructs us from getting the rice, it is threatening the lifeline of the Co-Prosperity Sphere. Paddy fields in French Indochina and Thai were like virgin territory left [uncared for] in nature . . . We can expect that rice production there will definitely increase.[83]

Conclusion

This chapter demonstrates how concerns about food supply shaped Japan's political and military policies from 1932 to 1941. In the early 1930s, mainland Japanese peasants envisioned Manchuria as a new world of hope, with boundless lands and fertile soil. Policymakers saw Manchuria as the promised land of bumper harvests and the key to the guaranteed food autarky of the empire. A state project of agricultural emigration to Manchuria thus took shape to turn Manchuria into Japan's new imperial granary. However, the project failed to help the empire achieve its food autarky. Manchuria became dependent on the inner-empire food supply system that quickly collapsed when the Second Sino-Japanese War broke out in 1937.

From 1937 to 1941, as Japan continued sending settler-farmers to Manchuria while fighting a protracted war with China, the empire became hungrier, particularly for rice. After the shock of unprecedented droughts in 1939 and 1940, the hungry wartime empire moved south hoping to secure a new granary. In early 1942, after occupying French Indochina, the Japanese wartime government drew a new blueprint for food supplies in the Greater East Asian Co-Prosperity Sphere.[84] Following colonial Korea and Taiwan, the new territory in the south officially became the third rice supplier in the wartime Japanese empire.

As argued in this chapter, Japan's quest for food autarky, to a great extent, fueled its agricultural emigration project in Manchuria and later its war-planning efforts during World War II. These events illustrate how anxiety over food shortages can serve as a motivating force for a state's decision-making in politics and military action. In exploring the Japanese case, this study aims to dialogue with the increasing scholarship that investigates the role of food broadly in the making of modern world history.

NOTES

1. Monbushō kōnai shakai kyōikukai, *Shōnen kokka tokuhon* (Tokyo: Shakai kyōikukai, 1932): 38.
2. Monbushō kōnai shakai kyōikukai, *Shōnen kokka tokuhon*, 4–5.
3. Monbushō kōnai shakai kyōikukai, *Shōnen kokka tokuhon*, 41–43. *Mizuho no kuni* is an ancient name for Japan, meaning literally the land of vigorous rice and metaphorically the land of rice harvest. *Koku* is a traditional Japanese unit of volume for rice. One *koku* equals approximately 180 liters, with an average weight of 150–160 kg.
4. Regarding the discussion about food autarky in 1920s Japan, see: Go Kitano, "Nihon no dairiku seisaku to bōkokurei mondai," *Shigaku zasshi* 119, no. 9 (2010): 1551–74.
5. For discussion of anxiety related to food-supply and its impact on societies in world history, see: Alan F. Wilt, *Food for War: Agriculture and Rearmament in Britain before the Second World War* (New York: Oxford University Press, 2001): 1–51. More studies examine wartime management of food supply and transforming food culture on the home front, see, for example, Belinda J. Davis, *Home Fires Burning: Food, Politics, and Everyday Life in World War I Berlin* (Chapel Hill: The University of North Caroline Press, 2000): 237–46; Katarzyna J. Cwiertka, *Cuisine, Colonialism and Cold War: Food in Twentieth-century Korea* (London: Reaktion Books, 2012): 86–91; Ian Mosby, *Food Will Win the War: The Politics, Culture and Science of Food on Canada's Home Front* (Vancouver: UBC Press, 2014): 133–61.
6. Yusuke Takeuchi, "The Shifting Axis of Specialization Within the Japanese Empire: A Study of Railway Distribution of Cereals in Colonial Korea," in *Economic Activities Under the Japanese Colonial Empire,* ed. Minoru Sawai (Berlin: Springer, 2016): 51–76; Minoru Ōmameuda, *Kindai nihon no shokuryō seisaku: taigai izon beikoku kyōkyū kōzō no henyō* (Kyoto: Mineruva shobō, 1993): 263–333; Minoru Ōmameuda, "Senji shokuryō mondai no hassei," in *Kindai nihon to shokuminchi 5,* ed. Sōji Takasaki (Tokyo: Iwanami shoten, 1993): 177–98.
7. Cecilia Y. Leong-Salobir, *Food Culture in Colonial Asia: A Taste of Empire* (New York: Routledge, 2011); Elizabeth M. Collingham, *Curry: A Tale of Cooks and Conquerors* (Oxford: Oxford University Press, 2006); Elizabeth M. Collingham, *The Taste of War: World War II and the Battle for Food* (New York: Penguin Press, 2017).
8. Hayato Ōtani, *Nihon no kiki* (Tokyo: Moriyama shoten, 1931): 1.
9. Kazushige Todaka, *Kiki kaki nihon kaigun shi* (Kyoto: PHP Publishing, 2009): 25.
10. "Beika no sanraku kara nōson kyōkō jyōtai ni tenraku, chōya no dai mondaika sen," *Yomiuri Shimbun,* September 28, 1930. "Nōson kaku kaikyū no sangai shujusō," *Yomiuri Shimbun,* October 4, 1930; "Dai hōsaku to fu keiki," *Asahi Shimbun,* October 5, 1930.
11. Kyōchōkai, *Shōwa rokunendo ni okeru Hokkaido Tōhoku chihō no kyōsaku gaiyō* (Tokyo: Kyōchōkai, 1932): 9–12.
12. Fumio Yamashita, *Shōwa Tōhoku dai kyōsaku* (Akita-shi: Mumyosha Shuppan, 2001): 60–65.
13. "Kiga semaru ko ni sukui no shisha, tōhoku no kesshoku jidō kyūsai ni

monbushō ga shisatsuin haiken," *Yomiuri Shimbun*, November 29, 1931; "Jidō ga taisō chū batabata taoreru," *Asahi Shimbun*, December 9, 1931.

14. Yamashita, *Shōwa Tōhoku dai kyōsaku*, 83–94; "Kyōsaku ni tsukekomu musumekai no aku shūsenya, aomori chiho deha ni san en no tetsuke de," *Asahi Shimbun*, December 26, 1931; "Moguri shūsendan kyōsaku chi no jijo he mashu," *Yomiuri Shimbun*, January 31, 1933. For recent studies of correlation between rice production decrease, rural economic crisis and the increase of "daughter trafficking," see: Yutaka Harada and Susumu Annaka, "Musume no miuri ha shōwa kyōkō ki ni fueta no ka," *WINPEC Working Paper Series No. J1410* (June 2015): 23, http://www.waseda.jp/fpse/winpec/assets/uploads/2015 /07/5b470002101e3b8927c86e34d6fbcd2b.pdf.

15. Shinichi Kitaoka, *The Political History of Modern Japan: Foreign Relations and Domestic Politics*, trans. Robert D. Eldridge and Graham Leonard (New York: Routledge, 2018): 122–24.

16. "Tainichi keizai fūsa wo kakoku ni yōkyū se yo, chin shi kan daihyō ni kunden," *Asahi Shimbun*, January 24, 1931.

17. "Tainichi keizai fūsa seigan, beikoku no yūryokusha jū shi ga daitōryō ni," *Asahi Shimbun*, February 21, 1932.

18. Tomosaburō Takagi, *Keizai dankō kowaru ni tarazu: tōa monrō shugi he bakushin* (Tokyo: Chikura shobō, 1932): 76–7.

19. Ōtani, *Nihon no kiki*, 41.

20. Ōtani, *Nihon no kiki*, 74.

21. Ōtani, *Nihon no kiki*, 41, 74.

22. "Keizai fūsa kowaru ni tarazu, shokuryō hin hiryō tetsu mo jikkyū," *Yomiuri Shimbun*, February 5, 1932; Takagi, *Keizai dankō kowaru ni tarazu: tōa monrō shugi he bakushin*, 77, 90–100.

23. "Kajyō jinkō wo manmō he ijyū, nōrinshō de taisaku chōsa," *Asahi Shimbun*, March 27, 1932.

24. For study of anxiety over the population problems and its connection with the food problems in early twentieth-century Japan, see: Sidney Xu Lu, *The Making of Japanese Settler Colonialism* (Cambridge: Cambridge University Press, 2019): 183–233.

25. "Manmō he manmō he, afure deru imin no gun," *Yomiuri Shimbun*, March 27, 1932.

26. "Manshū imin hi nado takumu tūka yosan," *Yomiuri Shimbun*, August 5, 1932.

27. "Manshū imin seisaku no kahi, kakugi de toki naranu gekiron, takushō rikushō nōshō to zōshō teishō no tairitsu," *Yomiuri Shimbun*, August 17, 1932.

28. "Inokori shokuryo jisshi no ken," 17 September 1932, C04011294800, Manju dai nikki (fu) 132/2, June 1 to 11, JACAR, Tokyo, Japan.

29. "Manshū imin jikkō ni kan suru ken," 23 May 1933, B02030710200, Teikoku no tai manmō seisaku kankei ikken, JACAR, Tokyo, Japan.

30. "Ōtani Sonyu shi no manshū imin jigyō no zenbō oyobi Ōmura mantetsu fuku sōsai no manshū hoku chū shi kaihatsu nituite," July 1938, B02030922400, Nihon gaikō kyōkai kōen shu dai go kan, JACAR, Tokyo, Japan.

31. Shinzō Araragi, *Manshū imin no rekishi shakai gaku* (Ōtsu: Kohrosha, 1994): 45.

32. Jōji Asada, "Manshū nōgyō imin to nōgyō tochi mondai," in *Kindai nihon to sho-kuminchi 3*, ed. Hideo Kobayashi (Tokyo: Iwanami shoten, 1993): 77–78, 80–88.

33. "Ōtani Sonyu shi no manshū imin jigyō no zenbō oyobi Ōmura mantetsu fuku

sōsai no manshū hoku chū shi kaihatsu nituite," B02030922400, JACAR, Tokyo, Japan.

34. Takumushō takumu kyoku, *Manshū imin dai ikki keikaku jisshi yōryō* (Tokyo: Takumushō takumu kyoku, 1937): 1–2.

35. Minami-Manshū tetsudō, *Manshū no nogyo imin* (Dairen: Minami-Manshū Tetsudō, 1932): 7–8.

36. "Kore ha fukuin, shokuryō Mondai ni kōmei. Manmō no shusanhin kara kōhi demo miru demo," *Asahi Shimbum,* January 23, 1933.

37. Nō shōmushō nōmu kyoku, *Kome ni kansuru chōsa* (Tokyo: Dai nihon nōkai, 1912): 241; Noboru Harada, *Manshū kaihatsu jūgo nen shi* (Tokyo: Kaigai keizai tsūshin sha, 1921): 205–6; Minami-Manshū tetsudō shomubu chōsa ka, *Wagakuni jinkō Mondai to manmō* (Dairen: Minami-Manshū tetsudō, 1928): 240.

38. Sueharu Kawamoto, *Manmō wo ikani subeki ka* (Tokyo: Meiji daigaku shuppan bu, 1931): 51.

39. Minami-Manshū tetsudō, *Manshu no nogyo imin,* 7–8.

40. Minami-Manshū tetsudō, *Manshu no nogyo imin,* 15–35; Toa keizai chōsakyoku, *Honpō ni okeru kome no jukyū zuki manshū ni okeru kome* (Tokyo: Toa Keizai chōsakyoku, 1932): 2, 114; Iichi Kasai, *Manshūkoku ijū shishin* (Tokyo: Naigaisha, 1932): 23.

41. "Shiken imin kaihatsu to chian iji wo sōken ni ninatte nozomi wo san nen go no seikō ni jikyū jisoku no funtō," *Asahi Shimbun,* September 15, 1933; Osaka Mainichi Shimbun sha, *Senji keizai haya wakari 11* (Osaka: Osaka Mainichi Shimbun sha, 1939): 69.

42. "Manshu no beisaku," *Chigaku Zasshi* 50, no. 6 (1938): 299.

43. "Manshu no beisaku," 299.

44. "Manshu no beisaku," 300.

45. Nōrinshō nōmukyoku, *Nōji kairyō shiryō 61: komugi yōran* (Tokyo: Dainihon nōkai, 1940): 68–69.

46. Tōyō kyōkai, *Tōyō kyōkai chōsabu chōsa shiryō 12: Manshūkoku nōgyō* (Tokyo: Tōyō kyōkai, 1940): 51.

47. Tōyō kyōkai, *Tōyō kyōkai chōsabu chōsa shiryō,* 51

48. Yukio Ozaki, *Manshū seisaku ni kan suru ikensho nami ni sankōsho* (1932): 2–3.

49. Ozaki, *Manshū seisaku ni kan suru ikensho nami ni sankōsho,* 3.

50. Chikai Shimakage, *Manshū imin no jissō* (Tokyo: Gendai panfuretto tsūshin sha, 1935): 7.

51. Tōyō kyōkai, *Tōyō kyōkai chōsabu chōsa shiryō 12: Manshūkoku nōgyō,* 20–1; Motoaki Kondō, *Kyōryoku naikaku no taibō to kaobure* (Tokyo: Seiji Kōronsha, 1936): 8–9.

52. Osaka Mainichi Shimbun sha, *Senji keizai haya wakari,* 68–69; Ōmameuda, "Senji shokuryō mondai no hassei," 182.

53. "Manshūkoku de bei senbaisei jisshi, jūyō nōsanbutsu tōsei no daiichi kaitei," *Yomiuri Shimbun,* June 6, 1937.

54. "Manshū sangyō kaihatsu gonen keikaku kōyō," 1937, A09050546900, Shōwa zaisei shi shiryō 6/68, JACAR, Tokyo, Japan.

55. Investment to put in increasing rice production in the five-year plan was 28.2 million yen, only second to the amount invested in soybean. "Manshū sangyō kaihatsu gonen keikaku kōyō," A09050546900, JACAR, Tokyo, Japan.

56. Manshū ryōkoku kabushiki kaisha, *Manshū ryōkoku yōran* (Shinkyō: Manshū ryōkoku kabushiki kaisha, 1939): 100.

57. Xiang Chen, "The Changing Process of Agricultural Policy in Manchukuo during the Sino-Japanese War," *Kan Higashi ajia kenkyū senta nenpō*, no. 6 (March 2011): 77, https://niigata-u.repo.nii.ac.jp/?action=repository_uri&item _id=6979&file_id=20&file_no=1.

58. Ōmameuda, "Senji shokuryō mondai no hassei," 184–86.

59. Daiyamondo sha, *Daiyamondo keizai tōkei nenkan shōwa jūroku nen ban* (Tokyo: Daiyamondo sha, 1940): 432.

60. Ōmameuda, "Senji shokuryō mondai no hassei," 184–86.

61. Manshū ryōkoku kabushiki kaisha, *Manshū ryōkoku yōran*, 117; Daiyamondo sha, *Daiyamondo keizai tōkei nenkan shōwa jūroku nen ban*, 598; "Otōto bun no tabemono wo, nōsō nōsan kakujū no hōfu," *Yomiuri Shimbun*, August 17, 1939; Minami-Manshū tetsudō Tokyo kaisha, *Tōa ni okeru busshi jikyūryoku chōsa so no san: manshū no bu (toku hi)* (Tokyo: Minami-Manshū tetsudō Tokyo kaisha, 1940): 18.

62. Janet Hunter, "Nature, Markets and State Response: The Drought of 1939 in Japan and Korea," *Australian Economic History Review* 50, no. 1 (March 2010): 80–90.

63. Daiyamondo sha, *Daiyamondo keizai tōkei nenkan shōwa jūroku nen ban*, 513.

64. Daiyamondo sha, *Daiyamondo keizai tōkei nenkan shōwa jūroku nen ban*, 512.

65. Daiyamondo sha, *Daiyamondo keizai tōkei nenkan shōwa jūroku nen ban*, 514.

66. Daiyamondo sha, *Daiyamondo keizai tōkei nenkan shōwa jūroku nen ban*, 514.

67. "Senmai hyaku gojū man koku inyū: nai-sen-man aida ni sankaku bata sei," *Asahi Shimbun*, December 13, 1939.

68. "Shōwa jūgo nendo shotō ni okeru chōsen shokuryō shigen ni kansuru ken," January 16, 1940, C01004823100, Mitsu dai nikki S15–8–18, JACAR, Tokyo, Japan.

69. Manshū imin kenkyū kai, *Nihon teikoku shugi ka no manshū imin* (Tokyo: Ryūkei Shosha, 1976): 90.

70. "Manshū imin keikaku dai i ki ha jū man nin wo koyu," *Asahi Shimbun*, February 26, 1941. Manshū imin kenkyū kai, *Nihon teikoku shugi ka no manshū imin*, 90.

71. Daiyamondo sha, *Daiyōhin no hanashi* (Tokyo: Daiyamondo sha, 1939): 1–2.

72. "Taiwan ni okeru beikoku mondai wo meguru fuon kōdō ni kansuru ken," 13 May 1940, C01004837900, Mitsu dai nikki S15–9–19, JACAR, Tokyo, Japan.

73. "Shōwa jūgo nendo shotō ni okeru chōsen shokuryō shigen ni kansuru ken," 16 January 1940, C01004823100, Mitsu dai nikki S15–8–18, JACAR, Tokyo, Japan.

74. Naozo Masuo, *Daiyōshoku to konshoku no hanashi* (Shinkyō: Manshū ryōkoku kabushiki kaisha, 1939): 5–25; George Ōsawa, *Manshū shokuyō dokuhon: dairiku nihon no tadashii shokumono* (Tokyo: Nihon shokuyō kenkyūsho, 1939): 14–20.

75. "Hakumai ni sayōnara mondō," *Asahi Shimbun*, October 7, 1939; Daiyamondo sha, *Daiyōhin no hanashi*, 181–82; Kokumin seishin sōdōin chuō renmei, *Senji gakusei dokuhon* (Tokyo: Nihon seinen kyōikukai shuppan bu, 1938): 110–1.

76. "Chōsen mai no migawari ni gaimai," *Asahi Shimbun*, February 7, 1940.

77. "Nijūni nen buri ni shimin no shokuzen he gaimai," *Asahi Shimbun*, March 12, 1940.

78. "Gaimai no kufū: atarashi takikata shōkai," *Asahi Shimbun,* June 10, 1940.
79. Correspondence from Kuga to Arita, 27 June 1940, B09041292500, Rangon mai, Honpō beikoku seisaku kankei zakken vol. 1, JACAR, Tokyo, Japan.
80. Correspondence from Fukui to Konoe, 27 March 1941, B09041292500, Rangon mai, Honpō beikoku seisaku kankei zakken vol. 1, JACAR, Tokyo, Japan.
81. Correspondence from the military attaché to Akira Mutō, 7 December 1940, C01004833900, Taimai kaitsuke ni kansuru ken, Mitsu dainikki, JACAR, Tokyo, Japan.
82. Nanpō sakusen ni tomonau kokunai shokuryō handan, March 1941, C12120405000, Kinkyū sensō junbi kenkyū kankei shorui tsuzuri, JACAR, Tokyo, Japan.
83. "Nanpō ni hōko, shokuryō jikyū ken kakuritsu gosu. Sakuya, Yukawa chōkan hōsō no yōshi," *Yomiuri Shimbun,* November 13, 1941.
84. "Kyōeiken nai no shokuryō keikaku Shigemasa sōmu kyokuchō hōsō, nanpōbei nihon ni yūsen kyōkyū," *Yomiuri Shimbun,* April 17, 1942.

CHAPTER 6

"We Don't Need Red Tape, We Need Red Meat"

A Comparative Overview of the Fight against Black-Market Meat in Australia, Canada, Great Britain, and the United States during World War II

LESLIE A. PRZYBYLEK

It was late March, 1945 and Alois Vondich wanted in on the wartime black-market meat trade in western Pennsylvania.[1] Each day for three weeks, he set out with an old truck, a bundle of cash, and "a little persistence" to see how much meat he could round up in the industrial districts around Pittsburgh.[2] Ranging within a thirty-mile area, Vondich visited wholesale grocers, community markets, back alley dealers, and even a turkey farm that an enterprising proprietor had converted to a cattle slaughterhouse.[3] After a slow start caused by Easter (the holiday demand for meat was so great that little was available for new customers), Vondich hauled in more than a ton of black-market meat.

But all was not as it seemed. "Alois Vondich" was really Ray Sprigle, an investigative journalist for the *Pittsburgh Post-Gazette*, and his meat-gathering exploits ended up as a seven-part series that ran on the front pages of the *Post-Gazette* and twenty-two other newspapers in April 1945, when it also appeared in *Time* magazine.[4] Sprigle's account emerged in a politically charged climate fueled by debate over a national meat shortage and the perceived failures of the much-maligned Office of Price Administration (OPA)—the federal agency that oversaw rationing in the United States.[5] Senate hearings convened during this time estimated that 80 to 90 percent of the beef Americans consumed, especially in large cities, was acquired illegally.[6] All of this was in response to what one home economics editor called "the worst meat shortage we here in America have ever known," warning consumers not to "connive" with black marketeers to get what they wanted.[7]

Meat supply issues fueled black markets and impacted United States diplomacy, contributing in March of 1945 to significant reductions in the quota of American meat allocated for lend-lease aid to Great Britain, as much as 87 percent less.[8] Critics blamed price control, accusing the meat industry of engineering shortages to provoke change.[9] One U.S. Army quartermaster acknowledged that even the armed forces were having trouble supplying meat, noting that drought in Australia and New Zealand also contributed to the supply woes.[10]

A Matter of International Debate

While this drama played out in the American press, on March 30, 1945 in Canada, the *Ottawa Citizen* ran an editorial damning the situation in the United States. The paper accused individuals below the southern border of inflaming opinion against Canada for "withholding" meat, and decried the whole thing as an "artificial shortage," lamenting it was "far from an inspiring picture of human nature" at Easter.[11] The *Saskatoon Star-Phoenix* also addressed the matter, acknowledging the "pressure of the black market" in the States but noting that British newspapers "have pointedly reminded the Americans that the people of Britain still have many war hazards to contend with."[12] Clearly implying that Americans had nothing to complain about, the writer addressed the fear this raised for Canadians: that meat rationing in Canada, suspended since March 1944—thanks to a meat surplus and limited shipping space to Britain—might resume.[13] He lamented, "Already, some American papers have been commenting upon the apparent abundance of meat supplies in this country while their own butcher shops are nearly empty."[14]

To American eyes, the Canadians had it good. Accounts of American crowds surging across the border to go meat shopping in Canada, especially around Detroit, enjoyed extensive coverage in the Canadian press.[15] Many Canadians believed their system worked better. "Canadian Food Situation Envy of the Americans," pronounced an editorial written by Canadian hockey legend Lester Patrick, who spent "several months in each and every one of the war years" in a major eastern American city (clearly New York, where he coached the New York Rangers and managed

Investigative reporter Ray Sprigle posed for a photo with some of his black-market meat in 1945. *Courtesy Senator John Heinz History Center, Detre Library and Archives, Ray Sprigle Papers and Photographs.*

Madison Square Garden).[16] He wrote, "Very little is heard of the black market in foodstuffs in Canada, but I can assure you that such a market does function in the United States—and in a very objectionable manner."[17]

Other Allied Powers also criticized the situation. In March, Australia's *Sydney Morning Herald* added its voice to the chorus. In an article titled "U.S. Meat Muddle," the *Morning Herald's* correspondent, writing from

Washington, DC, castigated the United States for one of the "worst muddles in the history of supply planning."[18] Acknowledging that American per-capita meat consumption would be reduced in 1945, the article nonetheless asserted that American consumers, blessed with high incomes and other abundances, were not suffering. In contrast, the paper noted that British citizens faced much worse. But, the writer admitted, they enjoyed a benefit over the Americans, with a distribution system that was "better regulated":

> The gap between the meat supply available to those who can afford to use the black market and to the city dweller of moderate means who must trade in the legitimate market accentuates the unevenness of supply in America. Some American housewives simply cannot trade their ration points for meat.[19]

By early April of that year, the *Sydney Morning Herald* noted a bigger threat: "Americans have been slow to realize that you may begin with the almost innocent practice of buying black-market steak for a dollar a pound, and take a road that leads to dangerous abandonment of values."[20] This came from a nation with its own meat concerns: drought and the needs of Allies stationed in Australia and overseas threatened to cut the country's meat ration by 20 percent—a serious sacrifice in a meat-loving nation. Melbourne's *The Age* worried, "The Australian is so wedded to his large meals of meat . . . that he never thinks of, nor does he want, substitutes."[21]

This political food fight in the spring of 1945 highlighted the intertwined relationship between Canada, the United States, and Australia as they fought to manage wartime food supplies at home while supplying crucial sustenance to their own armies as well as the United Kingdom and other partners overseas. They compared themselves to each other, measuring successes and failures, Great Britain's plight always on the horizon. The pattern of this episode, with dramatic headlines from the United States countered by commentary from Canada and Australia, both making pointed references to Great Britain and the moral nature of the matter, captured the dynamic between them as they struggled with black-market meat during World War II. In truth, none were immune—Canada and Australia both faced battles with black markets. By August 1945, it was Canada's turn to worry, as the United States, having addressed the meat shortages of the spring, announced a possible suspension of meat rationing just as the Canadian government debated its return, timing some warned would make Canada's black-market situation "almost incontrollable."[22]

A Chapter Outside the Accepted Narrative

Studies of food and its role as weapon and propaganda during World War II have received increasing attention from scholars since the 1990s, when the publication of works such as Amy Bentley's *Eating for Victory* (1998) and Harvey Levenstein's *The Paradox of Plenty* (1993) paved the way for wider recognition of the topic. Since then, a rich selection of books, articles, and theses across the United States, Canada, Great Britain, and, to a lesser extent, Australia have explored many food-related themes, including the politics of rationing, gender stereotypes, the origins of convenience foods, and the introduction of new tastes to national palates during World War II.[23]

Yet until recently, studies of black markets in Allied nations connected with foodstuffs during World War II remained uncommon. Such episodes contradicted popular narratives of the war. With a few exceptions, it was only in the 2000s that new studies emerged exploring less admirable sides of the home-front experience.[24] This stands in stark contrast to coverage during the 1940s, when reams of paper and thousands of words were devoted to the scourge of black markets, black-market meat most glaringly. During that time, government agencies amassed volumes documenting and studying how to combat the problem. They collected court and federal hearing testimonies and gathered evidence from civilian informants, governmental agencies, and consumer surveys. Until recently, much of this documentation remained difficult to access unless it was republished in other formats. Much of it has yet to be fully analyzed.[25]

For consumers, black market concerns played out most visibly in the press and popular media. Sensational headlines attracted readers and shaped coverage. So too did press affiliations with various political and business concerns. Such accounts, including much of the material explored in this overview, played to an audience. The media rarely shied away from dramatizing events, epitomized by Ray Sprigle's undercover investigation. Nonetheless, such coverage accurately captured the atmosphere surrounding public debate about the issue, a reality reflected in the tone taken by governmental attempts to sway people to comply through the use of tools such as propaganda films, which featured the same tabloid flavor.

A comparative overview of the struggle over black-market meat during World War II in Australia, Canada, Great Britain, and the United States reveals key patterns shared by these Allies as they confronted the control of a food with deep symbolic meaning for consumers. "Meat" in this context meant red meat, primarily beef steak, as well as pork, lamb, and veal. Specifics varied by nation, but most rationing systems excluded a variety of lesser meat products such as sausages, bologna, and organ meats, as well as small game and animals such as rabbits.[26] Some citizens showed great ingenuity in locating alternate meat sources, none more so than in Great Britain, where the situation was most extreme. In one famous example, a gentleman in London enjoyed off-ration meat from deceased animals at the London Zoo, including antelope, giraffe, crocodile, and elephant.[27] Most people were less adventurous, and campaigns to increase the popularity of organ meats fell flat in the United States, where these delicacies were not part of culinary tradition.[28]

As home economists and nutritionists endlessly reminded people, consumers had access to alternate protein sources, including beans, peanut butter, soybeans, and cheese as well as non-rationed meats. But black markets addressed desire, not need. Whether British, Canadian, American, or Australian, people wanted red meat. Apart from sugar, no rationed food caused such home-front turmoil, whether shortages were real or imagined.[29] No food was so coveted by soldiers and workers. Psychology lurked behind the desire. Studies in the United States showed that eating red meat helped citizens feel well-fed—it preserved morale.[30] Eating certain kinds of meat conveyed status. Especially for male workers and fighting men, it was the "consummate symbol of virility."[31] The image of a thick steak or joint of beef became shorthand for what civilians were giving up in order to ensure victory. It also fed a sense of national identity. A writer for the *Australian Women's Weekly*, preparing that nation for meat rationing, warned, "Australians may feel the pinch of rationing a little more . . . than Canadians and Americans because we are normally bigger meat eaters."[32] The scarcity of meat prolonged World War II's impact after the fighting ceased. Meat rationing remained in effect in Canada until 1947, Australia until 1948, and Great Britain, where it was the last item removed from ration lists, until 1954. Meat rationing might have lasted longer in the United States, but Truman abolished it in 1946 due to new fears surrounding black markets and to partisan political charges that price control equaled communism. So polarized was the U.S. debate over meat that strike actions undertaken by the American meat industry shaped the 1946 Congressional elections and ultimately brought down the Office of Price Administration (OPA).[33] For Canada and Australia, the war's end increased black-market activity, as war-weary citizens and butchers grew tired of shortages and resisted further sacrifice.

Divergent Responses from the War's Beginning

Black markets for meat developed early in World War II as Allies imposed government control over their economies, beginning with Great Britain in 1940. While Britain's Minister for Food, Lord Woolton, wrote that "there was little or no black market activity" in England during the war, calling it "a tribute to the British people," reports of black-market activity emerged by 1939.[34] The situation became so bad by the winter of 1941–42 that a parliamentary proposal considered flogging black marketeers. Some suggested the death penalty.[35] By 1941, thieves specialized in stealing and reselling food, and their meat offerings could be dangerous. In some cases, meat contaminated with tuberculosis and livers classified as "unfit for human consumption" made their way into the food chain.[36] Britain aggressively pursued scofflaws, sending undercover agents to enter shops and test merchants' willingness to break ration laws. The maximum penalty was fourteen years imprisonment.[37] While enforcement efforts continued throughout the war, British officials and the media tried to put a positive spin on the matter, and they largely succeeded. A syndicated news article written by a London correspondent that ran in Canada and the United States in 1943 epitomized this. Titled "How Britain Beats Black Market," it proclaimed the success of these efforts, noting that the extent of British networks was "very small."[38]

The nation that garnered the most dramatic headlines was the United States, and here the comparison with Canada was instructive. Both witnessed the emergence of black markets prior to imposing meat rationing in March 1943. In the United States, illegal activity evading OPA price ceilings for beef emerged by 1942, mere months after the bombing of Pearl Harbor. This occurred especially in New York City, where beef from small Kosher slaughterhouses escaped early OPA regulation.[39] Reports also emerged in cities such as Akron, Ohio, where critics charged that inconsistency in price ceilings (there was no ceiling on meat purchased for the military or lend-lease shipment) meant that large packers chased higher profits selling meat to the government, forgoing sales to small industrial cities and thereby encouraging black markets.[40] By spring 1943,

rumors surfaced around the Great Lakes that black marketeers were vis-
iting rural dairy herds to buy cattle for slaughter, further inflaming the
situation.[41]

Like Britain, the Canadian government initially hesitated in acknowledging that black markets existed, although suspicions of illegal selling
emerged in Vancouver by 1942.[42] Ironically, the trade relationship between
Canada and the United States exacerbated this. Canadian ranchers had
long preferred selling their cattle in the lucrative U.S. market. Through
early 1942 they continued doing so, even as government officials argued
that the "only morally acceptable outlet" for Canadian agricultural products was Great Britain.[43] By 1943 in cities such as Montreal, estimates
placed as much as half of the meat supply on the black market.[44]

While Canada and the United States witnessed the start of black-
market activity at roughly the same time, their trajectory of civic response
diverged as the war progressed. In the United States, people quickly perceived the issue as reminiscent of prohibition during the 1920s. Black
marketeers were called "meatleggers" and headlines touted the revival
of "bootleg days." Some early reports even alleged the involvement of Al
Capone's gang in the meat rackets.[45] Judging by how openly black markets
persisted in the United States, a lingering sense of public cynicism about
official rules remained. By the time Ray Sprigle rounded up his ton of
meat in Pittsburgh in 1945, government officials had been trying futilely
to combat the situation for three years.

On the other hand, when a series of incidents in British Columbia,
Ontario, and Quebec brought attention to black-market activity in
Canada in 1943, the Canadian press quickly denounced it as treason and
sabotage.[46] "Are farmers and retail merchants going to 'sabotage' Canada
and sell out the meat industry for the sake of a few dollars profit?" asked
the *Vancouver Sun*.[47] Officials emphasized that buying illicit meat endan-
gered public health. "You might be buying meat that was dead a long time
of natural causes before it was cut up for steaks and roasts," warned the
Windsor Star.[48] Of course, agencies in the United States issued similar
messages, with increasing urgency as the war progressed. But in contrast to a population that seemed disinclined to fully heed warnings, the
Canadian public listened. While support for rationing hit a low in 1943,
it rebounded, and the majority of Canadians complied with ration laws
throughout the war.[49] But black-market activity did continue. Montreal,
long known as a vice capital, garnered an especially bad reputation for
running afoul of the Wartime Prices and Trade Board (WPTB), Canada's

version of the OPA.[50] While new scholarly evidence demonstrates that discriminatory WPTB policies in Quebec contributed to the perception of lawlessness, the idea's wide acceptance suggests enough black market activity occurred nationally for the accusations to have public resonance.[51] And black market activity likely recurred after meat rationing was reintroduced in September of 1945, an act that elicited waves of protests, including more than nine thousand coal miners walking off the job in Alberta and British Columbia, and a violent "meat ration revolt" among butchers in Montreal.[52]

A Larger Ration on the Other Side of the World

Initially, Australia enjoyed a respite from the drama playing out elsewhere. A women's magazine writer, returning to Australia in 1943 after spending six years in England and Canada, remarked, "I shall never forget my first meal at an Australian hotel. . . . When it came I thought they had given me my whole week's meat ration in one meal."[53] With a landmass nearly the size of the United States but with fewer people, Australia had meat supply enough to assist other Allies. American writers in 1943 reminded people that Australia and New Zealand supplied more beef to U.S. troops than the United States supplied to the lend-lease program.[54]

But while Australia did not begin meat rationing until January 1944, the experiences of Great Britain and other Allies were clearly on people's minds as rationing of tea and sugar was introduced in 1942. Australian authorities worried outwardly about black markets. Articles explaining what they were and how to prevent them appeared by 1942.[55] *The Age* in Melbourne warned, "Investigations show that black markets began in Britain as soon as rationing, price control, and limitations of supply were established," noting that authorities were "continually unearthing intricately organized 'black markets' throughout Britain, especially in the big cities."[56] In 1943, the government instructed the Australian High Commissioner in London to examine Britain's response to black markets, preparing for the inevitable.[57]

Once rationing was announced, Australian officials emphasized that their meat ration was larger than that of Britain, the United States, or Canada.[58] But as the war progressed and Australia's obligations to Great Britain and the U.S. military presence on its shores grew, the Australian people witnessed further reductions, first in February and then in May of 1945.[59] Reports clearly indicated that black-market activity had emerged in cities such as Victoria and Sydney. Commenting upon the newest reductions and an anticipated shortage of meat, a butcher in Sydney noted, "There is no shortage of meat provided you are willing to pay black-market prices for it."[60]

Perceptions of Inequity and an Urban Divide

The history of black markets shared by these nations underscored significant dangers for national morale. In part because black markets were perceived as an urban problem, they fed suspicions of inequity in resource distribution, creating a sense of social divide. While black-market transactions could take place anywhere, and rural suppliers were crucial to the system, cities dominated investigations and headlines— New York, Montreal, Sydney, London, Vancouver, Pittsburgh. In places such as Sydney, the worst reports emerged in the old urban core.[61] This was logical: a greater concentration of people meant a greater demand for meat where customers were willing and able to cheat the system or pay higher prices, including war workers flush with more income than many had ever seen before. Reports in Canada suggested that urban areas often ran short of meat by the end of the work week—sending consumers on a mad dash for what the *Toronto Star* called the "week-end scramble for meat"—in contrast to rural small towns, where meat was more easily found closer to the source.[62]

Large urban centers provided greater anonymity. They were also more likely to have criminal networks in place to exploit the system—an idea personified in the United States by reports of involvement from Al Capone's gang. Urban black markets also underlined tensions between cultural communities. In New York, rumors about black markets swirled around Kosher slaughterhouses. In Canada, fury was aimed at Montreal, a francophone city in a nation where French- and English-speaking populations clashed; French-speaking Canada never trusted the Wartime Prices and Trade Board (WPTB).[63] A sense of entitlement also underscored differences of perspective in prioritizing individual desires over community needs. Describing Montreal's situation, a correspondent noted the "appalling acceptance" of black markets, adding: "There is a feeling that an honest man who does his duty gets all the dirt and none of the gravy; it is a struggle between integrity and a sense of being a sucker."[64] In Pittsburgh, where Ray Sprigle spotlighted the brazenness of urban operations, this sense rang through letters sent by readers. One disgruntled person wrote: "How much of this give, give, give, and do without do you think the American people will stand," signing their letter "No Name" because "apparently this is no longer the U.S.A."[65]

"You and Others Like You": A Battle Drawn along Gender Lines

Some also viewed the preference for steaks and pork tenderloin, meats pursued on the black market, as symbolic of larger societal changes, a loss of tradition and a speeding up of daily life, with more women working outside the home. In the Canadian propaganda film *The Main Dish* (1943), a family butcher addressed the challenge of customers' increasing demand for steak by lamenting that in his younger days, "women spent more time and gave more thought to cooking. . . . Today, a great number of women know little about meat cuts. Thinking of a quick meal, if they can't buy steaks or pork tenderloin, they are at a loss."[66]

This pointed to another defining aspect of the battle against black markets: the fight followed clearly demarcated gender lines, as did so much of rationing. On an operational level, the architects of black-market meat activity were men—butchers, grocers, drivers, meat packers, back alley dealers, cattle suppliers, and slaughterhouse workers. It took a confederacy of men to operate these illegal networks. Men's appetites for meat shaped public dialogue and civic debate. In Australia, concern over the lack of access to meat for miners and other workers prompted protests and strikes.[67] In U.S. industrial communities such as Pittsburgh, family traditions based on ensuring meat for the working man's plate had long led women and children to sometimes go without so the primary breadwinner could eat.[68] Additionally, defense production demanded meat. The U.S. Department of Agriculture film *Home on the Range* (1942), shows scenes of civilian shipyard workers as the narrator proclaims that ranches are producing "Steaks and roasts, short ribs for these chaps building Liberty Ships."[69]

But if men ate meat, women prepared it, and the onus of securing a righteous supply for the family table without resorting to black markets fell on them. As multiple scholars have shown, national propaganda campaigns urging compliance with rationing guidelines aimed streams of posters, magazines, and advertisements at women.[70]

This remained true of campaigns against black marketing, where women were stereotyped as the primary offenders.[71] Women were not

A wartime demonstration on meat "extending" methods in Washington, DC; note the audience mainly of women. *Courtesy Library of Congress, Prints and Photographs Division, Farm Security Administration—Office of War Information Photograph Collection.*

just encouraged to support the rules, they were depicted as complicit if they did not. In British and U.S. films against black marketing, they were equated with criminal defendants. In *It's Up to You!* (1942, U.S.) and *Prices Unlimited* (1944, U.S.), female characters set out to purchase more steak than allowed, only to be persuaded by some supernatural experience (a personified conscience or time travel experience, akin to the tale of Ebenezer Scrooge) to rethink their desire.[72] In the propaganda courtroom dramas *Partners in Crime* (1942, UK; also shown in Canada and Australia) and *Black Marketing* (1943, U.S.), women's purchases of black-market meat are juxtaposed with criminal trials.[73] In the end of both, a court figure—the judge in *Partners in Crime* and the prosecuting attorney in *Black Marketing*—speaks directly to the camera, urging audiences to consider the impact of their actions. In *Partners in Crime* the link is especially explicit, as the film appears to end, then shows an audience in the theater, spotlighting two women, one of whom, it is implied, has just made a black-market purchase. The judge breaks the fourth wall within the film, noting the nature of the film in response to the two women, then turns and speaks directly to the camera, addressing "you and others like you" who have benefited from black-market activities: "Let those of you consider just exactly who and what you are and whether you are any better than common criminals, parasites, plagues on the body of a community at war."[74] The message is blunt and unmistakable, and it was aimed at women.

As the first film expressly aimed against black markets, Britain's *Partners in Crime* was especially important. The film set the tone of expectation in British Commonwealth nations like Australia and Canada and appeared in the United States as well.[75] It is difficult to imagine the U.S. courtroom drama *Black Marketing* being made without awareness of the British film, although the American film goes into more convoluted detail about the conspiracy of men scheming to make the markets work, a reflection of the gangster films after which it is patterned. The "bumbling men" motif appeared in other American popular media, where, again, the black market was regarded with more humor and cynicism than in the Commonwealth nations. The radio show *Fibber McGee and Molly* featured a plot in which Fibber unwittingly buys tainted meat from a back-alley dealer, to Molly's great chagrin.[76] And in the wartime comedy film *Rationing* (1944), a jovial grocer played by Wallace Beery finds himself enmeshed in a black-market meat ring through misadventures involving his town nemesis, the head of the local ration board.[77]

While women are portrayed as culprits in such propaganda films, they also serve as the public's watchful eye, voicing criticism of the black market, whether as a young girl talking back to her elder in *Partners in Crime*, a woman's conscience in *It's Up to You!*, another customer in *Black Marketing*, or as women themselves (witnessing the reality of a black-market universe) in *Prices Unlimited*. While the Australian film *Give Us This Day* (1943, AUS) does not fit neatly into this model—it features battlefield scenes of a starving soldier, provoking different emotions—it too presents a woman as the voice of reason. As two affluent diners sit in a restaurant cajoling their waitress, "you could get us a steak if you tried," one of them laments that he has not tasted steak in six days. The waitress responds by reminding him, and thus all Australians, "there are a lot of men in New Guinea who haven't tasted steak in six months."[78]

In the end, while efforts to counter black-market meat in Great Britain, Canada, the United States, and Australia met with varying degrees of success, it was a fight that outlasted World War II. The spring of 1946 brought more dramatic headlines as postwar food supply issues lingered, impacting local and national economies. A sense of war-weariness pervaded these debates as Allies wrestled with the expectations of their citizens versus the needs of war-torn Britain. Australian butchers and meat salesmen asserted in August 1946 that "meat was the one commodity which could not be successfully rationed" and the Premier of Queensland protested that meat was "one of the biggest rackets ever put over on people in this war."[79] In Windsor, Ontario, headlines in April and May of that year recounted a black market situation more extreme than anything seen previously, while further west, fears increased that black-market meat buyers were making inroads in Edmonton and Calgary, buying meat to sell illegally in the east and siphoning off food needed for Britain.[80] That year in the United States, President Truman first signed over more than one million dollars in March to help the beleaguered OPA fight the growing problem in black-market meat, then abolished all meat control measures in October.[81]

By this point, meat seemed to symbolize a world still trying to right itself, contrasted later in the decade when those steaks sizzling on backyard patio barbecue grills in America, Canada, or Australia epitomized a new suburban prosperity. There is much yet to be mined from the story of the wartime struggles with black-market meat by Allies whose efforts were closely intertwined as they sought to balance the needs of their citizens with a sense of the greater good. Hopefully, future scholars will find it an enticing dish to further cultivate.

NOTES

1. The chapter's title and reference to red meat is from *Prices Unlimited*, directed by Erle C. Kenton (Universal Pictures Company, U.S. Office of Price Administration and the U.S. Government Office of War Information, 1944).
2. Ray Sprigle, "Black Marketers Operate in Open Here Despite OPA," *Pittsburgh Post-Gazette*, April 13, 1945, 1.
3. "Black Market Expose Hits Canonsburg Area," *Daily Notes* (Canonsburg, PA), April 18, 1945, 1.
4. Martin Raymond "Ray" Sprigle served more than fifty years as a journalist. The Sprigle Papers are in the Detre Library and Archives, Senator John Heinz History Center, in Pittsburgh, PA. Sprigle's series ran April 13, 1945 through April 19, 1945. Twenty-two papers were reported by the North American Newspaper Alliance: Henry M. Snevily to Ray Sprigle, July 5, 1945, Sprigle Papers, Box 3, Folder "Black Market Meat Story"; "Meat Makes News," *Time* 45, no. 18 (April 30, 1945): 61.

5. By 1945, complaints against the OPA reflected the exhaustion of some U.S. consumers and industry lobbyists during a period marked by real shortages and a perception that the war in Europe was winding down. Initially, the OPA enjoyed strong consumer support. Newspapers, beholden to advertisers and political interests, were less enthusiastic. For a full account of the OPA and its impact, see: Meg Jacobs, "How About Some Meat? The Office of Price Administration, Consumption Politics, and State Building from the Bottom Up, 1941–1946," *Journal of American History* 84, no. 3 (December 1997): 910–41.

6. "House Group to Probe N. Y. Black Market Meat," *Daily News* (New York), April 3, 1945, 80; Marshall B. Clinard, *The Black Market, A Study of White Collar Crime* (Montclair, NJ: Patterson Smith, 1969, reprint of 1952 original): 127.

7. Glenna H. Snow, "Acute U.S. Meat Shortage Faces Housewives with Food Problem," *Akron (OH) Beacon Journal*, April 1, 1945, 4-B.

8. "Meat Ration Threat," *Sydney Morning Herald*, March 16, 1945, 3; "Meat Ration Cut Expected," *Marshfield News-Herald* (Marshfield, WI), March 17, 1945, 1; "Britain Faces Direst Food Crisis as U.S. Slashes Meat Supply 87%," *The Gazette* (Montreal, QC), March 19, 1945, 7.

9. "Meat Shortage was 'Planned' Senator Charges," *Harrisburg (PA) Telegraph*, April 24, 1945, 8; "Meat Shortage Blamed on Controls," *Ithaca (NY) Journal*, April 13, 1945, 5.

10. "Shortage of Meat Blamed on Black Market, Drouth [*sic*]," *Journal Herald* (Dayton, OH), April 6, 1945, 6.

11. "The Advent of Spring," *Ottawa Citizen*, March 30, 1945, 16.

12. "Britain's Food," *Saskatoon Star-Phoenix*, March 20, 1945, 9.

13. "Britain's Food," 9; Stacey Jo Anne Barker, "Feeding the Hungry Allies: Canadian Food and Agriculture During the Second World War" (PhD diss., University of Ottawa, 2008): 323–25.

14. "Britain's Food," 9.

15. "Detroiters Enjoy Shopping Bee in Windsor Stores but Tie-up at American Customs Takes Joy Out of It for Most of Them," *Windsor Star*, January 29, 1945, 3; "Detroiters Jam City Market, Stores Seeking Steaks, Chops," *Windsor Star*, March 3, 1945, 5.

16. "Canadian Food Situation Envy of Americans Says Lester Patrick," *Victoria Daily Times*, June 4, 1945, 9.

17. "Canadian Food Situation," 9.

18. A. D. Rothman, "U.S. Meat Muddle," *Sydney Morning Herald*, March 29, 1945, 2.

19. Rothman, "U.S. Meat Muddle," 2.

20. A. D. Rothman, "Lure of High Stakes on U.S.A.'s Black Market," *Sydney Morning Herald*, April 6, 1945, 2.

21. "Balanced Diet for Australians," *The Age* (Melbourne), April 17, 1945, 5.

22. Chester Bloom, "Fear Black Market Meat," *Saskatoon Star-Phoenix*, August 18, 1945, 4.; "U.S. Meat Plans Worrying Ottawa," *Winnipeg Free Press*, August 18, 1945, 1.

23. For example: Allison Carruth, "War Rations and the Food Politics of Late Modernism," *Modernism/modernity* 16, no. 4 (November 2009): 767–95; Lizzie Collingham, *The Taste of War and the Battle for Food* (New York: Penguin Press, 2012); Ian Mosby, *Food Will Win the War: The Politics, Culture, and Science of Food on Canada's Home Front* (Vancouver: UBC Press, 2014).

24. Among the earliest: Edward Smithies, *Crime in Wartime: A Social History of Crime in World War II* (London: Allen & Unwin, 1982). Jeffrey Keshen was first of the new crop, see: Jeffrey A. Keshen, "One for All or All for One: Government Controls, Black Marketing, and the Limits of Patriotism, 1939-1947," *Journal of Canadian Studies* 29, no. 4 (1994-95): 111–43; and Jeffrey A. Keshen, *Saints, Sinners, and Soldiers* (Vancouver, BC: UBC Press, 2004).

25. A crucial example was Marshall B. Clinard's 1952 U.S. study, *The Black Market: A Study of White Collar Crime.* Other than in the work of Clinard, a full consideration of the story of the U.S. wartime black market documented in the archives of the Office of Price Administration and other federal agencies has yet to be undertaken. In Australia, some records were not opened until they were requested for a student honors thesis. See: Timothy Blum, "Profits over Patriotism: Black Market Crime in World War II in Sydney" (BA honors thesis, University of Sydney, 2011).

26. In Canada, sausage was rationed, prompting such headlines: "Sausage Cries for Ration Freedom as Housewives Gang Up on Steak," *The Gazette* (Montreal, QC), June 10, 1942, 13.

27. Donald Thomas, *The Enemy Within*, 147–48. Postmortems proved the meat safe for consumption.

28. While American campaigns failed, organ meats had long been budget staples in working-class Britain and Canada. Mosby, *Food*, 146.

29. Women especially missed sugar. When asked in a July 1945 U.S. Gallop Poll which ingredient they most wanted, a third of Americans chose beef, but half said sugar. See: Bentley, *Eating*, 102–3. As for meat, Americans actually increased their consumption when assessed across all demographic groups. See: Jacobs, "How About Some Meat," 931.

30. Bentley, *Eating*, 94.

31. Bentley, *Eating*, 97.

32. Edna Moore, "How I Managed Family Meat Coupons in Canada," *Australian Women's Weekly*, November 13, 1943, 12.

33. Harvey Levenstein, *Paradox of Plenty* (New York: Oxford University Press, 1993): 99; Communism fears also emerged in Queensland, see: Kay Saunders, *War on the Homefront, State Intervention in Queensland 1938–1948* (St. Lucia, Queensland: University of Queensland Press, 1993): 130–31. For more on the 1946 "beefsteak elections" see: Jacobs, "How About Some Meat," 913–14, 932–39. The OPA was officially abolished on May 29, 1947.

34. Michael Tyquin, *A Bit on the Side: Price Fixing, Rationing, Profiteering and Black Markets in Australia and Britain 1939–1945* (Australia: Michael Tyquin, 2017): xxiii; Thomas, *Enemy*, 135.

35. Thomas, *Enemy*, 133–35.

36. Thomas, *Enemy*, 147.

37. Thomas, *Enemy*, 40, 135.

38. The article appeared May through June 1945, see: Tom Wolf, "How Britain Beats Black Market," *Fort Lauderdale (FL) Daily News*, May 8, 1943, 2; Tom Wolf, "How Britain Beats Black Market," *Times Colonist* (Victoria), June 5, 1943, 4M.

39. Ray Barret, "Holes in Rules Cause Black Market Beef," *Daily News* (New York), October 12, 1942, 2, 14; Ray Barrett, "OPA Ready to Stamp Out Kosher Beef Black Market, *Daily News* (New York), October 15, 1942, 4.

40. William V. Wallace, "'Black Market' in Meat Grows," *Akron (OH) Beacon Journal*, December 23, 1942, 1; "New Tips Show Akron Meat 'Black Market' Larger than Believed," *Akron Beacon Journal*, December 25, 1941, 1.

41. Buyers targeted herds near Lake Erie: "Meatleggers Buying Here," *Gettysburg Times* (Gettysburg, PA), April 14, 1942, 3.

42. Barker, "Feeding," 327; "Woman's Board Reports, 'Meat Black Market'" *Vancouver Daily Province*, December 9, 1942, 11.

43. Barker, "Feeding," 100, 175.

44. Keshen, *Saints*, 109.

45. "Operators of Meat 'Black Market' Revive Methods of Bootleg Days of Al Capone," *Moline Daily Dispatch,* (Moline, IA), January 29, 1943, 1; "Capone Gang Nibbling in Black Market," *Hammond Times* (Hammond, IN), February 16, 1943, 10.

46. See: "Treason," *Vancouver Sun,* April 13, 1943, 4; "Black Market in Meat Seen," *Calgary Herald,* April 21, 1943, 13; "Claimed Cattle Bought in the West," *Winnipeg Tribune,* April 23, 1943, 7; "Black Market Meat," *Nanaimo Free Press* (Vancouver Island), May 18, 1943, 1.

47. H. L. Ford, "Evils of Meat 'Black Market'," *Vancouver Sun*, March 1, 1943, 26.

48. W. L. Clark, "Black Market Meat," *Windsor Star*, April 13, 1943, 2.

49. Black, "Feeding," 327; Mosby, *Food*, 83, 85–86.

50. Black, "Feeding," 331–33; "Big Black Market Seen in Montreal," *Toronto Star*, January 28, 1943, 5; "Meat Black Market Brings 15 Dealers into Montreal Court," *The Province* (Vancouver), July 7, 1945, 13.

51. WPTB enforcement was more aggressive in Quebec, increasing violations, see: Mosby, *Food, 79*.

52. Mosby, *Food*, 80; "Meat Ration Revolt Flares; Gangs Close Montreal Shops," *Calgary Herald*, September 24, 1945, 1; "Butchers Open Today," *The Gazette* (Montreal, QC), September 28, 1945, 1.

53. Moore, "How I Managed," 12.

54. S. Burton Heath, "Lend-Lease Meat," *Manhattan Republic* (KS), April 15, 1943, 4.

55. "Black Market Causes / Public Asked to Help," *Sydney Morning Herald*, 11.

56. "Racketeering in Britain," *The Age* (Melbourne), February 14, 1942, 2.

57. Blum, "Profits," 43.

58. "Minister Explains Meat Ration," *Sydney Morning Herald,* January 8, 1944, 11.

59. "Section 3—Food / Clothing and Food Rationing," *Year Book Australia, 1944– 1945* (Australian Bureau of Statistics), accessed September 9, 2019, https://www .abs.gov.au/websitedbs/D3310114.nsf/home/year+book+products?opendocument.

60. "Meat Leakage," *The Age* (Melbourne), March 2, 1945, 3; "Less Fresh Meat Next Week," *Sydney Morning Herald*, March 3, 1945, 3.

61. Blum, "Profits," 10.

62. Barker, "Feeding," 199.

63. Mosby, *Food*, 78–79.

64. Barker "Feeding," 331.

65. Unnamed to Ray Sprigle, May 12, 1945, Sprigle Papers.

66. *The Main Dish,* The Knife & Fork Series, (Canada: National Film Board Canada, 1943).

67. "Miners Want More Meat," *Sydney Morning Herald*, January 18, 1944, 6; "Meat Ration Strikes Spread," *Sydney Morning Herald*, February 14, 1944, 6.

68. Margaret Byington, *Homestead: The Households of a Mill Town* (New York: Russell Sage Foundation, 1910): 64.

69. *Home on the Range*, directed by Tom Hogan (U.S. Department of Agriculture, 1942).

70. Bentley, *Eating*, 34–37; Mosby, *Food,* 68–69.

71. Bentley, *Eating*, 36.

72. *It's Up to You!*, directed by Henwar Rodakiewicz (U.S. Department of Agriculture, 1942); *Prices Unlimited*, 1944.

73. *Partners in Crime*, directed by Frank Launder and Sydney Gilliat, (UK: Gainsborough Pictures, Ministry of Information, 1942); *Black Marketing* (U.S. Office of War Information, Bureau of Motion Pictures, 1943).

74. *Partners in Crime*, 1942.

75. Philip K. Scheuer, "British War Shorts Drive Home Powerful Messages," *Los Angeles Times*, August 19, 1942, 15; "Six British Health Films Available to Audiences in Iowa," *Sioux City Journal*, April 25, 1945, 8-B.

76. *Fibber McGee and Molly*, show 430427, aired April 4, 1943, file 17, https://archive.org/details/FibberMcGeeandMolly1943/430427_Black_Market_Meat.mp3.

77. *Rationing*, directed by Willis Goldbeck, (U.S.: Metro-Goldwyn-Mayer, 1944).

78. *Give Us This Day*, directed by Ken G. Hall, (Australia: Department of Information, 1943).

79. "Policing Price of Meat," *The Age* (Melbourne), August 21, 1946, 5.

80. "'Black Market' Meat Trail Leads Here; Prosecutions Pending," *Windsor Star*, April 12, 1946, 5; Ray Martin, "Farmers Say Black Market Getting Meat," *Windsor Star*, May 17, 1946, 3; "Black Market Meat Buyers Said Spreading into West" *Edmonton Journal*, March 7, 1946, 1.

81. "OPA Gets Added Funds to Fight Black Market," *Tampa Bay Times*, March 23, 1946, 1; "Truman Abolishes Meat Controls," *Janesville Daily Gazette* (WI), October 15, 1946, 1.

CHAPTER 7

Food in the Counterinsurgency of the Malayan Emergency

Security, Hawking, and Food Denial

YVONNE TAN

Food serves an important role in Malaysia and Singapore as it celebrates multiculturalism and cultural collaboration in a society where race relations are usually points of contention.[1] In particular, food demonstrates the hybrid cultures that form within colonial communities; in the case of British Malaya, blending the tastes and ingredients from British colonizers and Malay, Chinese, and Indian communities while serving as an illustration of political power. The tumultuous historiography of food within Malaya, therefore, is not an expression of banal domesticity but rather of empire's enduring legacies.

The colonial figure of the street vendor gained widespread popularity during the late nineteenth to early twentieth centuries under British colonial control.[2] In fact, street hawking is still very popular even decades after Malaysian independence because it serves as a lucrative way for unskilled immigrants to make a living. Regulation of street hawkers first intensified under British imperialism and hawkers received greater scrutiny when food security was weaponized during the Malayan Emergency (1948–60) and hawkers were accused of harboring sympathies for the Communist guerillas within Malaya's New Villages. Thus, from the colonial era through the early Cold War, street hawkers were the focus of intense scrutiny among political elites, who sought to control and deny access to food.

As street hawkers occupies the precarious space between the public and the private, wherein they negotiate between authority and informal economic activity, they are easy targets for government force despite serving the vital need of creatively providing food for a population that has itself been the target of imperial aggression and military occupation. Symbolizing the issues of internal conflict, lingering colonialism, and counterinsurgency that came to dominate Malaysian life during the nineteenth and twentieth centuries, the hawker is usually an outsider (distinguished by race, religion, or political leanings). Taking into account Malaysia's resettlement programs and food insecurity, this chapter examines the weaponization of food in the colonial context and presents the street hawker as a crucial survival figure, not only for the hawkers' families themselves but for other workers in the nation dependent on the hawker for food and survival.

Food in the Informal Colonial Economy

Street hawking and urban vendors had long been part of the British Empire's cultural and culinary landscape. Dipesh Chakrabarty has discussed bazaars in British India as an important outdoor spatial complex usually thought of as a place of heat and dust, overflowing with crowds, dirt, and disease. Bazaars were interstitial spaces with their own structures and relationships of power that served as the meeting point of several communities. In colonial Britain, bazaars combined recreation and economic exchange, and their vendors and workers were generally marked as members of the lower classes.[3] Officials alleged that these public spaces posed a threat to public health and order, as well as enhancing the power of dialect clans and secret societies that controlled vendors. Enforcing discipline and regulating bazaars, therefore, became one of the chief ways that British colonials sought to regulate local economies and police the public sphere. The same pattern existed in the Malaysian equivalent of a bazaar (similar phonetically, called a *pasar*) with similar implications for social regulation and colonial control. One British visitor described the pasar as a chaotic, multiracial culinary spectacle:

> There is probably no city in the world with such a motley crowd of itinerant vendors of wares, fruits, cakes, vegetables, &c. There are Malays, generally with fruit; Chinamen with a mixture of all sorts, and Klings with cakes and different kinds of nuts. Malays and Chinamen always use the shoulder-stick, having equally balanced loads suspended at either end; the Klings, on the contrary, carry their wares on the head on trays. The travelling cook shops of the

Chinese are probably the most extraordinary of the things that are carried about in this way. They are suspended on one of the common shoulder-sticks, and consists of a box on one side and a basket on the other; the former containing a fire and a small copper cauldron for soup; the latter loaded with rice, vermicelli, cakes, jellies and condiments.[4]

These observations reveal the colonials' derogatory view of the spaces (especially towards the indentured laborers, who were here called "Klings" and "Chinese coolies"). And the "kaleidoscope" detailed by another British observer demonstrates their attitudes toward purity and pollution and layers of imperial racial logic and hierarchy:

Chinese Towkays in grey felt hat, nankeen jacket, and capacious trousers; Straits-born Babas as proud as Lucifer; easy-going Malays in picturesque sarong and baju; stately Sikhs from the garrison; lanky Bengalis; ubiquitous Jews in old-time gabardine; exorbitant Chetties with closely-shaven heads and muslin swathed limbs; Arabs in long coat and fez; Tamil street laborers in turban and loincloth of lurid hue; Kling hawkers scantily clad; Chinese coolies and itinerant vendors of food; Javanese, Achinese, Sinhalese, and a host of others—in fact, the kaleidoscopic procession is one of almost endless variety.[5]

There has always been a conflict over what constitutes public and private space, with frequent conflicts between colonial authority and occupiers of public space for informal economic activity. Within British India, *Halla* was a regular colonial practice (continued by the Indian national government) of sudden, violent police action aimed at clearing streets of hawkers and vendors whose presence was proscribed by law.[6] In 1887, Singapore passed Municipal Ordinance IX, allowing authorities to remove any "obstructions" along the five-foot ways, which were continuous roofed walkways along rows of shophouses. Soon after the introduction of the ordinance, the 1888 Verandah riots, where the police and peddlers clashed, ensued, lasting from February 20 to 22 of that year.[7]

In 1905 another bill was drafted to regulate hawkers through licensing and registration so that street hawking could be "brought under control."[8] Although the governor rejected this legislation, the bill demonstrates the continued tug and pull between hawkers and authorities into the twentieth century. Political elites and colonizers regarded hawking with skepticism, distrusting "the selling of food in a manner rendering it liable to contamination, and the fouling of streets and five-foot ways."[9]

For nearly a decade, there was no definite policy regarding hawking, simply sporadic activity against it by the police and municipal authorities until another governor of Singapore, Sir Cecil Clementi, attempted serious hawking regulation. He formed a committee involving various organizations, including the Municipal Health Officer, the police, the Superintendent of Town Cleansing, head representatives of the Chinese Chamber of Commerce, the Clerical Union, twenty Teo Chew Guilds, the Indo-Ceylon Club, and the Straits Chinese British Association. During this new wave of governmental scrutiny, Seow Poh Leng began to emerge as a champion of hawker's rights. Once a street peddler himself, Leng became a founding member of the Ho Hong Bank. Despite Leng's pleas for humane treatment, subsequent bills concerning street vendors were passed, included the licensing of eateries and coffee shops in 1913 and itinerant hawkers during both day and night in 1919. The clashes that centered on informal economy of food had only just begun and would soon be adopted as a weapon of war to be used throughout the twentieth century.

Cutting Tensions in Race:
Food in Guerilla Warfare and Beyond

On June 16, 1948, High Commissioner Edward Gent declared a state of emergency in Malaya against The Malayan National Liberation Army (MNLA), the military arm of the Malayan Communist Party (MCP). This began the tumultuous period of guerilla warfare popularly known as the Malayan Emergency, but which the MNLA called the Anti-British National Liberation War—a view of the conflict consistent with a wider independence struggle throughout the Southeast Asian region embroiled in larger geopolitical tensions of the Cold War.

The MNLA, also known as the Malayan Races Liberation Army (MRLA) or Malayan People's Liberation Army (MPLA), was a remobilization of the Malayan Peoples' Anti-Japanese Army (MPAJA), which was trained and armed by the British and played a crucial role during the late stages of World War II against Japanese occupation. When disbanded at the end of the war, the British persuaded MPAJA to surrender their weapons in exchange for economic incentives, although most did not voluntarily do so. By late April, the MCP began compiling lists of former MPAJA members who they committed for a sudden call-up. The estimated number of soldiers was around 5,800 with an additional 4,700 underground forces.[10] These guerilla recruits began to specifically target colonial resource extraction industries in Malaya, mainly tin mines and rubber plantations. Chinese laborers had come to Malaya to work as indentured laborers at these mines and plantations and were forced to defend the country against the Japanese during the Pacific War. During the postwar era, these ethnic Chinese laborers had to consider their political place within a divided country.[11]

Despite the end of the Pacific War, Malaya continued to experience political turmoil and food shortages. During World War II, the Japanese targeted the Chinese in areas of occupation, under an imperialist policy informed by the Second Sino-Japanese War, while favoring Malay cooperation. This, in turn, led to wartime discontent and mobilization by the Chinese. But what was most devastating was the rice prohibition during the war, in which rice stockpiles had to be declared to the Commercial and Industrial Section of the Japanese occupation government. Wartime rice production averaged only 35 percent of its requirements between 1920 and 1940. The resulting food shortages were compounded by the longstanding ethnic division of labor under British colonial rule, where non-Malays were prevented from cultivating rice in order to work for the profitable mines and estates owned by the British elite. At the same time, until 1930, governmental restrictions discouraged Malays from entering these sectors (such as mining and rubber production) as smallholders, to reduce competition with the interests of colonial capital.[12] These limits on food production, combined with rice-rationing during the Japanese occupation, led to high food prices and the emergence of black markets, and encouraged migration to the countryside to grow more food with the establishment of agricultural settlements, segregated along ethnic and linguistic lines. An unstable food supply, internal migrations, governmental restrictions over food production, and tensions over ethnicity and labor set the stage for the guerilla warfare and forced resettlement to come.[13]

The Malayan Emergency was largely influenced by Eisenhower's Domino Theory of 1954 that justified harsh foreign intervention to combat communist expansion, particularly in Southeast Asia.[14] For decades, U.S. policymakers fueled a brutal crackdown in the region, exemplified by the nineteen-year Vietnam War, the CIA-backed Indonesian mass killings by Suharto, twelve years of the Hukbalahap Rebellion, and the thirty-three years of the Malayan Emergency.

The Malayan Emergency, often referred to as Britain's Vietnam, was lauded as a counterinsurgency success, praised for its military tactics, and particularly applauded for the containment policy enacted by British General Sir Harold Briggs. British operations and implementation of the

Briggs Plan during the Malayan Emergency even informed the United States' armed conflict in Iraq and Afghanistan decades later.[15] Before Briggs's appointment in 1950 as Director of Operations, the MCP was winning the guerilla war in the jungle and had widespread public support.

The essence of the Briggs Plan, implemented in 1950, was to shift the frontlines from guarding the mines and estates, which the MCP targeted, to controlling the civilian population. British counterinsurgency relied on a forced resettlement program of rural peasants who provided support, intelligence, recruits, and most importantly, food to the MCP. More than half a million people in Malaya were resettled into 509 "New Villages" (Malay: *Kampung Baru*), a process that was completed quickly, by 1952, and affected almost half a million people—of whom 86 percent were ethnic Chinese, 9 percent Malay, 4 percent Indian, and 1 percent others.[16] The Briggs Plan entailed mass forceful evictions to guarded camps with imposed curfews and required residents to carry identity cards, causing disruption of individual lives, amid the backdrop of a guerrilla war, the larger geopolitical tensions of the Cold War, and the last vestiges of British imperialism.

The Briggs Plan brought about the resettlement of Malaya's rural population into the New Villages which meant distancing the population from their homes and the abandonment or transfer of property. Although the citizens were given new land in the New Villages, housing was substandard and the social amenities were lacking, which alienated residents from colonial authorities, even though they were not initially sympathizers of the Malayan Communist Party.[17] A typical New Village usually included public buildings such as a police post, pharmacy, school, community hall, livestock pens, cropland, and in villages under severe restriction, a communal kitchen, all enclosed by a wire fence.[18] The New Village houses, from which some who settled there have never moved out, can today be easily distinguished by the makeshift zinc panels used for roofs and walls.

The New Villages program uprooted residents' daily lives, along with their source of diet and income—a state of affairs that provided an opportunity for itinerant street hawking. These food vendors provided a crucial form of both subsistence and sustenance because of severe restrictions placed on New Villages' communal kitchens, inadequate rations provided by the British, and the lingering food shortages in a Malaya still recovering from Japanese occupation.

Katarzyna Cwiertka remarked on how "food management is a powerful example of the structural continuities between colonial and postcolonial" when speaking of the effects of the war in Korea, where food insecurity measures implemented by the Japanese continued well into the Cold War.[19] Cwiertka points out that the end of the war did not bring about a turning point or the end of food scarcity, but simply a perpetuation of war-induced hunger and disease. The events in Korea paralleled British Malaya with the resettlement of the MNLA's source of food during the New Villages program. British counterinsurgency strategies were managed by the District War Executive Committee and focused on denying food to the MNLA through village gate and field checks, which controlled food supplies and prevented food from passing between individuals. Women were not allowed to take packed lunches, for instance, in case the food was meant for the MNLA, while schoolchildren were regularly searched for food before being allowed to board the bus to school. A few kilometers from the compound, the bus then might be stopped by the MNLA, who were seeking recruits, money, or food before fleeing a nearby British patrol.[20] By October of 1953, intelligence and food denial operations were described as decisive weapons in anti-guerrilla warfare. The Briggs Plan involved a phased approach, relying on intelligence buildup, intensification of food control (including arrests of food suppliers and the destruction of food dumps) and, finally, exploiting the enemy's loss of morale due to reduced supplies and increased attacks and ambushes.[21]

The most detailed implementation and regulation of the Malayan Emergency concerned food itself. Food inspectors purchased all surplus rice and ensured that there were no surplus ration cards among retailers and in private houses. Officials also policed stocks of rice and other important commodities. People living inside food-restricted areas had to buy their food from a small number of licensed shops while rubber tappers and manual laborers were not allowed to take food out of their villages for a midday meal. If found supplying food to the MCP, villages were immediately punished with additional curfew regulations, reduced rice rations, closure of several rice dealers, and removal of all surplus rice, along with detentions and interrogations, all of which were carried out in the New Villages of Sungai Pelek, Selangor, and Tanjung Malim, Perak.[22]

The policing of food reached a point at which possession of food itself was criminalized, at one time carrying a penalty of up to five years' imprisonment and a five-thousand-dollar fine.[23] In some areas the British introduced an Operational Rice Ration that limited residents to just over half the normal ration. In the case of the Semenyih New Village, London's *Guardian* published secret file reports alleging that "British troops regularly strip-searched and abused women near the village of Semenyih during a 'food denial' operation,"[24] which triggered a government inquiry and nearly spiraled into a riot on January 12, 1956, followed by another disturbance on January 14. Of the 41 million dollars spent in 1951—provided by the United Kingdom Colonial Development and Welfare funds—only 0.02 million was allocated for agricultural aid and 0.36 million for medical and health requirements. A stark contrast to the 6.39 million dollars spent on the police buildings.[25]

Agent Orange, best known for its use in the Vietnam War, was first tested in the Malayan Emergency as part of the food denial campaign in the early 1950s. The use of Trioxane 2,4,5-T and 2,4-D (components of Agent Orange) and sodium trichloroacetate (STCA) was encouraged by Professor Blackman from the University of Oxford and Dr. Kearns at University of Bristol and spearheaded by Imperial Chemical Industries Limited (ICI).[26] These chemical weapons were used first and foremost "to destroy terrorists' crops in deep jungle by spraying from the air. Other chemicals besides sodium tricholoroacetate may be used but they all share the property of being harmless to human and animal life."[27]

Since the British colonial administration was convinced of the chemicals' safety, they were more concerned with the question of which crops to destroy. Increasingly cut off from urban settlements and their families, the MNLA was highly reliant on the Orang Asli, the indigenous hunter gatherers living in the depths of the jungle, whose livelihood was largely dependent on the forest. The Orang Asli provided some guidance for spraying defoliants, since British counterinsurgents contrasted the "orderly rows in the Chinese method, whereas the aborigines cultivate in a disorderly manner."[28] British authorities even hired Orang Asli to differentiate the owners of food cultivation plots, recruiting those who knew the jungle best to their side.

Agent Orange and STCA were used to wipe out food crops as a form of defoliant or herbicide and were also used along key roads and possible ambush points. Later, helicopters and fixed-wing aircrafts dispatched the defoliants onto crops like sweet potatoes and maize.[29] While deployment of these chemicals caused significant ecological and agricultural losses, estimates about the number of civilians and insurgents in Malaya affected by chemical warfare are unclear and were not publicized, as they would be in the Vietnam War.

By June of 1954, instructions for food denial operations included the role of police, Special Constables (operating as Area Security Units), Home

FOOD IN THE COUNTERINSURGENCY

Guard, information services, and psychological warfare, controlled by the Director of Operations.[30] The Emergency Food Denial Organization set up central cooking kitchen schemes to further prevent food getting to the MCP, as well as Operational Rice rationing, first established in May of 1954. According to this food-denial program, after collecting uncooked rice with a security escort, families would collect their rations as cooked rice, which was more difficult to smuggle.[31] These extensive measures, which involved mass resettlement, policing, and chemical warfare, were highly calculated toward the ultimate control of food as a weapon of war, which raised the profile of the street hawker as an essential source of food. Since food hawkers operated outside of tightly regulated governmental food sources, they became figures of scrutiny and distrust for government officials, leading to another devastating crackdown on food vendors.

Although the New Villages were not extensively implemented in Singapore, the Criminal Law (Temporary Provisions) Act (CLTPA) was introduced in 1955 to control the movement of food, supplies and information and remains in force today:

> Any person who demands, collects or receives any supplies from any other person in circumstances which raise a reasonable presumption that he intends or is about to act or has recently acted in a manner prejudicial to public safety in Singapore or the maintenance of public order therein or that the supplies so demanded, collected or received are intended for the use of any person who that first-mentioned person knows or has reason to believe intends, or is about, so to act, or has recently so acted, shall be guilty of an offence and shall be liable on conviction to imprisonment for a term not exceeding [ten] years.[32]

As the MCP operated mainly through trade unions in Singapore, performing strikes and protests before being driven into the jungles, illegal strikes and assemblies were banned under the act as well.

The Malayan Emergency was never thought of as an outright declaration of war. Instead, the Emergency operated by asymmetric warfare and avoiding armed confrontation, while winning popular support was a crucial goal on both sides. Britain's use of chemical and psychological warfare in counterinsurgency during the Emergency relied far more on monitoring food security and production than direct combat and guerilla war. The British "Hearts and Minds" campaign was one effort in garnering support and affinities for the imperial power and the new government that would emerge after independence. Another strategy in the New Village era was dropping airborne leaflets. By 1950, the British had dropped about 35 million leaflets—a central component of the psychological warfare of the time.[33] Food was also part of the propaganda campaign, as illustrated by the Safe Conduct Pass (pictured below), which displayed a happy and healthy Chinese family juxtaposed with a starving and sick MCP member. It also displays a warning in English, Malay, Jawi, Tamil, and Chinese to "Treat bearer [of the Safe Conduct Pass] well, give food and medical attention report to military or police officer" and displayed the image of a lifeline thrown to a drowning MCP member.

Throughout the early Cold War Era, the MCP and MNLA was comprised primarily of ethnic Chinese, creating a highly sensitive social divide. Malays were presented as national defenders while the Chinese as communist outsiders, a tension between these two communities that still persists today. Describing the Emergency, Sir Henry Gurney, the High Commissioner to Malaya, was likewise preoccupied with the ethnic aspect of conflict, calling it "the Chinese problem in Malaya." When he helped set up the Malaysian Chinese Association (MCA), he wrote that it was a "loyal" alternative, insisting "the answer [to the Chinese problem] was that the rural Chinese, the peasants, who are the real target, must first be protected."[34] In other words, residents poorest and closest to the jungle were thought to be most susceptible to MCP's message. The MCA, in fact, adopted a strategy quite similar to what Gurney advised and, in the process, raised millions for community projects in New Villages. Nevertheless, there was still little support for the party throughout the region. Police and military officers were provided with a booklet titled with Gurney's words, informing officers that the Chinese were used to authoritarian forms of government. Therefore, "they have no clear comprehension of the requirements and machinery of democratic institutions," and would remain loyal to China's Communist regime.[35]

By the middle of the twentieth century, street-hawking slowly reemerged in Malaya, with licenses provided to eating stalls and shops to sell poultry and vegetables. While vendors had to pay conservancy fees, street-hawking remained one of the few forms of employment outside of rubber tapping and smallholder farming. Many settlers actually held two occupations: a wage-earning activity (like food-hawking) in the morning and market gardening in the afternoon. Some families also raised pigs and chickens.[36] Street-hawking, therefore, was still work linked to immediate sustenance and "getting-by" agricultural concerns.

"1458, Safe conduct pass. Treat bearer well, give food and medical attention," from Department of Public Relations, United Kingdom, 1952. *Courtesy of Lee Richards, www.psywar.org.*

Although street-hawking is not as well explored as tin-mining or rubber-tapping, Ray Nyce, a Christian evangelist, gathered research in Malaya from 1957–61, particularly from Hakka dominant New Villages in northern Malaya and the "Valley Villages" along a ten-mile stretch of the Grik Road. He noted that the most common economic activities there were family-centric industries such as making incense sticks and food production. Nyce noted:

> Food production is another family occupation. One family in Village A makes sheets of dried bean paste to be sold in Chinese food stores for making soup. Bean paste is made by boiling small yellow beans in large iron pans until a thick skin is formed on top. The skin is

separated from the pan edges, sliced through the middle and each half peeled off the hot paste. The resulting sheets are hung on racks and dried until hard and brittle. The father sorts the beans and carries them to the oven in the back, the mother tends the fire under each of the twelve pans, and their son peels off the sheets of paste.[37]

Creative use of the rice rations and other cheap ingredients, inexpensive "poor man's" cooking, and the organization of the family as an economic unit, continue to be the hallmarks of eateries in the New Village areas today.[38] As small enterprises, each family commonly produced one product, such as bean curd, and other dishes commonly associated with New Village cooking, including noodles, beggar's chicken, yong tau fu, red bean paste buns, and many more dishes. Nyce, again observing New Village food production, explained that:

> Another family in the same village makes a kind of spongy pudding out of rice. It is put into small metal dishes and sold as an early morning meal to rubber tappers on their way to work. A table with large trays containing many small dishes of pudding is set up at about 5.30am near what is for this purpose the main intersection of the village. The selling is handled in turn by the mother and the grandmother, who are also in charge of washing the bowls. Most of the cooking and other work is done by the father. These three seem adequate for all the tasks concerned in the small industry. Such small family industries are found in every New Village. Other forms of hawking do not involve the whole family. There are usually several hawkers in each village.[39]

The regulated hawking industry slowly developed during the Emergency as more New Villages were declared to be "White Areas" free from association with the MCP, as opposed to heavily sanctioned "Black Areas" that were suspected to have ties to the MCP.[40] By 1955, MCP activity was moving closer to the Thai border and MCP members were cut off from most contact with their families. In 1950, Franklin Gimson, former Governor of Singapore, had once again established a Hawkers Inquiry Commission, which produced a report to deal with what were perceived as the problems of street hawking. The Singapore government hoped for a success story of street hawker resettlement into the permanent modern food courts and hygiene reforms. As a result, the report called street vendors "primarily a public nuisance to be removed from the streets" and noted the "disorderly sprawl of hawkers blocking up entire streets with a jumble of goods in defiance of all order and reason."[41] Meanwhile, in 1952 in Malaya, the Local Councils (Amendment) Ordinance established a local council body for each area, which supervised advertising, licensing of eateries, and hawkers in order to "regulate, supervise and license peddlers, hawkers and street traders and to prescribe streets or areas in which peddling, hawking or street trading shall be prohibited."[42]

Following the Emergency, 84 percent of hawkers in Singapore were Chinese, mostly from southeast China; Hokkien hawkers formed the largest group followed by Teochews, who often sold market produce, while the Hainanese sold cooked food.[43] During the years of high unemployment and food shortages that followed the Pacific War, food hawking was a lucrative source of income, particularly among the unemployed, since it required little capital and technical skills. In Malaysia, now separated from Singapore, the ethnic composition of street vendors in 1970 was only 4.4 percent Malay, while Chinese constituted 80.8 percent and Indian 14.8 percent. By the turn of the millennium in 2000, the composition of licensed street vendors had changed slightly to 31 percent Malay, 59 percent Chinese, and 9 percent Indian. This change was likely a result of the Department of Hawkers and Petty Traders (DHPT; established in 1986) which preferred to grant more licenses to the Malay population.[44]

Street vendors offered a variety of affordable food to a population continually subjected to bouts of hunger as food was weaponized during war and counterinsurgency. Yet the class of people who took on the occupation of street-hawking were continuously assigned to the lowest social strata and demonized as outsiders. In this way, the colonial mindset, which repeatedly criticized and demeaned the street vendor, returned throughout the twentieth century. The irony, however, was that the street hawker, though often maligned, satisfied the real needs for economic and nutritious sustenance. As one observer noted:

> It was precisely the migration of these largely working-class, young and under-employed Chinese to the urban kampong and the emergence of an autonomous way of life therein, which resulted in its being powerfully represented as a place of social danger. Tied frequently to the informal economy, many urban kampong dwellers lived beyond the pale of the social discipline of full-time employment. Such a person, to the authorities, was akin to a vagrant, who was "the most helpless, and therefore the most illuminating, of a large army of those outside the Establishment, among whom we may include the very poor generally, the criminals, the lunatics."[45]

The street vendor comes from a community that continues to operate on the fringes of economic development, industrialization, and modernity.[46] As residents of a normalized battleground of disloyalties, imprisonment, and surveillance and one of the last areas that experienced direct domination from the fading imperial power, New Villagers were civilian figures subjected to a war that was never declared, witnessing the tumultuous breakdown of colonial order while developing narratives of nationalist struggle and patriotic sacrifice. New Villagers continue to feel the lingering effects of the Malayan Emergency today, and many remain in their makeshift homes and maintain racial divisions that set clear boundaries between "natives" and "immigrants."

Modern-day street vendors in Malaysia and Singapore come from a new wave of migrants from the rest of Southeast Asia, who experience the same marginalization as previous generations of food-hawkers. In this way, history repeats itself, so much so that the Federal Territories Ministry in Malaysia has declared that there will be no more roadside traders in the city by 2020. Singapore has banned street vendors altogether, instead celebrating the licensed hawker centers. Recently, Prime Minister Lee Hsien Loong announced his intention to nominate Singapore's hawker culture for UNESCO's Representative List of the Intangible Cultural Heritage of Humanity, and was added to the list on December 2020. Paradoxically, the only time the street vendor is celebrated as a part of both nations' heritage is through its recognition by the Western world.

The original practice of street vendors offering cheap food and goods emerged from high rates of unemployment and individual deprivation, and street vendors adapted and grew in popularity in the twentieth century by providing necessary services unavailable through larger retail outlets. The British food denial campaign in twentieth-century Malaya exacerbated these circumstances, as food-hawking became an expression of weaponized of food security during the Emergency. Food hawkers provided sustenance and alleviated anxieties surrounding food and survival. New Villagers found themselves caught between the decisive tactics used against the MCP and suspicions of sympathies towards their cause. With food used to exercise political and economic pressure, hawking was one of the few occupations where individuals could work on their own account and provided convenience of movement in precarious times, making street vending an integral part of life in the New Village.

NOTES

1. Jean Duruz, and Gaik Cheng Khoo, *Eating together: Food, space, and identity in Malaysia and Singapore* (London: Rowman & Littlefield, 2015): 3.

2. Sheri Lynn Gibbings, and Fridus Steijlen, "Colonial Figures: Memories of Street Traders in the Colonial and Early Post-Colonial Periods" *Public History Review* 19 (2012): 63–85.

3. Dipesh Chakrabarty, *Habitations of Modernity: Essays in the Wake of Subaltern Studies* (Chicago: University of Chicago Press, 2002): 71.

4. John Cameron, *Our Tropical Possessions in Malayan India: Being a Descriptive Account of Singapore, Penang, Province Wellesley, and Malacca: Their Peoples, Products, Commerce, and Government* (London: Smith, Elder and Co., 1865): 65.

5. Arnold Wright, and H. A. Cartwright, *Twentieth Century Impressions of British Malaya: Its History, People, Commerce, Industries, and Resources* (London, Durban, Colombo, Perth, Singapore, Hong Kong, and Shanghai: Lloyd's Greater Britain Publishing Company, Ltd, 1908): 603.

6. Chakrabarty, *Habitations of Modernity*, 77.

7. Brenda Yeoh, *Contesting Space: Power Relations and the Urban Built Environment in Colonial Singapore* (New York: Oxford University Press, 1996): 250.

8. *Report of the Committee Appointed to Investigate the Hawker Question in Singapore* (Singapore: Government Printing Office, 1932): 1.

9. *Report of the Committee*, 2.

10. Timothy Norman Harper, *The End of Empire and the Making of Malaya* (Cambridge: Cambridge University Press, 2001): 145.

11. Cheah Boon Kheng, *Red Star over Malaya: Resistance and Social Conflict during and after the Japanese Occupation, 1941–1946* (Singapore: NUS Press, 2012): 265.

12. Paul H. Kratoska, "Rice Cultivation and the Ethnic Division of Labor in British Malaya," *Comparative Studies in Society and History* 24, no. 2 (1982), 280–282.

13. Examples of agricultural settlements include Shyonan Bahru at Endau, Johor for Chinese, Fuji-Go at Bahau, Negeri Sembilan for Eurasians and Catholics, and Bintang Island for Malays and Indians. On resettlement and the New Villages movement, see: Ray Nyce, *Chinese New Villages in Malaya: A Community Study* (Singapore: Malaysian Sociological Research Institute Ltd., 1973): xxxi.

14. The Malayan Emergency developed in two phases: the first phase (1948–60) is the main focus of this chapter. The second phase (1968–89) was also known as the Second Malayan Emergency in Malaysia. On the politics of the Cold War in Southeast Asia, see: Ang Cheng Guan, *Southeast Asia's Cold War: An Interpretive History* (Honolulu: University of Hawai'i Press, 2018): 140; Jack Henry Brimmell, *Communism in South East Asia: A Political Analysis* (Abingdon: Oxford University Press, 1959).

15. See: John Nagl's *Learning to Eat Soup with a Knife*.

16. As of June 30th, 1953, the population of forced resettlement stood at 570,838 in 546 New Villages with 67,930 to left to be resettled. CO1022/337 Federation of Malaya, *Progress report on the Development Plans of the Federation of Malaya, 1950–1952* (Kuala Lumpur: Government Printer, 1953): 48; Ray Nyce, *Chinese New Villages*, xli.

17. Lee Kam Hing, "A Neglected Story: Christian missionaries, Chinese New Villagers, and Communists in the Battle for the 'Hearts and Minds' in Malaya, 1948–1960," *Modern Asian Studies* 47, no. 6 (2013), 1981.

18. Ray Nyce, *Chinese New Villages*, L.

19. Katarzyna J. Cwiertka, *Cuisine, Colonialism and The Cold War: Food in Twentieth-Century Korea* (London: Reaktion Books, 2013): 80.

20. Akshita Nanda, "Village Boy Tells All on Malayan Emergency," *The Star*, 25 June 2012, https://www.thestar.com.my/lifestyle/features/2012/06/25/village-boy-tells-all-on-malayan-emergency/.

21. Anthony Short, *The Communist Insurrection in Malaya 1948–60* (London: Frederick Muller Limited, 1975): 144, 376–378.

22. Original Correspondence of the Southeast Asia Department, 1950–1956 [Hereafter, CO] 1022/55, 22/4/1952, 3; CO 1022/54, 21/5/1952, 21.

23. Short, *The Communist Insurrection*, 483.

24. Owen Bowcott, "Colonial Office Files Detail 'Eliminations' to Choke Malayan Insurgency" [online], *Guardian*, 18 April 2012, https://www.theguardian.com/world/2012/apr/18/colonial-office-eliminations-malayan-insurgency?intcmp=239 [accessed August 18, 2019], "Federation of Malaya Political Report for January 1956," CO1030/33; Federation of Malaya, Report on the conduct of food searches at Semenyih in the Kajang District of the State of Selangor (Kuala Lumpur, 1956).

25. CO1022/337 Federation of Malaya, 21, 48.

26. CO1022/26 The use of chemicals in clearing under-growth near ambush points and destroying terrorist crops in Malaya 1951–1953, 16/11/1951, 5, 13, 93.

27. CO1022/27, 9/6/1953, 12, 20.

28. CO1022/27, 9/6/1953, 12, 20.

29. CO1022/27, 24/3/1953, 33.

30. Short, *The Communist Insurrection*, 378.

31. Tan Teng-Phee. "'Like a Concentration Camp, Lah': Chinese Grassroots Experience of the Emergency and New Villages in British Colonial Malaya," *Chinese Southern Diaspora Studies* 3 (2009): 216–28, 225; Short, *The Communist Insurrection*, 485; Mahani Musa, "Women in the Malayan Communist Party, 1942–89," *Journal of Southeast Asian Studies* 44, no. 2 (2013), 247. Poisoning was a popular method of sabotage or espionage through food by women in the MCP camps, as most were assigned kitchen duties.

32. Singapore Statutes, Ordinance No. 26 of 1955, now Cap. 67, 2000 Rev. Ed, s. 3.

33. Ramakrishna Kumar, *Emergency Propaganda: The Winning of Malayan Hearts and Minds 1948–1958* (London: Routledge, 2013): 73.

34. CO 1022/148, 12/1951, 21

35. Records of Former Colonial Administrations: Migrated Archives (FCO) 141/7365, 4/1955, "Chinese co-operation the key to the Malayan problem," 13.

36. Hamzah-Sendut, "Rasah—A Resettlement Village in Malaya." *Asian Survey* (1961), 24.

37. Ray Nyce, *Chinese New Villages*, 62–63.

38. "Sungai Buloh new village well-known for SMEs and restaurants offering good food," *The Star* (Kuala Lampur), 20 January 2015, https://www.thestar.com.my

/metro/focus/2015/01/20/from-farms-to-factories-sungai-buloh-new-village
-wellknown-for-smes-and-restaurants-offering-good-fo.

39. Ray Nyce, *Chinese New Villages*, 63.

40. By the end of 1957, 3,471,500 people were living in White Areas, Ramakrishna Kumar, *Emergency Propaganda*, 175.

41. Azhar Ghani, "A recipe for success: How Singapore hawker centres came to be," *Institute of Policy Studies* 3 (2011), 2, 3.

42. Laws of Malaysia, Local Government Act 1976, 55.

43. Azhar Ghani, "A recipe for success," 1.

44. Sharit K. Bhowmik, "Street Vendors in Asia: A Review" *Economic and Political Weekly* 40, no. 22/23 (May 28–June 10, 2005), 2260.

45. Loh Kah Seng, "Black Areas: Urban Kampongs and Power Relations in Postwar Singapore Historiography," *SOJOURN: Journal of Social Issues in Southeast Asia* 22, no. 1 (2007), 21.

46. Ee-Tan Chow, "Chinese Resettlement Villages in Malaysia Get a Facelift, 60 Years after the First 'Temporary' Settlements Sprang Up," *South China Morning Post*, 22 August 2019, https://www.scmp.com/lifestyle/article/3023563 /chinese-resettlement-villages-malaysia-get-facelift-60-years-after-first.

PART II

Expanding Chronological Boundaries

CHAPTER 8

"To Calm Our Rebellious Stomachs"

*U.S. Soldiers' Experience with Food
during the U.S.–Mexico War*

CHRISTOPHER MENKING

Popular culture often portrays warfare as a series of dramatic battles and glory-filled moments. However, average nineteenth-century American soldiers spent much of their time either in camp or marching between camps. Battles proved scarce, so soldiers often spent time exploring nearby communities in pursuit of better-quality food to supplement their rations. Food was a primary point of contact between United States and Mexican cultures during the U.S.–Mexico War (1846–48) which brought more than fifty thousand American soldiers into Mexico, many of whom then tried Mexican food for the first time. It is important to note that Mexican food as it is known in the United States today was virtually unheard of across most of the United States in the 1840s and 1850s. This cultural interaction helped shape the postwar borderlands as the U.S.–Mexico War caused dramatic territorial shifts.

The goal of this chapter is to illustrate the role that the war played in helping spread Mexican food further across the continent and to demonstrate how the southwestern United States became a cultural hybridization of the two neighboring countries—a status evolving from the 1850s through the early 1900s, when Mexican food began its ascension to a dominant food style in the United States. Citizens from the United States had tasted Mexican food before, but the war presented the first chance for many U.S. men to try Mexican food as a collective experience. Just as the border moved in terms of land and people at the end of the war, so too did food move across these same borders. Understanding the transnational history of the Southwestern borderlands is crucial in understanding how soldiers experienced Mexican food during the war and how their culinary adventures traveled home with them afterward, laying the foundation for a future embrace of Mexican food. The war was not the only reason that people from the United States began to love Mexican food, but it did introduce tens of thousands to their first Mexican dishes.

The U.S.–Mexico War created a unique problem for the United States military, which needed to supply multiple armies thousands of miles from supply hubs while in a foreign country. The army's logistical network, controlled by the Quartermaster Department, did an admirable job transporting, equipping, and feeding thousands of soldiers that served. These soldiers traveled from New York to California to Mexico City and many places in between. The Subsistence Department procured food and worked in conjunction with the Quartermaster Department to deliver it to the armies in the field. This logistical hurdle necessitated the establishment of massive trade networks that crisscrossed North and Central America. The Quartermaster Department purchased steam and sail ships to ferry goods, hired teamsters and muleteers to carry goods overland, and hired private contractors to supplement the Army-owned portion of the trade network.[1]

Soldiers' rations varied throughout the war. While they received some food regularly, the quality and variety of army rations failed to satisfy the quartermaster's stipulations or the soldiers' appetites. The soldiers quickly solved this problem themselves by exploring the areas surrounding the camps to forage, buy, or steal food to supplement their rations. In addition to trying exotic new foods that sparked curiosity among all ranks of soldiers, learning a bit of Spanish helped the soldiers interact with Mexican citizens. Prior to the war, most U.S. residents had never lived or eaten apart from their local communities before. Wealthier men and women could travel, but the majority of nineteenth-century Americans were farmers and were thus tied to their land year-round. In one sense, wars represented a government-sponsored trip abroad to experience new foods and cultures, foreign lands, and different ways of life—as long as soldiers were willing to risk their lives for the cause of American imperialism.

There has been very little written on the relationship between soldiers and food in the context of the U.S.–Mexico War. While the importance of food in war is clear, very few historians have analyzed how wartime periods in the nineteenth century dealt with the more intimate relationship between a soldier and the food that they ate, even though virtually every diary, journal, or collection of letters from U.S. soldiers during the war with Mexico includes passages about food.[2]

There are several major works analyzing the relationship between food, soldiers, and the wartime experience, although the majority of these books are set in the twentieth century. Furthermore, there are no notable articles or books addressing food during the U.S.–Mexico War beyond the logistics of abstractly acquiring food for an army. At the forefront of the literature on food in the nineteenth century are William Davis's *A Taste for War*, Andrew Smith's *Starving the South*, and most notably Helen Zoe Veit's two-volume *Food in the Civil War Era*. These authors discuss food during the Civil War era, which would have shared similarities with the Mexican War era a decade earlier. While each adds an important contribution to the historiography, these works also demonstrate the dearth of books addressing the wartime food issues during the first half nineteenth century.[3]

Finally, the spread of Mexican foods north into what would become the United States started before the war and prior to the territorial acquisition, but the U.S.–Mexico War would accelerate the popularity of Mexican culinary traditions. Several books address the growth and spread of Mexican food, including Jeffrey Pilcher's *Que Vivan Los Tamales* and *Planet Taco*; Gregory McNamee's *Tortillas, Tiswin, & T-Bones*; and Meredith Abarca's *Voices in the Kitchen*. In addition, *Food Across Borders,* an edited volume, includes chapters on both the spread of Mexican food and the role of food in the military. These works lay the foundation for a more in-depth look at the relationship between the U.S.–Mexican War and food. The soldiers' wartime experiences are vital components to understanding how and why Mexican food has traveled the path it has to reach plates in the United States today.[4]

While not unanimously supported, the war proved popular among men wanting to test their mettle and to see Mexico. General Zachary Taylor's Army of Occupation fought in Northern Mexico including the battles of Matamoros, Monterrey, and Buena Vista. The Mexican people proved to be far more resilient than President Polk had predicted. Taylor's forces barely survived the brutal attack by an army led by Antonio López de Santa Anna during the Battle of Buena Vista. Fortuitously for the Americans, Santa Anna's forces retreated to deal with political problems in Mexico City, but not before debilitating Taylor's army.[5]

While Taylor fought in northern Mexico, General Stephen Kearny and Captain John Frémont led their forces to capture Mexican territory in the western portion of the continent. Kearny and Frémont, with aid from the Navy, secured Santa Fe and California with minimal fighting. Despite the success of United States forces in northern Mexico and the western territories, Mexico stood resolute in its resistance to the United States. Polk then turned to General Winfield Scott's proposed campaign to capture Mexico City. Scott launched a daring invasion of Veracruz, capturing the city and quickly pushing inland toward Mexico City, confronting Santa Anna at the Battle of Cerro Gordo. After the United States troops captured the city of Puebla, Scott's army marched toward Mexico City, culminating in September of 1847 at the Battle of Chapultepec.[6]

Although it would take several months of occupation before an agreement was reached, most of the fighting had ended between United States and Mexican forces. On 2 February 1848, United States and Mexican diplomats signed the Treaty of Guadalupe Hidalgo. The primary component of the treaty was the cession of a vast portion of Mexican territory. The cession of land had dramatic implications for both Mexico and the United States, both of which were forever changed by the war.[7]

The war's dramatic influences on the postwar United States and Mexico began during the war itself as soldiers interacted with new foods during their time Mexico. What soldiers experienced and how they interacted with a foreign population laid the foundation for an altered borderland after 1846. One of the driving forces for such contiguity as arose between United States soldiers and Mexican citizens was the soldiers' hunt for food.

The nineteenth-century United States Army was not known for providing appetizing rations to its soldiers. The army's goal was to keep the soldiers ready for combat and able to march—anything beyond base nutritional value meant an extra cost and a significant effort to deliver the supplies. The rations allotted to each soldier included "three-fourths of a pound of pork or bacon, or one-fourth a pound of fresh salt beef; eighteen ounces of bread or flour, or twelve ounces of hard bread, or one-fourth pound of cornmeal." Every hundred soldiers shared "two quarts of salt; four quarts of vinegar; eight quarts of peas or beans, (or in lieu thereof) ten pounds of rice; six pounds of coffee, and twelve pounds of sugar."[8] While this appears to be a rather generous daily ration, the reality is that the Quartermaster Department rarely delivered the amounts of foodstuffs outlined by the Subsistence Department's General Regulations. More often than not, the quartermaster worked with the available rations.

"TO CALM OUR REBELLIOUS STOMACHS"

Substitutions and partial rations became a way of life for the armies operating in foreign territory. This meant that the soldiers often resorted to obtaining their own supplements to the provided rations whenever the opportunities arose.[9]

Soldiers frequently wrote about the preparation of their rations, complaining that the quality of the rations was often wanting. Private Richard Coulter recalled the rations thus: "Our fare, raw flitch [bacon] principally fat, the rank taste killed with vinegar and crackers with scarcely sufficient water to wash it down." While regulations outlined bacon as an option, Coulter made clear that it was not the same mouthwatering fare he normally ate. Benjamin Franklin Scribner, a volunteer, also became "surfeited with bacon and hard moldy bread," and noted it proved tiresome eating the same unpalatable food each day. Coulter's problems are recorded over several months. He wrote he "had no provision but the boiled beef of last, without salt, which began to taste noxious, and so [he] tried some prickly pears, but after getting [his] lips and tongue full of the beard with which they [became] covered, gave it up." Due to limited access to salt while marching, rations prepared with fresh beef often spoiled quickly. An artillery officer, Robert Anderson, experienced some of this ostensibly fresh beef, which he concluded might "have been a spare cut from the rump of some poor donkey killed by one of our shells." Anderson welcomed the fresh meat the first night due to hunger, but the next day he "could not go it, like a second bad egg." These problems with rations drove the men to seek food elsewhere to make dining a more palatable affair.

The trend of bland, undesirable food was not unique to the army. During the early nineteenth century, health-reform movements changed the way many Americans understood what constituted healthy food. Notable proponents of these reforms such as Sylvester Graham, today remembered most for the Graham cracker that bears his name, pushed for bland, plant-based foods they felt would curtail the less desirable aspects of human nature. Graham argued that a bland diet would reduce violence, sexual promiscuity, and masturbation, and improve family life. By the time young soldiers destined for Mexico set off in the mid-1840s, Graham had already retired, but his supporters promoted a less rigid form of his program. The young men going to war most likely would have been exposed to their message, as Graham and other reformers targeted young men as their most important audience. However, as soldiers left home for war, they also departed from many social constraints American society placed upon them for behavior and diet, so it is likely that these reform movements did little to deter soldiers from trying new, flavorful food to supplement their rations.[10]

One of the most readily available options for purchasing supplemental rations came from United States merchants that the Quartermaster Department allowed to accompany the army into Mexico, particularly in the Northern Campaign. These merchants also served as intermediaries between the U.S. Army and the indigenous markets for goods and labor. American merchants provided few options for soldiers to supplement their rations, and these often cost the soldiers dearly as merchants sold goods at a premium during wartime. Many soldiers instead resorted to unsanctioned foraging when not on duty. During this war, quartermasters had orders to pay for all goods taken from Mexican citizens. Soldiers, however, chose to be a bit more liberal in their foraging. Frederick Zeh, a German immigrant who joined the U.S. Army, described vividly what drove the troops to forage on their own:

> Impatiently we waited for our longed-for provisions. To calm our rebellious stomachs somewhat, we had gradually tightened our saver belts down to the last notch. With a tremendous hurrah we greeted the commissary wagon. What a bitter disappointment after three days of strain and severe deprivation! The entire supply consisted of a pound of flour per man. It was assumed we would make a meal of this without fat or salt...Those of us who still had money—and there were few who did—looked elsewhere for food. Meanwhile, our more forbearing comrades tried to boil watery dumplings while others cooked pancakes, using [for grease] the stumps of tallow candles they found. We were hungry enough to consume even the coarsest of items.[11]

Private Coulter and comrades resorted to hunting cows, which they skinned and quartered to make up for rations not delivered. Armies function better when soldiers eat quality food.[12] A hungry or malnourished soldier could not fight as effectively. Add in decreased morale for poor quality rations and the army further decreases its effectiveness. Soldiers took this situation into their own hands, boosting both morale and health.[13]

The soldiers foraged in surrounding towns, farms, and ranches as often as possible, sometimes with official sanction but more often without. The hunting parties were indiscriminate in their choice of game, including fowl, cattle, wolves, land turtles, and snakes. Scribner recorded that once a seven-foot-long rattlesnake was served for dinner. Another volunteer, A. C. Pickett, concluded that armadillo was "good and well flavored." When accessible, fishing was a great favorite of the soldiers as it not only provided fresh food but also served as recreation. Foraging, hunting, and fishing consumed the men's time when they camped too far from a town or city and also provided a needed supplement to their rations.[14]

However, when camped close enough to an urban center, United States troops took full advantage of all the available foods at markets, restaurants, and street vendors. In these towns and cities, American soldiers interacted with Mexican citizens and society for the first time. Often the different styles of vendors, markets, and foods created a measure of culture shock for the men. Early in the war, after the capture of Matamoros along the Río Grande, Brevet Major Philip Barbour wrote that the brave Mexican families that remained north of the Río Grande "are now reaping the reward of their wisdom in so doing by selling our Camp poultry, milk and vegetables." Thomas Barclay recalled that "the Mexican market women will flock to the quarters of the soldiers, their best customers." A volunteer, J. Jacob Oswandel, wrote of "the Mexican huckster women [who] came around our quarters wanting to sell us *tortos, fritillos, fritura,* etc." For many Americans, the torta style sandwich, fritters, and empanadas (fried pies) shared some similarities with dishes back home, but with an emphasis on portability. The Mexican market women additionally served as a curiosity to many United States soldiers because their actions in the public sphere differed greatly from what many soldiers were used to regarding their own female family members, who handled food preparation within the home rather than in public. Combine that with the new types of food the women offered, and Mexican markets seemed like a truly foreign culture to them.[15]

The various markets across Mexico—the town bazaars full of stalls and vendors selling all types of goods—captivated the imaginations of the soldiers who experienced them. The variety of goods available, the size of the markets, and the quality of food impressed many of the American troops. Robert Anderson seemed particularly enamored with the markets of Mexico, writing at length about each one he visited. The fresh meats— beef and pork—always caught his eye, and he even noticed the regional variations that favored one over the other. The different varieties of peppers and beans amazed Anderson and many other soldiers. The markets carried fish, turtles, rice, corn, raisins, onions, garlic, multiple varieties of potatoes, and numerous breeds of tomatoes.[16] The single most frequently mentioned aspect of the markets was fruit. The soldiers consistently commented on their amazement at how much fruit was available and in season throughout the year. The multitude of melons, pears, apples, apricots, plums, oranges, lemons, limes, and bananas left the soldiers scrambling to buy as many as they could. During the occupation of Mexico City at the end of the war, the soldiers exacted a "fruit toll" on the market vendors before allowing them to enter the market. Coulter concluded that "this kind of tariff during the day amounted to about three gallons of milk, and oranges, apples, pears, bananas, sweet potatoes, pulque, etc. in abundance." It seemed the toll amounted to whatever quantity the soldiers needed that day. Neither strictly sanctioned nor forbidden, such tariffs demonstrated the soldiers' desire for quality food with fruit being a main goal.[17] Ralph Kirkham sums up what many soldiers felt about the markets in the larger Mexican towns and cities they occupied when he wrote of the markets in Jalapa: "In the way of supplying the table, there is everything to be had."[18]

The experiences in the towns provoked comparisons between Mexico and home. The rhetoric of the war attacked Mexico as a nation.[19] In the 1840s, the American soldiers saw particular dishes and drinks as markers of civilization. Two of primary signals were ice cream and mint juleps. George Gibson considered these "luxuries in our country" as important components of comfort and civilization in the inhospitable deserts of New Mexico. For George Wilkins Kendall, one of the first American war correspondents in history, the arrival of ice cream and mint juleps in Matamoros represented "a long step toward civilization—and their back tracks will never be discovered."[20] Both Gibson and Kendall, while born in the northern U.S., spent large portions of their lives in southern society, learning the cultural significance of drinks like mint juleps. The production and storage of ice in the American south also represented a significant technological development: iceboxes or icehouses that enabled the storage of foodstuffs, the creation of ice cream, and the supply of crushed ice for juleps throughout the summer months. The strong influence of southern culture certainly played a role in the perceptions of civilization held by these two men. Furthermore, the familiarity of the food available dictated how modern and civilized a city appeared to the soldiers. Oswandel noted that at Christmas he enjoyed "a supurb gobbler, stuffed with bread, and eggs, and a bunch of venison with apples sauce, in the benighted land of the Aztecs. Is this not evidence of the progress of civilization?" Despite these jingoistic views on the relative civilization of

Mexican towns, the soldiers continued to try food foreign to their palates and began to taste flavors and spices wholly new to them.[21]

As the soldiers marched throughout Mexico, they did so in dual capacities, first as soldiers focused on battle and conquest, second as young men touring a foreign country, hoping to see and taste everything they could. Although soldiers sought food to supplement their rations for nutritional and palatable reasons, there was also a degree of tourism involved, as these men traveled across vast portions of Mexico through many different regions.[22] Corn was not foreign to most Americans, but the way Mexicans prepared it surprised many soldiers. The Army quartermasters welcomed entry into the Mexican corn-producing regions because it meant access to local food supplies. The Army's bakers made bread half flour, half cornmeal, and the field armies created mills that could be transported to grind the corn wherever the army camped. At its peak, General Taylor's army in northern Mexico operated about a dozen mills.[23] Private Coulter recorded his first introduction to the creation of tortillas at a local farm, "Here [we] first learned the manner of making these corn cakes which are called 'Tortillas.' The corn is boiled in an earthen jar. Smashed on a stone roller, patted into cakes with the hand and baked on a hot stove. They taste of the cob and are very flat, no salt being used." The flat bread challenged what many American perceived as corn-based bread.

While tortillas were novel to the soldiers, tamales seemed completely foreign. Robert Anderson described his first taste of a tamale, "The other morning I was offered, seemingly as a great treat, one of their dishes, a little pork cut into fine pieces, rolled in cornmeal dough, and boiled well covered by a corn shuck. It tasted pretty well, and I answered their enquiries by telling them it was *muy bueno.*" The soldiers proved willing to embrace new foods, even if unsure as to their provenance, many times impressed by what they tasted. Just as enjoyable to the soldiers was the chance to use some of the Spanish words they picked up while in Mexico.[24]

One of the most entertaining interactions with Mexican food recorded during this period comes from Frederick Zeh when he tasted what he called *picante* and other soldiers called *chili Colorado*. Often served with tortillas, Zeh's picante consisted "of a red broth with suspect meat leftovers of every possible kind and thinly sliced cactus floating in it." The cactus was most likely *nopales* or prickly pear cactus, typically sliced thin and cooked into a dish called *nopalitos*. Zeh's account of his first bowl of this dish left a lasting impression on him.

I dined after the fashion of the Mexicans, sitting on the pavement nearby. So, for a starter, I was served *picante* in a wooden bowl, unwashed but licked clean, along with a big spoon made of the same material. My hunger pangs made be oblivious to the flavor until the bowl was emptied and a pause followed. Then I suddenly felt a burning sensation in my throat and palate, such that I could not open my mouth to quench the infernal fire. After I caught my breath again and had wiped the tears from my eyes and the sweat of anxiety from my brow, I took heart and consumed the less spicy beans and dry *pan de maíz* for dessert.

Soldiers experienced a level of spice not common in the United States during this period. Despite the discomfort, many returned for more of these spicy dishes rather than eat the rations provided at camp.[25]

The last consistent foodstuffs mentioned by soldiers serving in Mexico were three beverages not common in the United States: *pulque, aguardente,* and Mexican hot chocolate. Chocolate existed in the United States, but in Mexico, it was served as a morning beverage alongside various pastries typically dipped in the chocolate. Some of the chocolate was spiced with cinnamon or a hint of red pepper. *Pulque,* a fermented sap of the agave plant, and *aguardente*, a fermented sugarcane juice, caught the attention of many soldiers who were simultaneously curious to try new drinks and to get intoxicated. The soldiers had mixed feelings about these drinks, but few were too discerning if they were the sole or cheapest alcoholic drinks available. Soldiers spent much of their time in Mexico looking for or imbibing alcohol. Drunkenness became such a problem during the occupation of Mexico City that alcohol was forbidden to be sold to soldiers and much of the available alcohol was kept under armed guard.[26]

As noted above, the experiences of these soldiers during the U.S.–Mexico War marked the first large-scale interaction between United States citizens and Mexican cuisine. The food most often eaten and described by soldiers was the food of the common people that was readily available and inexpensive to purchase. The diaries and letters cited here carried the first wave of Mexican food culture back to the United States as soldiers shared these memorable interactions with friends and family back home. In the years following the war, 1848–60, the first cultural mixing occurred along the border of Texas and Mexico. While the Tex-Mex known in the late twentieth century was still to come, a mixing of culinary styles did occur as more Anglo-Americans moved to South Texas to take advantage of economic opportunities supplying Army depots along the Río Grande. The borderlands regions served as a hybridization of culture, creating something not completely Anglo-American but not solely Mexican either.[27]

Following the war, stories of the food tasted in Mexico traveled back with the soldiers. Many of the stories entered the American consciousness through the very quotes discussed in this chapter. Travelogues and diaries of U.S. soldiers were published and sold across the country in the years following the war. Slowly, Mexican food began to spread across the United States, starting first in the American Southwest. However, Mexican food was often a hard sell to many Anglo-Americans because of its association with low socioeconomic status and Native American traditions. Rather than fight an uphill battle, many early Mexican restaurants branded themselves instead as "Spanish" to be more palatable to Anglos. Such "Spanish" restaurants often retained some dishes that spoke to the *mestizo* culinary traditions that mixed Spanish and Native American food over several hundred years. Many also modified some spicier dishes to be more agreeable to Anglo patrons, who tended to prefer milder dishes. Regardless of the name change or dish modifications, Mexican food staples such as tacos began to spread across the nation by the early twentieth century.[28]

The U.S.–Mexico War was an important step in introducing North Americans to Mexican food. From tortillas to tamales, abundant fruit to the spiciest peppers, the war brought more Americans into contact with these dishes and flavors than ever before. Beginning first along the borderlands of South Texas, New Mexico, and California, a culinary mixing emerged as Anglo-Americans and Mexican Americans lived together in these regions. This caused both culinary traditions to evolve and embrace aspects of the other. While racism and socioeconomic discrimination continued after the end of the war, it would be Mexican food that first began to tear down some cultural barriers and force many Anglo-Americans to at least acknowledge the importance of Mexican culture through its food. Without the war with Mexico, the spread of Mexican food into the United States would not have occurred for decades, until more Americans could have afforded to travel as tourists to their southern neighbor. Warfare in all its horror provides forced interactions between societies and cultures that otherwise never would have occurred, and which almost always have interesting and unexpected outcomes wholly unrelated to combat or the causes of the war itself. It is these curious results that begin to reconcile some of the brutality of war and show that two countries, once at war, can live together and create something new, if only through food.

1. Erna Risch, *Quartermaster Support of the Army: A History of the Corps, 1775–1939* (Washington, DC: Center of Military History, United States Army, 1989): 237–63; James A. Huston, *The Sinews of War: Army Logistics, 1775–1953* (Washington, DC: Office of the Chief of Military History, United States Army, 1966), 125–36.

2. Some historians have analyzed the soldiers experience during the U.S.–Mexico War, including Bruce Winders, *Mr. Polk's Army: The American Military Experience in the Mexican War* (College Station: Texas A&M University Press, 1997); James McCaffrey, *Army of Manifest Destiny: The American Soldier in the Mexican War, 1846–1848* (New York: New York University Press, 1992); Paul Foos, *A short, offhand, killing affair: Soldiers and Conflict during the Mexican–American War* (Chapel Hill: University of North Carolina Press, 2002).

    These authors do an excellent job of analyzing the experience of the soldiers but lack a thorough investigation of U.S. soldiers' experiences with Mexican food.

3. William Davis, *A Taste for War: The Culinary History of the Blue and the Gray* (Mechanicsburg, PA: 2003); Andrew Smith, *Starving the South: How the North Won the Civil War* (New York: St. Martin's Press, 2011); Helen Zoe Veit, *Food in the Civil War Era: The North (The South)* (East Lansing, MI: Michigan State University Press, 2015).

4. Jeffrey Pilcher, *Que Vivan Los Tamales: Food and the Making of Mexican Identity* (Albuquerque: University of New Mexico Press, 1998); Jeffrey Pilcher, *Planet Taco: A Global History of Mexican Food* (Oxford: Oxford University Press, 2012); Gregory McNamee, *Torillas, Tiswin, T-Bones: A Food History of the Southwest* (Albuquerque: University of New Mexico Press, 2017); Meredith Abarca, *Voices in the Kitchen: Views of Food and the World from Working-Class Mexican and Mexican American Women* (College Station: Texas A&M University Press, 2006); Matt Garcia, E. Melanie DuPuis, and Don Mitchell, eds., *Food Across Borders* (New Brunswick: Rutgers University Press, 2017).

5. David M. Pletcher, *The Diplomacy of Annexation: Texas, Oregon, and the Mexican War* (Columbia: University of Missouri Press, 1975): 139–71, 273–351; Peter Guardino, *Dead March: A History of the Mexican–American War* (Cambridge, MA: Harvard University Press, 2017): 31–70, 78–81, 81–82, 134–42, 147–55; K. Jack Bauer, *The Mexican War, 1846–1848* (New York: Macmillan, 1974): 1–105; John S. D. Eisenhower, *So Far From God: The U.S. War with Mexico, 1846–1848* (New York: Random House, 1989): 17–28, 19–70, 98–194.

6. Guardino, *Dead March*, 186–202, 247–50, 271–74, 317–18, 311–14; Bauer, *The Mexican War*, 127–200, 232–325; Eisenhower, *So Far from God*, 205–16, 253–344.

7. Pletcher, *The Diplomacy of Annexation*, 522–50; Guardino, *Dead March*, 325–40; Bauer, *The Mexican War*, 326–91; Eisenhower, *So Far from God*, 358–69.

8. United States War Department, *General Regulations for the Army of the United States, 1841* (Washington, DC: United States War Department, J. and G. S. Gideon, 1841): 261.

9. McCaffrey, *Army of Manifest Destiny*, 118; Risch, *Quartermaster Support*, 247–50; Huston, *The Sinews of War*, 133.

10. Adam D. Shprintzen, *The Vegetarian Crusade: The Rise of an American Reform Movement* (Westport, CT, 2006): 33, 36, 41, 46, 132; Jayne A. Sokolov, *Eros and Modernization: Sylvester Graham, Health Reform, and the Origins of Victorian Sexuality in America* (Rutherford: Farleigh Dickinson University Press, 1983): 13, 14, 144, 155.

11. Leroy Graf, "The Economic History of the Lower Río Grande Valley," (PhD diss, Harvard University, 1942:, 178; Frederick Zeh, *An Immigrant Soldier in the Mexican War*, ed. William Orr (College Station: Texas A&M University Press, 1995): 39.

12. Benjamin F. Scribner, *Camp Life of a Volunteer: A Campaign in Mexico, or a Glimpse at Life in Camp* (Austin: Jenkins, 1975): 16, 45–46; Richard Coulter and Thomas Barclay in *Volunteers: The Mexican War Journals of Richard Coulter and Thomas Barclay*, ed. Allan Peskin (Kent: Kent State University Press, 1991): 27, 28, 38, 70, 119; Robert Anderson, *An Artillery Officer in the Mexican War, 1846–7* (Freeport, NY: Books for Libraries Press, 1971): 116; Napoleon Jackson Tecumseh Dana in *Monterrey is Ours! The Mexican War Letters of Lieutenant Dana, 1845–1847*, ed. Robert Ferrell (Louisville: The University Press of Kentucky, 1990): 109.

13. Coulter and Barclay, *Volunteers*, 74.

14. Ralph Kirkham, *The Mexican War Journal and Letters of Ralph W. Kirkham*, Robert Miller, ed. (College Station: Texas A&M University Press, 1991): 38; Scribner, *Camp Life*, 26; Alexander C. Pickett, *A. C. Pickett's Private Journal of the U.S.–Mexican War*, ed. Jo Blatti (Little Rock: Butler Center for Arkansas Studies, 2011): 85; George Rutledge Gibson, *Over the Chihuahua and Santa Fe Trails, 1847–1848*, ed. Robert W. Frazer (Albuquerque: University of New Mexico Press, 1981): 16.

15. Philip Barbour and Martha Barbour, *Journals of the Late Brevet Major Philip Barbour . . . and his wife, Martha Isabella Hopkins Barbour: Written during the War with Mexico—1846*, ed. Rhoda van Vivver Tanner Doubleday (New York: G. P. Putnam's Sons, 1936): 25, 92; Coulter and Barclay, *Volunteers*, 226; J. Jacob Oswandel, *Notes of the Mexican War, 1846–1848*, eds. Timothy Johnson and Nathaniel Cheairs Hughes Jr. (Knoxville: University of Tennessee Press, 2010): 107; Anderson, *An Artillery Officer*, 203–5.

16. Anderson, *An Artillery Officer*, 164, 60, 61–62, 148.

17. Quoted in Coulter and Barclay, *Volunteers*, 193, 125, 150; Anderson, *An Artillery Officer*, 178, 25; Oswandel, *Notes of the Mexican War*, 251; Pickett, *Private Journal*, 127; Dana, *Monterrey is Ours!*, 140; Barbour, *Journals of the Late*, 95; Kirkham, *The Mexican War Journal*, 18, 22, 54, 78; Zeh, *An Immigrant Soldier*, 83; William Lytle, *For Honor, Glory, & Union: The Mexican & Civil War letters of Brig. Gen. William Haines Lytle*, ed. Ruth Carter (Lexington: University Press of Kentucky, 2009): 45, 49.

18. Kirkham, *The Mexican War Journal*, 10.

19. Guardino, *The Dead March*, 19–20, 39, 204, 294; Amy S. Greenburg, *Manifest Manhood and the Antebellum American Empire* (Cambridge: Cambridge University Press, 2005): 18–47, 96–105.

20. Gibson, *Over the Chihuahua*, 19; George Wilkins Kendall, *Dispatches form the Mexican War*, ed. Lawrence Cress (Norman: University of Oklahoma, 1999): 54; Kirkham, *The Mexican War Journal*, 10.

21. Oswandel, *Notes of the Mexican War*, 248; Anderson, *An Artillery Officer*, 16; Coulter and Barclay, *Volunteers,* 304; for more information on the significance of the mint julep, see: Joe Nickell, *The Kentucky Mint Julep* (Lexington, KY: University Press of Kentucky, 2003).

22. For more on soldiers as tourists during the U.S.–Mexico War, see: Andrea Boardman, "The U.S.–Mexican War and the Beginnings of American Tourism in Mexico," in *Holiday in Mexico: Critical Reflections on Tourism and Tourist Encounters* (Durham: Duke University Press, 2010): 21–53; Jeffrey Pilcher, "Coming Home to Salsa: Latino Roots of American Food," *American Latino Theme Study: Food,* https://www.nps.gov/heritageinitiatives/latino/latinotheme study/food.htm.

23. Dana, *Monterrey is Ours!*, 114, 118; Barbour, *Journals of the Late*, 67; Coulter and Barclay, *Volunteers,* 53, 120.

24. Coulter and Barclay, *Volunteers,* 50–51; Anderson, *An Artillery Officer*, 153, 261–63; Zeh, *An Immigrant Soldier*, 50; Jefferey Pilcher, *Planet Taco: A Global History of Mexican Food* (Oxford: Oxford University Press, 2012): 68.

25. Zeh, *An Immigrant Soldier*, 50; Gibson, *Over the Chihuahua*, 17; Pilcher, *Planet Taco,* 68.

26. Oswandel, *Notes of the Mexican War*, 105; Anderson, *An Artillery Officer,* 60, 62; Coulter and Barclay, *Volunteers,* 103, 192, 227; Kirkham, *The Mexican War Journal,* 98; Susanne Berthier-Foglar, "Gastronomy and Conquest in the Mexican–American War: Food in the Diary of Susan Magoffin," *Diálogos Latinoamericanos* 6, no. 10 (2005): 3–4.

27. Arnoldo De Leon, *The Tejano Community, 1836–1900* (Albuquerque: University of New Mexico Press, 1982): 62, 79; Thomas T. Smith, *The U.S. Army and the Texas Frontier Economy, 1845–1900* (College Station: Texas A&M University Press, 1999): 11; David Montejano, *Anglos and Mexicans In the Making of Texas, 1836–1986* (Austin, TX: University of Texas Press, 1999): 40–41.

28. Farley Elliott, "Racism Forced LA's Oldest Mexican Restaurants to Call Themselves 'Spanish': The City's Campaign of Whitewashing Dates to the 1800s," *LA Eater*, April 15, 2019, https://la.eater.com/2019/4/15/18311604/spanish -cafes-mexican-food-los-angeles-whitewashing-history-el-cholo-belmont-café.; Jeffery Pilcher, "Tex-Mex, Cal-Mex, or Whose Mex? Notes on the Historical Geography of Southwestern Cuisine," *Journal of the Southwest* 43, no. 4 (Winter, 2001): 659, 660, 668, 670; Joseph A. Rodríguez, "Becoming Latinos: Mexican Americans, Chicanos, and the Spanish Myth in the Urban Southwest.," *Western Historical Quarterly* 29, no. 2 (Summer, 1998): 167.

CHAPTER 9

Food, Hunger, and Rebellion

Egypt in World War I and Its Aftermath

CHRISTOPHER S. ROSE

On Thursday, October 24, 1918, sixteen people—eleven women, four children, and a police officer—were killed in a stampede at the cereals market in Rod-el-Farag, Cairo.[1] Rod-el-Farag, the main grain port on the Nile, was an obvious site for the Cereal Merchant's Association's twice-weekly market. Normally held Thursdays and Saturdays, the association had voted to reduce the market frequency to once per week—on Mondays—effective October 28. The public market's manager, Barakat Bey, mistakenly believed that the change took effect immediately and had not telephoned as usual to ask for additional police officers to assist with crowd control. As an estimated crowd of five thousand people—mostly women, many accompanied by children—gathered and waited past the normal start time, rumors about the market's closure began to circulate. Because of recent scarcity in the availability of wheat, the primary staple of the Egyptian diet, people were anxious about whether there would be enough for everyone waiting and when the gates finally opened, panic ensued. The crowd surged forward, trampling those that fell and crushing the police officer to death against a wall. The tragedy earned significant public attention: the press denounced Barakat Bey, the government took direct control of grain distribution, and collecting funds for the families of the victims became a cause célèbre among the Egyptian elite. The Rod-el-Farag incident attracted attention because it involved fatality, but it was not an isolated incident. Egypt's major cities had been experiencing a shortage of wheat throughout the summer and fall, contributing to widespread unrest that culminated in a nationwide uprising the following year (a point addressed later in this chapter). The Rod-el-Farag riot demonstrated the anxieties among poor Egyptians over the availability and affordability of food during World War I—a problem largely ignored by the Anglo-Egyptian government.[2]

At the outbreak of the war in 1914, the Anglo-Egyptian government introduced policies intended to control inflation in the price of foodstuffs and to ensure a constant supply for the civilian market.[3] The policies were an abject failure, accomplishing neither goal and exacerbating the already precarious financial situation of the peasantry (often referred to as *fella-heen*).[4] Wartime inflation in the cost of basic commodities far outpaced the rise in wages. Most Egyptians could not afford to buy enough food by the end of 1916, and supply shortages became common in early 1918. The war's end did not bring economic relief; wholesale and retail price indices continued to rise throughout the winter of 1918–19. Additionally, malnutrition presented a public health issue during the war; between December 1914 and December 1918 nearly two hundred thousand people died of infectious diseases. Even if only a small percentage of these deaths can be attributed to complications from hunger and malnutrition, they would still surpass the death toll from combat actions (just under fifteen thousand).[5]

In March of 1919, a nationwide uprising brought the country to a standstill for two months, with riots in major cities, the destruction of rail and telegraph lines, and attacks on British troops and government infrastructure throughout the Nile Valley. A British parliamentary commission convened under Lord Milner acknowledged "unfortunate incidences" during the period of the war that "shook for a time" Egyptians' "confidence in our justice and good will, and were pre-disposing causes of the savage outbreak of anti-British feeling in the spring of 1919." However, the commission's conclusion—in particular, the recognition that there were multiple contributing factors—was supplanted by an official national historiographical project sponsored by the Egyptian monarchy, which attributed the Egyptian Revolution of 1919 to the thwarting of nationalist aspirations by the British government ahead of the Versailles conference, and to a widespread rally of patriotic support in support of independence from Britain.[6]

Over the past several decades, Egyptian and foreign historians have questioned this narrative, noting that the peasantry—normally (if simplistically) considered an apolitical demographic—widely participated in the uprising. While agents representing national political movements did organize in rural areas, peasants frequently attacked rail and telegraph lines, and a number of independent or autonomous rural collectives were declared during the uprising. As Kyle J. Anderson has pointed out, this behavior suggests more of a desire to sever ties with the nation rather than to reify it.[7] The peasantry was largely illiterate and left few written records of their own, leaving Egyptian and colonial government archival records, the (censored) wartime press, and accounts written by urban political elites as the primary sources through which a history from below must be constructed. Projects have so far examined organized labor, guilds, and the urban poor, but the rural peasantry has only begun to emerge with the environmental-medical turn in scholarship.[8]

In 1992, Ellis Goldberg suggested that peasant participation in the uprising could be partially attributed to the food scarcity that occurred in 1918 and the fear that hunger would continue in 1919.[9] While witnesses to the Milner Commission acknowledged food scarcity as a source of discontent among the peasantry, Goldberg's remains the only scholarly study to examine it. In this chapter, I argue that the situation was more dire than Goldberg described. Food supply issues began within the first few months of the war, and peasant families were unable to afford enough food to subsist by the winter of 1916—two years earlier than originally proposed. As noted above, while the stampede at Rod-el-Farag was the only food riot to involve fatality, it was not an isolated incident; there was considerable anxiety over food security in the summer and fall of 1918. When political organizers ventured into rural areas the following spring, they almost certainly had their work cut out for them as they found the peasantry simmering with anger over five years of inflation, food scarcity, and hunger.

The "Primary Needs" Tariff

Egypt, nominally an Ottoman province, had been under the control of British advisors since 1882 to ensure its financial solvency. It became a British protectorate in December of 1914, after the Ottoman Empire joined the war on the side of the Central Powers. The Anglo-Egyptian government implemented a tariff regime on "primary need commodities," intended to prevent profiteering and guarantee supplies by fixing an official price for which goods had to be sold in the market. The tariff system was ineffective for three reasons. First, the government did not develop mechanisms to ensure the distribution and availability of the goods on the tariff list throughout Egypt; they relied instead on existing local organizations to carry out the work. When fluctuations in price occurred, these local organizations tended to sell to the markets that earned them the most profit.[10] Second, prices on the official lists did not take into account the cost of raw materials, even if those materials were also tariffed. Profiteering was widespread, but vendors found to be selling at elevated prices were fined so lightly that prosecution did not serve as a deterrent.[11] Third, commodities whose costs were unresponsive to price controls—as was the case with wheat and bread from the beginning, and with meat and sugar from mid-1916—were usually removed from the tariff list and their prices allowed to float, exacerbating market volatility. While the tariff system reflects E. P. Thompson's laissez-faire model of the moral economy, the situation was not, in fact, laissez-faire: colonial records make clear that the government's primary concern was provisioning the hundreds of thousands of Imperial and Dominion troops that began arriving in Egypt in December of 1914, with civilian needs considered a far lesser priority.[12]

While demand for agricultural products remained steady, agricultural production dropped an average of 2.8 percent each year between 1914 and 1918. This decline is attributable to the collection of both human and animal labor for the Egyptian Labor Corps (ELC), the suspension of outside investment in agricultural projects and the halting of projects in progress, and the near cessation of Mediterranean trade due to the German U-boat campaign. ELC recruitment began in 1915 with fairly modest numbers but was ramped up in the spring of 1917 for the beginning of the Palestine campaign; an estimated 325,000 Egyptians worked in military service between March of 1917 and June of 1918.[13] The majority of recruits came from the agricultural sector, but "men were taken wholesale without any regard as to whether they were more use at home or not. Labour from poorly inhabited districts was taken where it could not be spared."[14] The ELC's consistent year-round wages proved attractive for laborers, especially those from middle and upper Egypt where agricultural work was more seasonal. While agricultural labor wages held somewhat steady during the war, the minimum ELC wage was raised 25 percent in 1917 and most recruits earned more than the minimum based on their skill and where they were stationed. Private and industrial landowners throughout Egypt complained that workers were leaving in the middle of the agricultural season to join the ELC.[15] In 1917, the government acknowledged that civilian wages had not risen in line with inflation and that "the rise of wages has so far not been sufficient to enable the [peasant] to live and clothe himself and his family, as he was able to do before the war."[16]

Agricultural products and food were transported longer distances by railroad, however, beasts of burden—camels, donkeys, mules, and horses—were necessary for the critical stage of transportation from the farm to the local market and thence to the train station. The military began requisitioning pack animals from villages to move supplies and troops; the number of camels in rural Egypt dropped by 15 percent between 1914 and 1916.[17] The requisitioning of rail stock, watercraft, and the restriction of civilian navigation on the Nile further increased the cost of transporting food to market.[18] The increase in demand coupled with the decrease in available labor and imports led to inflation, which at first rose gradually but then began to increase exponentially at the end of 1916. The retail index based on the average price of a basket of commodities more than doubled over the course of the war; most foodstuffs doubled or tripled in price. Further, the official indices obscure the fact that many commodities could not actually be purchased at the officially tariffed price.[19]

The majority of the Egyptian population were peasants employed in agriculture, of whom at least one-third owned no land; the majority of landowning peasants held less than five faddans (roughly five acres).[20] Such small plots were insufficient to shield their owners from inflation and food scarcity; British officials calculated that peasants who worked three or less could not produce enough food or income to support a family, and had to either rent more land or send part of their family to work on a large estate in order to make ends meet.[21] Most small landowners were indebted to private lenders specializing in high-interest short-term loans used to purchase seed, which were repaid with the sale of the seasonal harvest. Any personal subsistence farming would have to come at the expense of raising more lucrative cash crops. This was encouraged by the Ministry of Agriculture, for whom cotton production was the basis of Egypt's financial solvency.[22] The debt situation was amplified in the spring of 1915 when the seasonal cotton sale was delayed while buyers waited for coin to be shipped out from England.[23] The Ministry of Finance decided to deal with its own cash shortage by proceeding with the annual tax collection, despite the fact that most peasants usually paid their taxes with cotton revenues. Most peasants had to take out a second seasonal loan to pay their taxes in 1915, which erased most of their income for both that year and the next. The press lamented that "a few months ago [the peasant] was one of the most contented souls in the land, but to-day he is a man with a grievance."[24]

Food Security

In the early years of the war, most complaints about food prices were lodged by vendors who felt that they were being deprived of profits as a result of the tariffs. In June of 1915, there were complaints that the price of bread was rising, even though the cost of flour was falling. Concerns were also raised about the availability of fruit, normally imported from Syria (now in enemy territory), and, indeed, by the spring of 1916, some fruits were selling for more than twice the average daily wages of an agricultural worker.[25] In mid-September of 1916, the Anglo-Cypriot government banned the exportation of livestock, cutting off the supply of mutton to Egypt.[26] Supplies of cattle and sheep were available in Anglo-Egyptian Sudan, but transport problems and required quarantine inspections posed problems, especially after the appearance of foot-and-mouth disease in 1916. In October, the official tariff on meat was raised by 20 percent.[27] This increase was unpopular with wholesalers and butchers; in late October a number of Alexandria butchers went on strike, complaining that wholesale prices (which were unregulated) were so high that they could not earn a profit selling meat at the official tariff price.[28] In a lengthy editorial to the *Egyptian Gazette*, an anonymous "major meat supplier" asserted that "talk of a meat famine is nonsense." The writer dismissed the idea of "hardship to the [peasant]," stating that "meat is certainly not his staple food."[29] However, a thriving black market in proteins developed in the major cities during the war.[30] Meat from overworked or diseased animals that had already died was sold into the black market from military bases or slaughterhouses. In the fall of 1918, the legal sale of horsemeat was authorized in Alexandria as a stopgap measure to address the high cost of meat.[31]

Supplies of cooking oil were constantly short throughout the war. Most Egyptians used cotton seed oil, which was produced in plentiful quantities locally, for cooking. In the spring of 1918, with the U-Boat campaign in the Atlantic and a boll weevil infestation in the Carolinas having an adverse effect on English oil supplies, the British government requisitioned the entirety of Egypt's cotton seed production.[32] When the British High Commissioner in Egypt protested on the grounds that the oil was needed for civilian use—one of few such instances during the war—the Foreign Office relented "on the understanding that arrangement may be cancelled at any time and that cotton seed so delivered to local crushers shall consist as far as possible of lower grades of quality."[33] Despite this, cotton seed oil became scarce and prohibitively expensive by late spring 1918: "It must be understood . . . that people are unable to purchase the oil tariffed as above even at double the prices."[34] Industries that also depended on the cotton seed production were heavily impacted. The price of soap suffered the most, with prices increasing more than 300 percent between 1914 and 1918.[35]

Most concerning was volatility of the cost of wheat, which constituted the main staple of the Egyptian diet; the average Egyptian consumed over 80 percent of their daily calories in the form of bread.[36] With the Anglo-Egyptian government's focus on profit, locally grown wheat was exported for sale, while cheaper and lower quality wheat was imported for domestic consumption, usually from India.[37] With the onset of the war, imports plummeted, but a record amount of wheat was exported from Egypt in 1915.[38] After objections were raised, the export of wheat was prohibited, but wheat defied attempts at price control.[39] It was included in the initial tariff system introduced at the onset of the war, then removed in early 1915 following complaints that prices were too high. It was then added again in early November of 1916 amid a four-day strike by Cairo's bakers, who complained that they were losing money on the sale of bread.[40] When Cairo's municipal commission acquiesced to the bakers' demands, bakers in Bani Suwayf and Alexandria also threatened to strike, resulting in the tariff being canceled yet again.[41]

The Supply Control Board

By early 1918, it had become clear that more centralized oversight was needed to overcome the labor, transportation, and distribution issues that were believed to be causing inflation and scarcity in the food market. The government established the Supplies Control Board (SCB) to assume control over the tariff list, to oversee the collection of crops by the Ministry of Interior, and to run district markets in order to guarantee the availability of commodities at the official price. The SCB stumbled right out of the gate. When proposing amounts to be requisitioned from each governorate and district for the spring 1918 harvest, calculations were made based on the expected productivity of each area based on the previous year's production but were not revised based on actual production. The governor of Cairo, Mahmoud Sidqi, explained the complications this caused:

> Specified amounts were collected . . . and in many cases a village was ordered to produce a larger quantity than it possessed, with the result that the inhabitants had to make up the deficit by purchasing at a higher price than what they were paid by the Army, thus incurring great loss.[42]

Profiteering remained widespread. George Reisner testified to the Milner Commission that market prices were higher than the requisition prices, so village overseers (*'umdas*) were anxious to collect as much grain as possible in order to resell the excess for their own benefit.[43] In parts of upper Egypt, some planters refused to sell grain at the tariff rate on the grounds that they were losing money, resulting in a standoff with government officials, who eventually seized the crop by force.[44]

The failure of the SCB's first harvest season had more devastating effects when, for the first time during the war, the supply of wheat to Egypt's major cities faltered in mid-1918. Cities were entirely dependent on wheat imports from outside; until the SCB was established, these markets had fetched the highest prices (usually in contravention of the tariff), but with the new oversight system in place, vendors looked for buyers who were willing to pay higher prices. Despite constant reassurances from the SCB that there was an ample supply of wheat, reports of shortages and price gouging were often published adjacent to the SCB's statements. In September of 1918, a "bread famine" was reported in Alexandria; *Al-Ahram* newspaper reported that the city had received less than a quarter of the flour needed to meet the its consumption needs.[45] *Al-Ahaly* reported that the wheat market in Behera governorate—which supplied Alexandria's eastern suburbs—was also empty.[46] The SCB blamed profiteers for the supply shortage; the press observed that wheat was being diverted to Alexandrine bakers who "are in a position to pay special prices," while poor, and even middle class, neighborhoods did not get enough flour to meet demand.[47] One paper reported that "Alexandria, as regards its bread, is now living from hand to mouth."[48]

In early October, the supply of grain to other major cities, including Cairo and Suez, also became unreliable.[49] SCB Director Ross Teller shuttled back and forth between Alexandria and Cairo to try to manage the crisis; in both cities, the local cereal merchants' associations passed resolutions (in Teller's presence) to expel any member from their ranks who was found to be profiteering.[50] On October 8, 1918, the SCB took full control of distribution in Alexandria, requiring that all grain be imported to and distributed from the Mina al-Basal market; violators were threatened with severe punishment.[51] On October 17, the Qalyubiya district (in the Nile delta) followed suit, making it a felony to export grain from the governorate without permission, and threatening violators with a military trial.[52] In Cairo, where local markets were still under the control of the Cereal Merchants' Association, bakers tried to deal with the crisis by producing smaller loaves of bread in order to serve more customers.[53] The SCB directed the Giza district to supply Cairo with additional wheat; Giza replied that it had been without wheat for days, and was itself unable to purchase additional wheat from neighboring Bani Suwayf.[54] The SCB announced a centralized distribution system for Cairo, modeled on that of Alexandria, to take effect on October 28; in a twist of tragic irony, the notice was published the same day that the fatal stampede took place at Rod-el-Farag.[55] Public reaction toward the SCB and the market's owner (who was never charged over the incident) was furious. Even after the tragedy, the Cairo press reported in early November that grain supplies had not been delivered "for the past several days," and two more governorates in the Nile delta completely ran out of wheat.[56]

In late October, an apparent slowdown by bakers frustrated over the strict enforcement of the tariff and the resultant slim profit margin abruptly brought the bread crisis back to Alexandria, although the city had ample grain.[57] For several weeks, bakeries were "besieged by large numbers of men, women, and children, for the most part natives, and in front of every bakery there were disturbances owing to the rush of the people to get served."[58] Some bakers began selling unprocessed flour to allow customers to make their own loaves at home, resulting in long lines at communal ovens.[59] The supply crisis did not ease until the end of the year, by which point public confidence in the SCB had mostly evaporated. If the end of the war had brought expectations that the situation would start to improve as imports resumed from abroad and business returned to prewar norms, these were dashed as prices continued to climb throughout the winter and into the spring of 1919, with no relief in sight.

The Hungry Peasant

Dr. W. H. Wilson from the Egyptian School of Medicine presented a memo to the Milner Commission in 1919 that described the challenges of the cost of living in wartime Egypt.[60] Wilson had set out to investigate the question of whether "a man in regular employment at the ordinary rate of wages" would be able to "provide sufficient food for himself and a small family, taking as the basis of the necessary expenditure on food the official retail prices of foodstuffs" as of May 1, 1918—the date the SCB tariffs became effective. Wilson determined the maximum amount that a hypothetical man who supported a family of four making a slightly-higher-than-average wage could afford to pay for enough wheat and durum (semolina) to provide his family with adequate nutrition. The SCB's initial tariff set the cost of wheat 80 percent higher than Wilson's threshold, and the cost of durum 73 percent higher. At the height of the wheat crisis in the summer of 1918, vendors were selling wheat for 121 percent above Wilson's threshold and durum for 96 percent above, both in contravention of the tariff.[61] The price of wheat and durum increased another 30 percent between April of 1918 and May of 1919.[62] However, price data from the government statistics reveals that the officially tar-iffed prices had been unaffordable for most Egyptians for two years. In November of 1916, wheat prices were already five percent above Wilson's threshold; in December of 1917, the price was 162 percent higher. While Wilson considered the SCB's tariff controls a direct cause of the 1919 uprising, it is clear that neither of the wartime price control systems guaranteed affordable commodities to the poorest Egyptians, as they were theoretically designed to do.[63]

Wilson further suggested a link between malnourishment and the high incidence of infectious diseases during the last year of the war, noting that

> underfeeding lowers the resistance to disease in as admitted fact, and in it may possibly be found an explanation for the very high mortality from influenza during the past year (1918–1919) and for the excessive death-rate in Cairo and Alexandria, where . . . the deaths in many weeks of 1918 and 1919 considerably exceeded the births in number.[64]

During the war, reported cases of most epidemic diseases in Egypt increased substantially over pre- and postwar levels, and at exponentially higher rates than combat-related deaths.[65] The Spanish influenza pandemic alone killed over one percent of the population of Egypt between October and December of 1918, when food supplies were at their scarcest and most expensive.[66]

Rebellion

In early March of 1919, when demonstrations in Alexandria began over the arrest and exile of three nationalist leaders who had demanded Egypt's right to represent itself at Versailles, a spark was lit. Years of frustration exploded in the fields and streets of nearly every settlement in the Nile valley, directed squarely at the Anglo-Egyptian government. As the uprising began in March of 1919, Zifta, a small agricultural village in the delta, declared its independence from the rest of Egypt; it was one of the districts that had run out of wheat in the fall of 1918.[67] Zifta's independence lasted barely two weeks and was forcibly ended by Australian and New Zealand Army Corps (ANZAC) troops. It and other areas that declared autonomy are usually treated as historical anomalies.[68] However, these rebellions, along with peasants who attacked rail and telegraph lines throughout Egypt, can be seen as an attempt to sever the tentacles through which the state was able to actively intervene into their lives.[69]

It took the appointment of Field Marshall Edmund Allenby as Special High Commissioner and the abolition of martial law in early May to bring the violence of this period to an end. In December 1919, a parliamentary commission under Lord Milner was appointed to find the causes of the uprising. Commission member Sir Owen Thomas observed that

> the chief cause of the recent trouble in Egypt is an economic one . . .
> the ground was prepared therefore for the political agitator in the
> towns by the scarcity and dearness of food . . . the price of food to a
> townsman who is dependent upon a wage which has not increased
> in proportion to the cost of living is sufficient cause for rebellion in
> most countries.[70]

In the Anglo-Egyptian government's parliamentary report for 1920, Sir Paul Harvey, the financial advisor, admitted that the wartime price control systems had done "rather more harm than good" but, like Thomas, insisted that the peasantry were an apolitical class led astray by agitators using economic instability as a rallying cry.[71] Likewise, in his memorandum to the commission, Judge J. F. Kershaw partially laid blame on the peasants themselves:

> I need not enter here into the causes of discontent of the fellaheen . . .
> They are temporary and directly caused by the War. The Army had
> to be fed and supplied. The fellah, having no national feeling, was
> not willing to make sacrifices for national defense.[72]

A number of witnesses identified the failure of the Anglo-Egyptian government to adequately provide for the civilian population during the war as one of the chief causes of the 1919 uprising; most, however, continued to blame intermediaries or agitators. R. S. Patterson observed that the method of food collection "was to requisition five times as much as the army required, and to sell back the surplus at enhanced prices to the original vendors," although he attributed this to "the country having been denuded for military purposes of its English inspecting staff, [so that] the collection of cereals had to be left in the hands of native officials, with the result that corruption was rife and large fortunes were illicitly acquired."[73]

Mahmoud Sidqi, the governor of Cairo, theorized that

> had British control been stricter, a potent cause of the unrest among the fellaheen could have been removed. . . . Similarly, in 1918 . . . in connection with the shortage of wheat, which threatened to cause of famine in the cities . . . if the Egyptian officials had secured the Army requirements from the rich cultivators instead of the poor (or had followed any other just system of collection) the fellaheen would not have been tempted to show their discontent.[74]

Sidqi suggested that the government subsidize the purchase of supplies for large landowners, to be paid for with an incremental tax: "Such a measure would ease the burdens of the fellaheen. The result of this will be that the Egyptians will become contented."[75]

This is, in fact, how the crisis ended in 1920. When the SCB began to guarantee wheat prices by using government subsidies, rather than relying on artificial price controls, inflation fell sharply, with prices finally returning to prewar levels the following year. The memories of wartime suffering endured, with politicians airing grievances over Anglo-Egyptian neglect of public health and welfare well into the 1920s, but were dampened as memories faded and the official history was incorporated into the national educational curriculum beginning in the 1930s.[76] Examining the politics around food and its environmental-medical effects allows us to understand the wartime experience of the poorest Egyptians and allows historians to gain a more complex understanding of early twentieth-century Egyptian history.

NOTES

1. "Egypt's Food. Wheat Distribution in Cairo. A Sad Tragedy. Fatality of Printed Notice," *Egyptian Gazette* (Alexandria), October 26, 1918, 4.
2. "The Native Press. Wheat Distribution Fatality," *Egyptian Gazette*, October 28, 1918; "Ḍaḥāyā Rawḍ Al-Faraj Wa Aʿānat ʿAlāyhim," *Al-Ahrām* (Alexandria), October 27, 1918.
3. "Loi no. 6 de 1914 ordonnant la Taxation des Tarifs Maxima des Denrées et Articles de Première Nécessité," August 16, 1914, Egypte, Ministère de Finances, *Recueil des documents relatifs a la guerre publiés au "Journal Officiel" du 3 Août 1914 au 31 Juillet 1915*, Imprimerie Nationale, Le Caire, 1915, 23–25.
4. The peasantry is often referred to interchangeably as *fellahin* ("tillers"). Since the latter is technically an occupational title, I use "peasant" to clarify that I am referring to members of the lowest socioeconomic class, regardless of their employment.
5. *General Annual Report of the British Army 1912–1919*, Parliamentary Paper XX, Cmd. 1193, 1921, pt. IV, 62–72; Christopher S. Rose, "Implications of the Spanish Influenza Pandemic (1918–1920) for the History of Early 20th Century Egypt," *Journal of World History* 32, no. 4 (2021).
6. Yoav Di-Capua, "Talking History: 1906-1920," chap. 2 in *Gatekeepers of the Arab Past: Historians and History Writing in Twentieth-Century Egypt* (University of California Press, 2009).
7. Kyle J. Anderson, "The Egyptian Labor Corps: Workers, Peasants, and the State in World War I," *International Journal of Middle East Studies* 49, no. 1 (February 2017): 19.
8. Joel Beinin and Zachary Lockman, *Workers on the Nile: Nationalism, Communism, Islam, and the Egyptian Working Class, 1882–1954* (Cairo: American University in Cairo Press, 1998); Joel Beinin, *Workers and Peasants in the Modern Middle East* (Cambridge: Cambridge University Press, 2001); John T. Chalcraft, *The Striking Cabbies of Cairo and Other Stories: Crafts and Guilds in Egypt, 1863–1914* (Albany: SUNY Press, 2012).
9. Ellis Goldberg, "Peasants in Revolt—Egypt 1919," *International Journal of Middle East Studies* 24, no. 2 (1992): 261–80.
10. Egypt, *Report to the Financial Advisor on the Work of the Supplies Control Board from March 1918 to February 1919* (Cairo: Government Press, 1919): 1.
11. "The Native Press. Leniency Towards Food Adulterers," *Egyptian Gazette*, July 11, 1918.
12. E. P. Thompson, "The Moral Economy of the English Crowd in the Eighteenth Century," *Past & Present*, no. 50 (1971): 76–136.
13. Anderson, "The Egyptian Labor Corps," 6.
14. John A. Scott, "Grievances of Fellahin," July 1919, FO 848/4, The National Archives of the UK (TNA).
15. Gen. Reginald Wingate, "Memo Re: Conversation between John Cecil and Harrari Pasha," May 26, 1917, FO 141/797/1, TNA.
16. Henry Haines, "Note to Wingate," September 23, 1918, FO 141/667/5, TNA.
17. Samīr Muḥammad Raḍwān, *Capital Formation in Egyptian Industry & Agriculture, 1882–1967* (London: Ithaca Press, 1974): 265.
18. Egypt, *Report on . . . the Work of the Supplies Control Board*, 2.

19. *Annual Statistical Reports,* 1914–22. Egypt. Ministry of the Interior. *Annual Report on the Work of the Public Health Department for 1922.* Cairo: Government Press, 1925; Egypt. Ministry of the Interior. Department of Public Health. *Annual Report for 1916,* Cairo: Government Press, 1918; *Annual Report for 1917,* Cairo: Government Press, 1919; *Annual Report for 1918,* Cairo: Government Press, 1920; *Annual Report for 1919,* Cairo: Government Press, 1921; *Annual Report for 1920,* Cairo: Government Press, 1922; *Annual Report for 1921,* Cairo: Government Press, 1923; *Annual Statistical Report for 1914,* Cairo: Government Press, 1916; *Annual Statistical Report for 1915,* Cairo: Government Press, 1917.

20. Alan Richards, *Egypt's Agricultural Development, 1800–1980: Technical and Social Change* (Boulder: Westview Press, 1982): 95, ff180; Mahmoud Abdel-Fadil, *Development, Income Distribution, and Social Change in Rural Egypt, 1952–1970: A Study in the Political Economy of Agrarian Transition* (Cambridge: Cambridge University Press, 1975): 4; Roger Owen, *The Middle East in the World Economy, 1800–1914* (London: Methuen, 1981): 218.

21. Gabriel Baer, *A History of Landownership in Modern Egypt, 1800–1950* (London: Oxford University Press, 1962): 76.

22. Owen Thomas, "Agriculture," December 13, 1919, 2, FO 848/5, TNA.

23. Aaron G. Jakes, conclusion to *Egypt's Occupation: Colonial Economism and the Crises of Capitalism* (Palo Alto: Stanford University Press, 2020); 'Abd al-Rahman Rafi'i, *Thawrat 1919: Tarikh Misr al-Qawmi Min Sanat 1914 Ila Sanat 1921* (Cairo: Dār al-Ma'ārif, 1987): 89–92.

24. Richards, *Egypt's Agricultural Development, 1800–1980,* 88; "The Fellah and the War. A Warning to the Government. Causes of Discontent," *Egyptian Gazette,* October 21, 1914.

25. "The Native Press. A Fruit Famine?," *Egyptian Gazette,* July 30, 1915, 4; "The Native Press. Melons and Dancing Girls," *Egyptian Gazette,* July 1, 1916, 4; Goldberg, "Peasants in Revolt," 269.

26. "The Native Press. The Meat Crisis," *Egyptian Gazette,* September 12, 1916.

27. "Alexandria Meat Crisis," *Egyptian Gazette,* October 24, 1916, 4.

28. "Alexandria Meat Crisis."

29. "Egypt's Meat Crisis. State of Affairs in Cairo. No Cause for Alarm," *Egyptian Gazette,* November 2, 1916, 4.

30. "Egypt's Food. Horse-Flesh at Alexandria," *Egyptian Gazette,* November 18, 1918; Nefertiti Mary Takla, "Murder in Alexandria: The Gender, Sexual and Class Politics of Criminality in Egypt, 1914–1921" (Unpublished doctoral dissertation, University of California Los Angeles, 2016): 45–46; Nancy Elizabeth Gallagher, *Egypt's Other Wars: Epidemics and the Politics of Public Health* (Syracuse: Syracuse University Press, 1990): 12.

31. "Egypt's Food. Horse-Flesh at Alexandria."

32. Gen. Reginald Wingate, "Note to Foreign Office," January 16, 1918, FO 368/1899 /10448, TNA.

33. Gen. Reginald Wingate, "Note to Foreign Office," March 9, 1918, FO 368/1899 /41268, TNA.

34. Oil Consumer, "Egypt's Food. The Oil Crisis," *Egyptian Gazette,* July 19, 1918, 6.

35. John Todd, "The Uses of Egyptian Cotton Seed," *L'Egypte Contemporaine* 2 (1911): 209–21.

36. W. H. Wilson, "Cost of Living to the Poorer Classes in Egypt. Memorandum," April 19, 1918, 8, FO 848/4, TNA.

37. Egypt, *Report on . . . the Work of the Supplies Control Board*, 5.

38. Egypt. Ministry of Finance. Statistical Department, *Annuaire Statistique de l'Egypte 1916* (Cairo: National Printing Department, 1916): 141, "Tableau XV : Production et Consommation du Blé en Egypte, Saisons Agricoles 1909–10 à 1913–14."

39. "Egypt's Food. New Cereal Regulations. Prohibition of Export," *Egyptian Gazette*, December 13, 1916, 3.

40. "Prices of Foodstuffs. Wheat Slightly Reduced," *Egyptian Gazette*, November 9, 1916, 3.

41. "Egypt. Food. Cairo Bakers Win the Day. Two Commissioners Resign," *Egyptian Gazette*, November 17, 1916, 4; "Egypt's Food. Alexandria Tariff Commission. Bakers' Complaints. Police Supervision," *Egyptian Gazette*, November 27, 1916, 4.

42. Sidqi Pasha, "Memorandum to Milner Commission," n.d., 2, FO 848/4, TNA.

43. G. A. Reisner, "The Grievances of the Egyptians. The Fellahin. Memorandum," August 20, 1919, FO 848/4, TNA.

44. "The Native Press. So It Goes On!," *Egyptian Gazette*, September 6, 1918, 6.

45. "Akhbār Al-Iskandariyya," *Al-Ahrām*, September 26, 1918.

46. "Serious Position in Behera," *Egyptian Gazette*, September 25, 1918.

47. "The Bread Difficulty," *Egyptian Gazette*, September 25, 1918; "Akhbār al-Iskandariyya," *Al-Ahrām*, September 25, 1918.

48. The expression "from hand to mouth" appeared both in Arabic and English, in "Akhbār Al-Iskandariyya," *Al-Ahrām*, October 2, 1918; and "Egypt's Food. Alexandria Bread Crisis," *Egyptian Gazette*, October 2, 1918.

49. "Al-Qamḥ Fī al-Qāhira," *Al-Ahrām*, October 11, 1918; "Al-Qamḥ Fī al-Suways," *Al-Ahrām*, October 11, 1918.

50. "Niqābat Tujjār Al-Ghilāl," *Al-Ahrām*, October 14, 1918.

51. "Al-Ḥabūb Fi al-Iskandariyya." *Al-Ahrām*, October 8, 1918.

52. "Al-Mudīrūn Wa al-Tamwīn," *Al-Ahrām*, October 18, 1918.

53. "Egypt's Food. The Wheat and Bread Crisis," *Egyptian Gazette*, October 7, 1918.

54. "Al-Qamḥ Fī al-Jīza." *Al-Ahrām*, October 23, 1918.

55. "Maktab Tawzī'a Al-Ghilāl," *Al-Ahrām*, October 25, 1918.

56. "Egypt's Food. Bread Famine at Alexandria. The Shortage Becomes Acute," *Egyptian Gazette*, October 24, 1918, 6; "Egypt's Food. Wheat Distribution in Cairo. A Sad Tragedy. Fatality of Printed Notice."

57. "Akhbār Al-Iskandariyya." *Al-Ahrām*, October 29, 1918.

58. "Egypt's Food. Wheat Distribution in Cairo. A Sad Tragedy. Fatality of Printed Notice."

59. "Akhbār Al-Iskandariyya." *Al-Ahrām*, October 29, 1918.

60. Wilson, "Cost of Living."

61. Wilson, 8; "Egypt's Food. The Fellaheen and the Tariff," *Egyptian Gazette*, September 7, 1918, 6.

62. Wilson, "Cost of Living," 15, table VII.

63. Wilson, "Cost of Living," 12, tables I and II.

64. Wilson, "Cost of Living," 11.

65. *General Annual Report of the British Army 1912–1919*, pt. IV, 62–72.

66. Rose, "Implications of the Spanish Influenza Pandemic (1918–1920) for the History of Early 20th Century Egypt."

67. "The Unrest in Egypt. Latest Official Intelligence. Position in the Provinces," *Egyptian Gazette*, March 24, 1919.

68. Hussein A. H. Omar, "The Arab Spring of 1919," *London Review of Books*, April 4, 2019, https://www.lrb.co.uk/blog/2019/april/the-arab-spring-of-1919.

69. I reference Daniel R. Headrick, *The Tentacles of Progress* (Oxford University Press, 1988).

70. Thomas, "Agriculture," 2.

71. United Kingdom. Parliament, *Reports by His Majesty's High Commissioner on the Finances, Administration, and Condition of Egypt and the Soudan for the Period 1914–1919*, Egypt No. 1, Cmd 957, 1920, 3–4.

72. J. F. Kershaw, "Note on the Unrest," June 17, 1919, 2–3, FO 848/4, TNA.

73. R. S. Patterson, "Memorandum on the Grievances of the Egyptians," August 1919, 1, FO 848/4, TNA.

74. Sidqi Pasha, "Memorandum to Milner Commission," 2–3.

75. Sidqi Pasha, "Memorandum to Milner Commission," 6.

76. Gallagher, *Egypt's Other Wars*, 19.

CHAPTER 10

Tasting Recovery

Food, Disability, and the Senses
in World War I American Rehabilitation

EVAN P. SULLIVAN

The sense of taste was central to veteran rehabilitation and the experiences of disabled, wounded, and sick veterans in the United States after World War I. Nutrition was a vital component to healing wounds and illnesses, and diets could help or hinder the process. And the physical health of each soldier determined the delivery mechanisms of their meals either in mess halls or wards. Poor quality of food could and did create strains and animosity between U.S. Army patients and staff, thereby threatening to undermine the credibility of the entire process. Food, disability, and the senses therefore fused during World War I and highlighted how patients ate within the walls of the hospitals, and how they exercised power in their relationship with the state. Exploring the agency and gustatory experiences of disabled doughboys in the immediate aftermath of the war shows how individual men used their sense of taste to assert control over their healing experiences and thus subverted the top-down power structures within military hospitals.[1] By calling attention to insufficient and ill-prepared food, patient-staff interactions enrich our understandings of the food systems within the walls of the military hospitals.

Food was an essential component of the war years. For Europeans in particular, four long years of war put strains on military and civilian life and contributed to devastating food shortages in 1916–17.[2] Despite entering the war later than their counterparts, Americans still recognized the importance of feeding the population. In order to save more food for the troops, environmentally conscious individuals in cities across the country organized victory gardens. The U.S. Food Administration and various state Councils of National Defense politicized food consumption through compelling and vibrant posters that appealed in particular to women and children to convince them not to waste.[3] In states like New York, organizations like the Orange County Food Preservation Battalion equated saving food for the war effort to a form of patriotism.[4] The Food Administration's motto, "Food Will Win the War," demonstrates how food served as a positive and coercive means by which to shape the lived experiences of Americans.[5]

Coercive voluntarism not directly related to food policy shaped much of American society during the war years. Wartime obligations proved to be powerful motifs for citizens who—like organizers of victory gardens—sought to exert patriotism and give their service to the country at war. However, voluntarism sometimes took negative forms as well. For example, some hypervigilant groups such as the American Protective League (APL) pressured workers, "slackers," and immigrants to conform to patriotic ideals by, for example, getting rid of German language programs in schools.[6] World War I forced a reconceptualization of the meanings of citizenship through ideas, practices of patriotic voluntarism and civic obligation as seen through victory gardens and the APL.[7]

Coercive patriotism also brought many civilians into military service, and from their training camps, recruits recorded the world around them. This often included their gustatory observations. When the U.S. Army mobilized in 1917, thousands of soldiers entered training camps across the country. Robert Kirk Brady wrote to his parents from Camp Doniphan, Oklahoma that the camp held between twenty-five and thirty thousand troops and looked "like a big tent city."[8] In this environment, stateside recruits usually consumed around 4,761 calories daily.[9] Despite their large diets, food quality was not always good. Brady commented that though the camp is a fine place, "The water . . . has a funny taste."[10] Kenneth Gow of the 27th Division wrote of the poor nutrition of mess food: "We cannot get fresh vegetables or milk here. Milk is very scarce, and what you do get is like water . . . Nearly everyone's digestion is upset."[11] Training at Fort Slocum, New York, George Brown had similar experiences with the milk, which "didn't look much like Jersey milk and certainly did not taste like it. At first I thought we must be late & someone had put dish-water in the pail by mistake. I found out later that it was plain water with just enough condensed milk in it to make the right color."[12] Poor taste experiences were a regular aspect of training.

When not under direct fire, soldiers at the front could expect better quality food compared to what they had in training. Many in the American Expeditionary Forces (AEF) relied on canned beef and hardtack in combat and had daily rations of fresh meat and vegetables. The AEF's bakery in Is-sur-Tille baked around 750,000 pounds of bread every day. Mess officers served food directly or put it in insulated cans to transfer to the front.[13] Many soldiers had negative experiences with food while in France.[14] Several noted in correspondence the body weight they lost from the lack of calories compared to what they ate at home.[15] In World War I, therefore, Americans encountered varying degrees of food standards and tastes. States and organizations mobilized food for coercive patriotism on the home front that embodied broader tenuous negotiations between group powers of persuasion and popular demands for wartime participation.[16] And soldiers sometimes experienced a substantial caloric intake, but often through poorly prepared meals.

Yet soldiers had far more to worry about than food. World War I was devastating to bodies and minds, and newer technologies of killing, like artillery and gas, sent roughly two hundred thousand American soldiers home with amputations, respiratory issues, and other disabilities.[17] Seeking to avoid the large veterans pensions that followed the American Civil War, policymakers instead looked to rehabilitation and insurance payments.[18] Progressive Era reformers shaped rehabilitation, a program that sought to heal the individual medically as far as possible before discharge, and to provide industrial or agricultural training so as to avoid the veteran becoming a public charge.[19] The General Hospitals were therefore sites of social, economic, and physical healing.

Much of the important literature on food and the Great War does not extend to the experiences with hospitals and postwar disabilities.[20] In American hospitals, food production was one tool of rehabilitation promoted as a way to help heal the wounded. It joined a plethora of other vocational training programs such as business, telegraphy, education, mechanics, and massage.[21] Agriculture was a popular venture in U.S. Army rehabilitation, as officials reasoned the slow-paced nature of the work and its predominantly outdoor labor was therapeutic for most wounds or illnesses. This was in contrast to the hectic lives of cities and factory labor, which some imagined would be detrimental to sick veterans.[22] While state efforts at major land resettlement—a way to provide farmland for veterans—may not have been wholly successful, the publicity surrounding them accompanied robust agricultural programs in hospitals. One of the largest of these was at Fort Des Moines, which taught courses in farming, science-related fields, tractor mechanics, chicken-raising, and many other topics important to beginning an agricultural career. There, the Red Cross donated two tractors for the hospital, the American Poultry Association gave four hundred chickens, and Iowa State's Agricultural College provided plans for carpentry students to build poultry houses.[23]

Agricultural programs at places like Fort Des Moines, Walter Reed, and Fort McHenry were not solely for vocational training purposes. While the hospitals purchased some food from nearby towns, the food soldiers grew on site was sometimes used for the hospital mess, contributing to broader wartime conservatory efforts. Tuberculosis patients at the hospital in New Haven, Connecticut, for example, grew a garden, and Walter Reed had a vibrant greenhouse.[24] Patients at Lakewood, New Jersey grew food for the hospital while enjoying the fresh air that physicians argued was beneficial for their health.[25]

Military and rehabilitation officials therefore positioned growing food as beneficial not just for the institutions but also for healing. As mentioned, the products of reconstructive vocational healing sometimes ended up in the mess kitchens to feed the men in another component of the journey to recovery: eating. In the hospital mess areas, food was an important site through which wounded and sick soldier-patients negotiated their relationships with the American state. In many cases, they challenged officials for better quality gustatory experiences as central components of healing.

In October of 1918, an anonymous letter to authorities arrived at U.S. Army General Hospital No. 9 at Lakewood, New Jersey alleging the poor quality of the meals there. An investigation found that the soldiers made complaints that meats and fish were spoiled by inadequate refrigeration, and the bakery and kitchen were both dirty. A planned inspection that same month found the food was of excellent quality and the meal—made special for the inspector of course—was prepared well. Upon questioning, the patients said the food was often served cold, likely caused by the fact that staff served the food by placing the meals on plates to be carried out in batches into the mess halls, rather than allowing the men to help themselves. The mess officer argued there were simply not enough serving dishes to follow the latter course.[26] The soldier-patients who voiced concern about food reflected the fact that they held their state to a certain standard in their postwar recovery. Food was not just a means of caloric intake. It also carried with it social and emotional experiences and symbolized the level of care and concern the state gave to returning soldier-patients.[27]

Lakewood was far from alone in fielding complaints about food. Patients at other hospitals—including Fort McPherson, Cape May, and Evergreen in Baltimore—all encountered inadequate dietary procedures. And more general letters of complaint were by no means rare in postwar hospitals, where thousands of American soldiers entered rehabilitation. The soldiers' concerns and the Army's responses give valuable insight into patient's views on the food they ate, and into the hospital power structures in the aftermath of war, when men no longer served in battlefield roles. In August of 1919, Medical Corps staff at Fort McHenry addressed the situation there, as charges about the mess were arriving "in considerable numbers." The medical officer there took a decidedly defensive stance, assuring those concerned that the patients were fed well, and that most men were dissatisfied with confinement in the hospital and were simply appealing to public sympathy.[28] The broader patient-staff-familial negotiations reveal how each group viewed the role of the state in the healing process. At the same time, soldier-patients negotiated a rehabilitative atmosphere built on the assumption that disabilities, wounds, and illnesses could and would be cured, which in many cases went against the reality of war disabilities that continued long after the war ended.[29]

Fort McHenry's officer personnel remained skeptical after receiving notice of patient discontent. Though not only the soldiers voiced concern. The overall cleanliness of the hospital also came under acute scrutiny from inspectors, employees, and soldiers' family members who visited. E. Francis Briggs, a Reconstruction Aide who had recently been discharged, called attention to conditions there in a letter directed to the Surgeon General. She claimed to have seen staff sweeping wards while physicians dressed wounds without gloves or gowns and patients having to wear dirty uniforms while healing.[30] Hospital staff vehemently disagreed with the charges against their conduct.[31]

Despite administrative disagreements about the hospital, soldier-patients at Fort McHenry made clear that conditions were far from satisfactory, and administrators at least took the complaints seriously enough that they warranted inquiry. A patient there found the frankfurters he was served "were a trifle old—the coffee was weak and the string beans we had looked as though they were cooked in curdled milk." He and his fellow comrades joked about the milk: "They say that the way the milk is made is to take a pitcher of water and put a dime in the bottom. Then they pour milk into the water. As soon as the dime can't be seen it is called milk."[32] Upon subsequent inspections, the mess officer explained the condensed milk did consist of equal parts water and milk, until the hospital switched to fresh milk shortly after the soldier's complaint.[33]

The U.S. Army could have used condensed milk in hospitals for a variety of reasons. Around the turn of the century there was significant fear surrounding the beverage, as it often carried diseases like typhoid and diphtheria. The United States was beginning to see rapid public health benefits as a result of germ theory, including water purification and food inspection.[34] Yet public health did not go far enough when logistical concerns left much to be desired. As cities grew, for example, milk production stretched further from urban environments, and the travel time from farm to customer increased. The milk often lacked temperature control required to keep it cool on the voyage.[35] Army hospitals also frequently struggled to maintain working iceboxes, which made storing milk a challenge.

The hospital at Jefferson Barracks, Missouri gives evidence of some difficulties the U.S. Army had in securing safe milk even without obtaining it from relatively far sources. This site had a modern dairy plant with well-constructed stables and a cooling system for the milk. The hospital kept a herd of over forty cattle and maintained a dairy to supply milk to the men there until around 1923, when the post veterinarian found almost all of the cattle had tuberculosis. The dairy had to get rid of the herd so as not to spread disease to the sick and wounded there.[36] Condensed milk therefore provided a far safer alternative, especially considering one of the stated goals of rehabilitation was to cure illness or disability, not spread more.

Sergeant Isaac Anderson had complaints of a different sort about General Hospital Number 11 in Cape May, New Jersey. Anderson was sent there after coming down with rheumatism in France in the summer of 1918. He was unhappy with his experience there, claiming that he was being detained longer than necessary so the U.S. Army would not have to make his War Risk Insurance payments. He also argued that his condition was not improving, sanitary conditions there were "far from satisfactory," and that he was being half fed, at times with tainted meat. The Inspector General's investigation in August of 1918 into Anderson's claims is revealing. They found that sanitary conditions were indeed far from satisfactory. The plumbing was old, and on account of leakage, "pools of water stand on the floor in many places." The leaky and unsanitary iceboxes contributed to the puddles of water that collected on the floors. And their poor functionality meant that any food being kept in them went bad.[37]

Cape May's administration was partially to blame for Anderson's experiences. Colonel Brechemin, who was in charge of the hospital, failed to exercise supervision over the mess hall, and officers didn't make regular inspections of meals or the stored meat. In addition to poor administrative standards, the kitchen lacked sufficient numbers of experienced cooks. The inspector concluded that the hospital building was "entirely unsuited for a General Hospital."[38] In preparing for wounded and sick patients, the U.S. Army's reliance on the promise of curing and rehabilitating soldiers made securing poorly prepared structures like the hospital at Cape May a viable option. Anderson's complaints that he was too long in the hospital and fed tainted meat was one of few avenues by which he could control his healing environment.

War can impose extraordinary sensory burdens on human bodies, and Cape May was not isolated in its haphazard handling of food, as U.S. Army sanitary reports suggest.[39] And evidence indicates the quality of ingredients spans from unappetizing to rotten. The hospital at Camp Dix, New Jersey served food that was coarse and unappetizing, with "almost universal complaint from patients." While meals that arrived for ward patients at Fort McHenry were typically insufficient or sometimes burnt.[40] The hospital at Lakewood was the subject of patient complaints about tainted fish, where the iceboxes and cooking equipment were "dilapidated and in need of replacement."[41] General Hospital Number 1 in New York City served tainted hamburger steak to patients. And inspectors found the butter at Otisville, New York's hospital for tuberculosis patients "rancid and unfit for serving."[42] The unfitness of the food, often relating to inadequate equipment like iceboxes, sheds light on more entrenched issues that led to poor gustatory experiences for soldier-patients, primarily personnel and equipment.

One reason for the inadequate gustatory experience was the poor use of dietitians or other personnel in hospitals. Despite the fact that the military used dietitians before 1917, it was their service overseas during World War I that helped prove their efficiency in nutritional science. The American Red Cross recruited dietitians as civilian employees of the U.S. Army Medical Department, where they served domestically and with the American Expeditionary Forces. Those who inhabited this role— predominantly women—strived to improve the nutritional health of the nation and its soldiers and veterans.[43]

Despite employing dietitians at Lakewood and other hospitals to address special diets, these professionals "played a rather minor role" and were there usually to supervise the preparation of food rather than to plan meals. The mess officer at Lakewood fared little better, having "little technical competence" in dietary science in comparison to his dietitian counterparts.[44] Women dietitians often found themselves with a wealth of expertise, but in an anomalous position without adequate authority.[45] Reports from military hospitals across the country reflect this fact. Otisville's hospital served inadvisable heavy diets to sick soldiers due in part to the mess officer writing the menu rather than the dietitian. Hospitals such as Fort McHenry and Boston Hospital both requested more dietitians for their staff.[46] In September of 1919, the inspector at the U.S. Army hospital in Oteen, North Carolina reported the need for more dietitians, and that those already there were being paid half of what far less qualified civilian cooks were paid in the same location.[47] Hospitals therefore relied heavily on civilian cooks, who, in cases like that of Lakewood, struggled to feed a population of over one thousand soldiers while relying on merely small numbers of cooks who "lacked practical experience in cookery."[48]

And while dietitians at Oteen suffered from inadequate pay in subordinate positions, those at Fort Bayard had to use the same kitchen as regular cooks, rather than working in a special diet kitchen that many other hospitals had. In this case, the failure to provide a diet kitchen reduced efficiency in cooking for soldiers who needed light diets to heal from various illnesses.[49] In Carlisle, Pennsylvania, many bed patients received a full diet that was too heavy, because of this type of inadequate kitchen situation.[50] The one hospital with a proficient record in hiring and using dietitians was the Base Hospital at Camp Wheeler, Georgia, which employed a mess officer, a senior dietitian, and six assistant dietitians.[51] However, Camp Wheeler was an outlier, as most military hospitals kept women dietitians largely subservient to far less qualified male civilian cooks.

Another reason for the poor taste and experience of eating in rehabilitation hospitals after the war was the lack of sufficient equipment. In the mess halls, soldier-patients either stood in line for service or had food delivered to their tables using dishware that was often chipped and usually poorly washed. Many hospital kitchens handwashed plates and silverware, and because of the small numbers of workers in the kitchen, tableware was not always properly cleaned. Inspectors regularly found knives, forks, and plates greasy or unsightly.[52] Clean utensils were particularly important, as one officer stated in the midst of the influenza epidemic, so as not to transfer bacteria to other patients.[53] If it wasn't the plates and utensils that contaminated the patients' gustatory experiences, it was the dirty tables they ate on, as was the case in Fort McHenry and Colonia, New Jersey.[54] The environment of eating was important, as historian Rachel Duffett argues about the British Expeditionary Forces, because in the face of so much disorder in war "decent table manners and clean cutlery assumed an even greater importance."[55] So too did clean cutlery make a difference in tasting recovery for soldiers struggling to heal from their war wounds or illnesses.

Organizing the arrival of patients and serving techniques proved problematic as well. Some hospitals had regulations that prohibited patients from going to eat until they were summoned and forbade "lounging in the hall-ways or porches before meals."[56] In the mess hall itself, the medical department sought control over the aural atmosphere, arguing, "Loud talking, rattling of dishes, and banging of chairs are disturbing to the sick."[57] Staff, however, had trouble upholding the rules, specifically surrounding patient lines for food, which caused long wait times and confusion. At the general hospital in Richmond, Virginia, for example, the lack of a coherent system for dispatching patients to the mess halls "resulted in a staggering to breakfast and a large number of patients . . . waiting in line outside of the mess hall for a chance to get inside for breakfast." Many of the soldiers were dressed only in their pajamas on cold mornings.[58] Fort McHenry had similar problems, leading to men on crutches allegedly having been forced to stand in lines for close to an hour.[59] Therefore some issues came not from the taste of the food, but instead from the mechanisms of serving.

Not all patients could travel to the mess halls, as many were too ill or wounded, and instead ate in the wards. Ward service was often as haphazard as mess hall service. While many hospital kitchens had food carts for transport, they often either did not work properly or did not travel well. The Biltmore, North Carolina hospital was the exception. It had electrically heated carts that worked well. Fort Ontario used fourteen large carts, but they were too heavy to travel far. And Fort McPherson's carts quickly became unserviceable.[60] Sometimes the problems with the carts had less to do with efficiency and more to do with hospital layout. At the hospital in Richmond, the carts could not withstand the irregular graveled walkways from the kitchen to the wards.[61] As a result, the food regularly arrived cold. Patients in the wards in Fort McHenry, for example, ate their food cold and, because of a lack of plate-ware and tables, the trays were placed on the floor instead of on tables and the food served from the floor."[62]

U.S. Army rehabilitation hospitals therefore inadequately prepared and administrated food production for sick and disabled soldier-patients. Medical officers underutilized and underpaid dietitians in the organization and cooking of meals. And there was a general lack of equipment spanning from forks and knives to trays and food carts. Civilian cooks, who were also lacking in numbers, put out cold food on often greasy or dirty plates to patients who waited in long lines. The realities evident in the sanitary reports lend legitimacy to patients' sensory complaints about the meals they ate and the power they projected toward the state whose responsibility it was to care for them after the war.

Examining World War I food in rehabilitation from the perspective of disability and sensory studies helps one understand the social history within the walls of American hospitals as well as agency at all levels of healing. Patient experiences and sanitary reports show that many aspects of hospital cleanliness and preparation were lacking, and not all patients had the same access to food. Similar to soldiers in the hectic trench and camp environments, patients recovering from oftentimes-horrific war wounds had little control over their postwar wounded world within the large bureaucratic military structures.[63] The sense of taste in these environments therefore was a crucial site for soldiers to negotiate their rehabilitation after the World War I.

Policymakers envisioned a system of retraining that took in wounded soldier-patients and dispensed industrial worker-civilians. Yet the men returning from war did not stand passive to the mechanics of mobilization or demobilization, and patients who complained about their taste experiences joined a broader history of veteran discontent after the war.[64] Much like in training, they recorded their encounters with food. Patients commented on the poor quality and quantity of food and drink, taking power into their own hands with regard to their healing. In the hospitals in particular, food was important not just for nutrition and healing but also for maintaining high morale. The long-term repercussions of war disabilities went against rehabilitation's presumption that these disabilities could be cured quickly. Hospitals meant to be temporary sites of healing did not always invest in kitchen appliances and staff, leading to poor quality food. Recognizing their place in the recovery process, soldiers exercised their patient power and complained, taking to task the state that mobilized them for war in the first place.

NOTES

1. For a discussion of the importance of sensory history in war, see: Mark M. Smith, *The Smell of Battle, the Taste of Siege: A Sensory History of the Civil War* (New York: Oxford University Press, 2015); Nicholas J. Saunders and Paul Cornish, eds., *Modern Conflict and the Senses* (New York: Routledge, 2017).
2. For a discussion of food and politics in Europe, see: Belinda J. Davis, *Home Fires Burning: Food, Politics, and Everyday Life in World War I Berlin* (Chapel Hill: University of North Carolina Press, 2000); L. Margaret Barnett, *British Food Policy During the First World War* (New York: Routledge, 2014).
3. Robert N. Gross, "'Lick a Stamp, Lick the Kaiser': Sensing the Federal Government in Children's Lives during World War I," *Journal of Social History* 46, no. 4 (2013): 976.
4. Sarah E. Wassberg, "Preserve or Perish: The Orange County Food Preservation Battalion and Food Conservation Efforts in New York State during the Great War, 1917–1919," (MA thesis, University at Albany, 2015): iii.
5. Helen Zoe Veit, *Modern Food, Moral Food: Self-Control, Science, and the Rise of Modern Eating in the Early Twentieth Century* (Chapel Hill: The University of North Carolina Press, 2013): 14; For a discussion on food and/or coercive voluntarism in the United States during World War I, see: Veit, *Modern Food, Moral Food;* Jennifer D. Keene, *Doughboys, the Great War, and the Remaking of America* (Baltimore: The Johns Hopkins University Press, 2001); Christopher Capozzola, *Uncle Sam Wants You: World War I and the Making of the Modern American Citizen* (New York: Oxford University Press, 2008); Nancy K. Bristow, *Making Men Moral: Social Engineering During the Great War* (New York: New York University Press, 1996).
6. Capozzola, *Uncle Sam Wants You,* 183; Evan P. Sullivan, "American Anxiety and German-Americans in New York State during the First World War," *Past Tense Graduate Review of History* 4, no. 1 (Spring 2016).
7. Capozzola, *Uncle Sam Wants You,* 20.
8. Robert Kirk Brady Letter to Folks, October 7, 1917, The State Historical Society of Missouri, http://digital.shsmo.org/cdm/compoundobject/collection/wwi/id/1155/rec/4.
9. Jennifer D. Keene, *World War I: Daily Life through History* (Westport, CT: Greenwood Press, 2006): 45.
10. Robert Kirk Brady Letter to Folks, October 7, 1917, The State Historical Society of Missouri, http://digital.shsmo.org/cdm/compoundobject/collection/wwi/id/1155/rec/4.
11. Kenneth Gow, *Letters of a Soldier* (New York: H. B. Covert, 1920): 147.
12. David L. Snead, ed., *An American Soldier in World War I* (Lincoln: University of Nebraska Press, 2006): 12–13.
13. Keene, *World War I,* 152.
14. Malnutrition, for example, was common among British soldiers during World War I. See: Walter Gratzer, *Terrors of the Table: The Curious History of Nutrition* (New York: Oxford University Press, 2005): 4.
15. David M. Kennedy, *Over Here: The First World War and American Society* (New York: Oxford University Press, 2004): 209.
16. Capozzola, *Uncle Sam Wants You,* 210.

17. John M. Kinder, *Paying with Their Bodies: American War and the Problem of the Disabled Veteran* (Chicago: University of Chicago Press, 2015): 5.

18. Beth Linker, *War's Waste: Rehabilitation in World War I America* (Chicago: University of Chicago Press, 2011): 2.

19. Jessica L. Adler, *Burdens of War: Creating the United States Veterans Health System* (Baltimore: Johns Hopkins University Press, 2017): 27–29. For a discussion on disability and rehabilitation in World War I, see: Adler, *Burdens of War;* Kinder, *Paying with Their Bodies;* Linker, *War's Waste;* David Gerber, *Disabled Veterans in History* (Ann Arbor: University of Michigan, 2012); Ana Carden-Coyne, "Ungrateful Bodies: Rehabilitation, Resistance and Disabled American Veterans of the First World War," *European Review of History* 14, no. 4 (2007); Joanna Bourke, *Dismembering the Male: Men's Bodies, Britain, and the Great War* (Chicago: University of Chicago Press, 1996); Deborah Cohen, *The War Come Home: Disabled Veterans in Britain and Germany, 1914–1939* (Berkeley: University of California Press, 2001).

20. See: Rachel Duffett, *The Stomach for Fighting: Food and the Soldiers of the Great War* (Manchester: Manchester University Press, 2012).

21. "What About the Farm?" *Carry On: A Magazine on the Reconstruction of Disabled Soldiers and Sailors* 1, no. 6 (March 1919): 23.

22. William J. Wright, "Vocational Training in Agriculture for Disabled Soldiers and Sailors," *American Journal of Care for Cripples* 8, no. 1 (January 1919): 31–32.

23. "A Brief Historical Sketch of Physical Reconstruction Work at U.S. General Hospital #26, Fort Des Moines, IA," RG 112, Series NM 31 (K), Box 266, Folder 353.91–1: General Hospital #26 (K) 1918, U.S. National Archives.

24. "What About the Farm?," 22–23.

25. T. B. Kidner, "Guiding the Disabled to a New Job," *Carry On: A Magazine on the Reconstruction of Disabled Soldiers and Sailors* 1, no. 3 (September 1918): 21.

26. Director of Military Intelligence to the Surgeon General, "Bad Food for Wounded Soldiers, Genl. Hospital No. 9, Lakewood, N.J." October 15, 1918, RG 112, Series NM 31 (K), Box 218, Folder 720.1-General Hospital #9, Lakewood, NJ (K); Colonel D. C. Howard, "Memorandum for Secretary of War," November 2, 1918, RG 112, Series NM 31 (K), Box 218, Folder 720.1-General Hospital #9, Lakewood, NJ (K), U.S. National Archives.

27. Duffett, *The Stomach for Fighting,* xi–2.

28. D. C. Howard to James Weir, August 12, 1919, RG 112, Series NM 31 (K), Box 184, Folder 330.14–1 U.S.A. Gen. Hosp. #2, Ft. McHenry, Md., U.S. National Archives; D. C. Howard to the Commanding Officer, August 4, 1919, RG 112, Series NM 31 (K), Box 184, Folder 330.14–1 U.S.A. Gen. Hosp. #2, Ft. McHenry, Md., U.S. National Archives.

29. See: Annessa C. Stagner, "Defining the Soldier's Wounds: U.S. Shell Shock in International Perpsective," (PhD diss., University of California, Irvine, 2014): 1–3.

30. E. Frances Briggs to the Surgeon General, "Concerning: Conditions at General Hospital No. 2" January 9, 1920, RG 112, Series NM 31 (K), Box 184, Folder 330.14–1: U.S.A. Gen. Hosp. #2, Ft. McHenry, Md., U.S. National Archives.

31. Lt. T. J. Leary to the Commanding Officer, "Report," January 21, 1920, RG 112,

Series NM 31 (K), Box 184, Folder 330.14–1: U.S.A. Gen. Hosp. #2, Ft. McHenry, Md., U.S. National Archives.

32. Representative Julius Kahn to General Ireland, July 31, 1919, RG 112, Series NM 31 (K), Box 184, Folder 330.14–1: U.S.A. Gen. Hosp. #2, U.S. National Archives.

33. S. J. Scott to D. C. Howard, August 7, 1919, RG 112, Series NM 31 (K), Box 184, Folder 330.14–1: U.S.A. Gen. Hosp. #2, U.S. National Archives.

34. Nancy Tomes, *The Gospel of Germs: Men, Women, and the Microbe in American Life* (Cambridge: Harvard University Press, 1999): 6; Lois N. Magner, *A History of Infectious Diseases and the Microbial World* (Westport: Praeger, 2009): 46.

35. Kendra Smith-Howard, *Pure and Modern Milk: An Environmental History since 1900* (New York: Oxford University Press, 2014): 12.

36. P. R. Hawley to the Corps Area Commander, "Sanitary Report on Jefferson Barracks," November 15, 1923, RG 112, Series NM 31(N), Box 160, Folder 721–1 (Jefferson Bks. K), U.S. National Archives.

37. "Report of investigation concerning the treatment of Sergeant Isaac J. Anderson, Company A, 117th Supply Train, 42nd Division A.E.F., now in General Hospital No. 11, Cape May, New Jersey," August 23, 1918, RG 112, Series NM 31 (K), Box 223, Folder 330.14–1: U.S.A. Gen. Hosp. #11, U.S. National Archives.

38. "Report of investigation concerning the treatment of Sergeant Isaac J. Anderson, Company A, 117th Supply Train, 42nd Division A.E.F., now in General Hospital No. 11, Cape May, New Jersey," August 23, 1918, RG 112, Series NM 31 (K), Box 223, Folder 330.14–1: U.S.A. Gen. Hosp. #11, U.S. National Archives.

39. Paul Cornish, Nicholas J. Saunders, and Mark Smith, "Introduction," in *Modern Conflict and the Senses,* eds., Nicholas J. Saunders and Paul Cornish (New York: Routledge, 2017): 4.

40. Major W. S. Shields, "Extracts from Reports of Sanitary Inspectors Made during the World War, Volume I," 150, RG 112, Series NM20–29A, Box 408, U.S. National Archives.

41. Director of Military Intelligence to the Surgeon General, "Bad Food for Wounded Soldiers" October 15, 1918; Colonel D. C. Howard, "Memorandum for Secretary of War," November 2, 1918, RG 112, Series NM 31 (K), Box 218, Folder 720.1: General Hospital #9, U.S. National Archives.

42. Major W. S. Shields, "Extracts from Reports of Sanitary Inspectors Made during the World War, Volume I," p. 150, RG 112, Series NM20–29A, Box 408, U.S. National Archives.

43. Patricia M. Hodges, "Perspectives on History: Military Dietetics in Europe during World War I," *Journal of the American Dietetic Association* 93, no. 8 (August 1993): 897–900.

44. Major R. G. Hoskins to the Surgeon General, "Nutritional conditions in U.S. Army General Hospital #9, Lakewood, N.J." October 3, 1918, RG 112, Series NM 31 (K), Box 218, Folder 720.1-General Hospital #9, Lakewood, NJ (K), U.S. National Archives.

45. R. G. Hoskins to Col. W. H. Smith, "Memorandum for Colonel W. H. Smith," September 14, 1918, RG 112, Series NM20–29A, Box 407, Folder 720.1–1: Food—September 1918, U.S. National Archives.

46. Major W. S. Shields, "Extracts from Reports of Sanitary Inspectors Made during

the World War, Volume I," 84, RG 112, Series NM20–29A, Box 408, U.S. National Archives.

47. Shields, "Quotations from Reports of Sanitary Inspections," 27.

48. Major R. G. Hoskins to the Surgeon General, "Nutritional conditions in U.S. Army General Hospital #9, Lakewood, N.J." October 3, 1918, RG 112, Series NM 31 (K), Box 218, Folder 720.1: General Hospital #9, U.S. National Archives.

49. Shields, "Quotations from Reports of Sanitary Inspections," 5.

50. Shields, "Extracts from Reports of Sanitary Inspectors," 151.

51. Shields, "Quotations from Reports of Sanitary Inspections," 79.

52. Shields, "Extracts from Reports of Sanitary Inspectors," 86 and 150.

53. The Surgeon General to the Chief of the Embarkation Branch, "Sterilization of Mess Kits, Dishes and Utensils Aboard Troop Ships," October 26, 1918, RG 112, Series NM20–29A, Box 406, Folder: unmarked, U.S. National Archives.

54. Shields, "Extracts from Reports of Sanitary Inspectors," 267–68.

55. Duffett, The Stomach for Fighting, 18.

56. Colonal Edger, "Memorandum #9: Regulations Governing Patients in Hospital," January 23, 1919, RG 112, Series UD-8, Box 1159, Folder: Hospital Regulations, U.S. National Archives.

57. "Regulations for the Mess," January 26, 1918, RG 112, Series NM 31 (K), Box 300, Folder 300.9–1: Gen. Hospital #40 (K), U.S. National Archives.

58. Shields, "Quotations from Reports of Sanitary Inspections," 78.

59. Thomas Bell to Representative Julius Kahn, July 30, 1919, RG 112, Series NM 31 (K), Box 184, Folder 330.14–1: U.S.A. Gen. Hosp. #2, U.S. National Archives.

60. Shields, "Quotations from Reports of Sanitary Inspectors," 42–43.

61. Shields, "Quotations from Reports of Sanitary Inspectors," 78.

62. Shields, "Extracts from Reports of Sanitary Inspectors," 150.

63. Duffett, The Stomach for Fighting, 233.

64. Keene, Doughboys, 7; Stephen R. Ortiz, Beyond the Bonus March and GI Bill: How Veteran Politics Shaped the New Deal Era (New York: New York University Press, 2010): 8.

CHAPTER 11

Culinary Nationalism and Ethnic Recipe Collections during and after World War I

CAROL HELSTOSKY

In an era when global tastes and cuisines are commonplace, the introduction and hybridization of diverse ingredients is hardly remarkable. Whereas geographic borders are sometimes contested, our culinary borders are decidedly porous. We consume universal "fast" foods, such as pizza, tacos, and sushi, which have national points of origin but are consumed by populations around the world. Consumers consciously embrace new foods and culinary techniques through tourism, migration, travel (virtual and real), and a broadly shared food consciousness created and sustained on social media platforms. Food historians agree that the United States has a lengthy history of embracing diverse cuisines, although the acceptance of foreign foodways has frequently been halting and often met with resistance.[1] The complex exchange and promotion of food practices by immigrant groups has been well documented in food studies literature. Ethnic restaurants consciously promoted the variety and taste of exotic cuisines so as to attract curious customers. Nonimmigrant entrepreneurs consciously appropriate, manufacture, and distribute foreign foods so that consumers can enjoy new food products. And while nationalist, ethnic, and racial tensions over food have emerged at different times, the United States has witnessed a vibrant, profitable, and mostly peaceful blending of food traditions from many countries.

Food habits, preparation techniques, and tastes do not exist in isolation. The paper trail of American foodways—cookbooks and domestic economy manuals—reveals that there was both acceptance of and resistance to blending diverse cuisines. Many eighteenth-century recipe books reflected the British origins of their authors. In the nineteenth century, cookbooks reflected culinary traditions of German as well as British immigrants. While Indigenous, African, southern European, and East Asian culinary traditions coexisted with western European ones, the majority of published cookbooks promoted British and German recipes at least until the years following World War II era. Cookbooks offer an imperfect but telling lens through which to understand foodways in the United States. Recipes for meat dishes, particularly those with beef, dominated alongside recipes for breads, root vegetables (potatoes, carrots, parsnips, turnips), cakes, custards, and other sweets. While there was an occasional recipe for a French or—rarely—an Italian dish, American cookbooks were far from cosmopolitan or international until after World War II, a period of great culinary transformation in the United States and around the world.[2] Cookbooks that promoted alternative lifestyles like vegetarianism and naturalism sometimes featured recipes for dishes prepared by Italian, Indian, and Chinese cooks; such recipes were highlighted for their rejection of meat and their use of fresh vegetables, seasonings, and spices.

This chapter argues that World War I was a significant moment in the history of U.S. cookbooks, as evidenced by several publications that touted the health and economic benefits of foods from European nations other than Britain or Germany. Indeed, World War I comprised a dramatic chapter in food history. As the war dragged on, governments became more aware of the need to balance military and civilian resources and thus encouraged consumers to eat less through propaganda initiatives and, as conditions worsened, by rationing foods in short supply. While soldiers were fed a largely monotonous but protein-heavy diet, civilians were challenged to think differently about food as they had to feed their families with less protein, fat, and sugar.[3] This challenge became an onerous task in countries like Germany and Austria, where chronic shortage meant coming up with substitutions for familiar foods or going without and even protesting when conditions became unbearable.[4] In some nations, the war brought to the fore a more experimental attitude toward cuisine and thinking about what was good to eat. Consumers in Britain and France drew culinary inspiration from their colonies and imported inexpensive foods from the United States—foods like corn, wheat, and pork. Although the United States would not militarily enter the conflict until 1917, citizens were encouraged to adopt thrifty and simple food habits early in the war. Cookbooks and cooking pamphlets encouraged consumers to think and cook differently. Several works encouraged consumers to adopt the cooking habits and meal plans from other allied nations, looking to Italy, Belgium, and Russia for culinary inspiration.

These books predate the broader acceptance of ethnic food in the United States after World War II and thus challenge our understanding of when and how the cultural transmission of food habits occurred, especially when it came to the acceptance of European cuisines that were not British or German. Wartime exigencies made possible the elevation of simple and inexpensive dishes. These cookbooks introduced readers to new ingredients and emphasized simple carbohydrates as well as fresh fruits and vegetables as the foundations for building healthful and satisfying meals. While these books put forward new ways of thinking about food preparation and consumption, they also put forward new visions or understandings of culinary nationalism. American readers were encouraged to think about the plight of other nations such as Belgium when they prepared daily meals. Thus, readers understood how their decisions as consumers impacted their health as well as the health and well-being of consumers from other nations. Readers were also encouraged to think about national cuisines in positive ways, as healthful and economical alternatives to an American diet built on wheat bread, corn, dairy products, and beef. Lastly, these cookbooks would have engendered a sense of pride among specific immigrant populations, given the public framing of ethnic foodways as a national good during wartime. World War I was a unique moment in the culinary history of the United States, one where national cuisines were organized, publicized, and discussed, both for their inherent value and for their utility to American citizens in a time of war.

In the postwar era, calls to economize in the kitchen were subsumed by postwar normalization in both Europe and the United States. Postwar affluence was uneven when it came to food and diet. Recovery in nations like Belgium and Germany took a significant toll on nutritional levels and health of vulnerable populations, particularly infants, children, and the elderly. New nations like Poland struggled with the declining health of vulnerable populations while famines decimated the populations of what were Russia's breadbasket regions. The United States, however, did not experience shortage, inflation, or near-famine conditions; rather, American agriculture emerged from the war stronger than ever and American consumers did not have to think about cutting back or going without.

In the interwar decades, the balance between feast and famine was a delicate and shifting challenge to government leaders, health care practitioners, and family providers. The simple and economical recipes from wartime cookbooks resurfaced, or more accurately, never went away, in European nations. The culinary nationalism first expressed in wartime American cookbooks resurfaced across the Atlantic in European nations that continued to tighten their belts after the war. Culinary nationalism manifested as pride in simple and economical cuisine was most prominent in fascist Italy (1922–45), where, under the reign of Benito Mussolini, food habits assumed great political significance. Ironically, the dishes promoted in the United States as cultural vehicles for internationalism became standards of the fascist "cooking of consent," intended to inspire Italians with pride and to foster greater economic independence.

The Search for Economy in Wartime

The need to provision millions of troops during the war challenged governments to balance resources between civilians and the military. This balancing act was easier for nations with vast empires, efficient bureaucracies, and access to maritime trade. As the war dragged on, civilians in many nations were encouraged to consume less. German and Austrian citizens resorted to consuming ersatz foods, rationing, and rioting when ration coupons no longer guaranteed adequate food supplies.[5] As the war dragged on, European consumers realized that they had to economize in order to survive. Wartime consumers tried new ingredients and preparation techniques in order to feed their families. Not surprisingly, in the context of wartime exigencies, consumers thought differently about the foods and dishes from other nations and cultures as potential solutions to the problem of dwindling food supplies. This openness to foreign culinary solutions had a history in the vegetarian and naturalist movements of the late nineteenth and early twentieth centuries. For example, the vegetarian theosophists in Britain examined and wrote about the vegetarian diets of India. In the United States, a national network of vegetarian food businesses catered to an international clientele. The Hercules Hygienic Supply House in Chicago, for example, corresponded in Esperanto with customers outside the United States.[6]

Reducing the consumption of meat and other more expensive food items was undoubtedly easier in nations where citizens were vegetarians by necessity because they could not afford meat. Thus, it would be easier for consumers in Italy to sacrifice meat than it would be for British or American consumers. Americans were known for their high levels of meat consumption, especially beef. Vast acreage for grazing cattle, in concert with the refrigerated railway car, brought beef to American tables, even those of the working class. European vegetarians were dismayed by Americans who subsisted on a "diet of beef, white bread, potatoes, pie, coffee, which seems to be a favorite among the American people . . . if vegetables are served at all, they are generally boiled in plenty of water, instead of being lightly steamed."[7] Naturalist and vegetarian movements across Europe and the United States promoted diets that were mostly or exclusively based on fruits and vegetables, but they frequently found themselves thwarted by folklore and superstitions about the unhealthful qualities of produce: strawberries, peaches, and cucumbers were thought to be poisonous; grapefruit was thought to have dangerous levels of quinine; tomatoes to cause cancer; lettuce to contain opium; and watermelons were thought to cause malaria.[8] Consuming a diet with less meat and more vegetables may have been recommended during wartime, but such a diet was alien or at least questionable for American consumers who were used to meat. Cookbooks highlighting the economy and healthfulness of foreign or ethnic cuisines were one way for American consumers to think about food and national identity in a time of war. These cookbooks demonstrated that fruits and vegetables would not cause disease and a reduction in meat consumption would not mean a sacrifice of taste or satisfaction. The skillful way cookbook authors blended recipes for the familiar with recipes for the new eased consumers into experimenting with ethnic cuisines during the war.

Ethnic Cookbooks in the Service of Economy

The war brought an outpouring of nationalist feeling in Europe. In the United States, first- and second-generation immigrants struggled to come to terms with the social, political, and cultural upheavals created by the conflict. Citizen efforts to express patriotic support for Germany and Austria were greeted with uncertainty at first, then condemnation within months of the war's start, as the press reported the fall of Belgium to German troops and detailed the atrocities committed there. In the first months of the war, some Americans who had been living in Europe found themselves attempting to feed millions of Belgians when back in the United States and fundraising campaigns to assist Belgians multiplied rapidly.[9] The *Belgian Cookbook*, published in 1915, was one effort to promote awareness of Belgium's plight while instructing American readers on how to economize on food costs without sacrificing quality or taste. Mrs. Brian Luck collected recipes from Belgian refugees in England in order to provide examples of Belgian cuisine for Americans.[10]

The book's message was that one should cook with empathy for the plight of Belgians. Yet not every recipe would have appealed to American consumers. Soups made with boiled cauliflower liquid may have been economical but were not necessarily appealing. And "starvation soup"— consisting of boiled pork bone, brussels sprouts, leeks, and cabbage—was likely in the collection to remind readers of the tremendous hardships their Belgian counterparts endured during the German blockade. Recipes for heartier fare appealed more to American readers interested in feeding families. Thick soups made with legumes and vegetables (potatoes, leeks, cabbage, and sometimes tomatoes) were occasionally flavored with meat, but meat was treated more like a condiment than a main ingredient. Several dishes underscored the way vegetables could substitute for meat. A dish called "Friday's feast," suitable for Lenten practices, consisted of cabbage and chestnut puree; preparation for the dish was time consuming but the ingredients were inexpensive, and the puree imitated a meat puree.[11] Stuffed vegetables also imitated dishes that had previously featured meat. Recipes that featured meat demonstrated how mutton could be made tender. Mutton and rabbit dishes predominated the meat section, while egg dishes and "made" dishes, or leftovers, outnumbered the meat dishes.

While the message of the *Belgian Cookbook* encouraged Americans to try a foreign cuisine out of empathy, other cookbooks used different rhetorical and culinary strategies. A joint Canadian and American project, *Allied Cookery: British, French, Belgian, Russian* was published to "aid the war sufferers in the devastated districts of France."[12] Authored by sisters Grace Clergue Harrison (who lived in the United States) and Gertrude Clergue (who lived in Canada) and published in 1916, the book combines characteristic American recipes with recipes from France, Serbia, Italy, and Russia, collected during the sisters' prewar travels and requested from the chefs of Montreal's clubs and hotels. The book's title and contents indicate that the Clergue sisters adopted a gentle approach to thinking about national cuisines under the umbrella of allied nations. They encouraged Americans to think more about French, British, Russian, Italian, and even Serbian cooking than about German or Austrian cuisine.

Organizing and categorizing recipes from eight nations (Britain,

France, Belgium, Russia, Italy, Serbia, Canada, United States) makes for an unwieldy definition of "allied" cooking. Unlike the *Belgian Cookbook*, which emphasized the simple cooking of Belgian farm wives, *Allied Cookery* strings together characteristic dishes of various nations and while most are simple and inexpensive, a few recipes involve extensive preparation and many expensive ingredients. The authors label the country of origin after each recipe, although in some cases, a recipe is attributed to a single individual, like a practicing chef. In the soup section, bouillabaisse and borscht have recognized ethnic or national origins while the origin of Serbian chicken soup is less precise, being a blend of chicken, carrots, and parsnips thickened with lard and cream. Alongside more complicated soups are simple ones like an Italian minestrone and French family soup. *Allied Cookery* differs from many of the wartime cooking collections in that it has lengthy sections for fish and meat, with recipes for more economical meats like mutton, but also complicated recipes for chicken and veal. In the fish section, there is one recipe for salmon teriyaki, which calls for shoyu and mirin, ingredients that were difficult to find outside of Japanese markets. It was suggested that cooks could substitute Chinese sauce (soy sauce) for shoyu and sauternes wine for mirin.

While readers might have recognized the Canadian (mutton pie) and American (fried apples) dishes, they would be less aware of French, Italian, or Russian dishes. *Allied Cookery* highlighted foreign recipes that stretched the main ingredient for family consumption. Recipes for Russian pirogi, a baked bread with sweet or savory fillings, featured combinations of rice, fish, eggs, and vegetables, all inexpensive and presumably accessible ingredients for American audiences. Italian dishes featured risotto, polenta, and ravioli. While readers would have recognized polenta as the Italian version of corn-meal mush, they were less likely to be familiar with risotto or stuffed pastas. Italian meat dishes used inexpensive cuts of meat or innards, extended and flavored with vegetables like tomatoes, onions, and peppers. Tripe Italian style layered strips of tripe with tomato sauce, cheese, and breadcrumbs. Readers expecting more familiar foods from British cuisine found recipes like old English plum pudding and Victoria scones, but also found recipes for Indian pilau (chicken, mango and onion stew served over rice) and several variations for curries (curries were based on a homemade curry powder consisting of red chili, coriander, and dagad phool or black stone flower, to which one could add cinnamon, baked garlic, scraped coconut, caraway seeds, cardamom seeds, and yellow or green pimentos).

The authors of *Allied Cookery* introduced less familiar dishes and ingredients to readers by interspersing recipes from foreign countries with recipes that represented the United States and Canada, suggesting broader culinary horizons based on military alliances. Unlike wartime cooking books that stress thrift and simplicity, *Allied Cookery* appealed to more status-oriented readers, as several of the recipes were contributed by Canadian chefs who interpreted sophisticated French dishes (blanquette of veal or crepes suzette, for example). Readers were also encouraged to think about economy by trying out humble foods from Italy, Russia, and Serbia. The humblest recipes were a culinary stretch for American readers during wartime. Readers were encouraged to use rice as a main ingredient in many of the recipes, and less familiar vegetables and ingredients were interspersed throughout the book. In contrast to the *Belgian Cookbook*, which suggested American readers attempt more economical foreign recipes out of a sense of solidarity or empathy, *Allied Cookery* reassured readers that they could still enjoy sophisticated dishes alongside humble fare.

As the number of military allies increased over the course of war, Italian Americans grew increasingly determined to demonstrate Italy's status as both nation and ally. Italian cuisine was relatively unknown outside of Italian immigrant communities in the United States and Italian recipes were seldom featured in cookbooks or domestic economy manuals before World War II, aside from an occasional reference to an Italian "paste" or macaroni, usually pasta dishes flavored with tomato sauce.[13] Mabel Earl McGinnis, publishing under the Italian-sounding pseudonym Antonia Isola, promoted Italian cuisine through simple recipes for pasta, rice, and polenta (served as fritters or cakes, with tomato or béchamel sauce) prior to World War I. Her recipes utilized produce familiar to Americans: pumpkin, tomatoes, celery, and string beans, and she provided instructions for substitutions for ingredients like parmesan cheese.[14] A handful of vegetarian cookbooks suggested Italian dishes because so many Italians were vegetarians by necessity, unable to afford meat, although the recipe suggestions in vegetarian cookbooks bore little resemblance to what was prepared and consumed in Italy or in Italian American communities.[15] For example, a recipe for Italian spaghetti in the 1922 *Lindlahr Vegetarian Cook Book* instructs readers to "put spaghetti in salted boiling water without breaking; boil about forty minutes; drain and put into a buttered baking dish, sprinkle with chopped onion and green pepper; cover with seasoned tomato juice, grate parmesan cheese over the top, and bake."[16] Given that the spaghetti was boiled for forty minutes and then baked, one assumes that this recipe took the meaning of pasta as "paste" quite literally.

Food historians point to the decades after World War II as a time when Italian and Italian American foods became universally popular, especially through culinary vehicles like pizza and pasta.[17] As evidenced by books like *Allied Cookery*, simple and economical Italian dishes were recommended for Americans during World War I, even though Americans were not facing extreme economic hardships. Julia Lovejoy Cuniberti's *Practical Italian Recipes for American Kitchens*, published in 1918, was a fundraising cookbook (proceeds from books sold went to aid families of Italian soldiers) that compiled and catalogued Italian recipes for Americans. This book predates better-known American cookbooks like Rosa Aiello's *La cucina casareccia napoletana pei golosi e buongustai*, published in the 1940s; Cuniberti produced and sold the book out of her home in Washington, DC, thus the book had limited circulation. It is however an extraordinary document of Italian culinary nationalism in the United States.

Julia Lovejoy Cuniberti was an American who married Italian-born Fernando Cuniberti; the couple moved between Washington, DC, and Janesville, Wisconsin, in the United States. Cuniberti's cookbook focuses on home-style cooking or *cucina casalinga*, as practiced by thrifty house-wives in Italy. In times of scarcity, simple meals served in Italy were very much in keeping with what the U.S. Food Administration advised for consumers: "The Italian housewife uses quantities of vegetables, many soups and made dishes containing only a small proportion of meat and that only the inexpensive cuts. Vegetable salads are a staple, while fresh or dried fruits, coffee, cheese and nuts are the regular dessert."[18] Indeed, Cuniberti's recipes emphasized little or no meat in most cases. Substitutions were encouraged, especially for readers who were unable to purchase Italian cheeses or uncommon Italian vegetables like zucchini squash. Most recipes contained a number of vegetables like vegetables alla Napolitana, an adaptation of a recipe from the Roma Pavilion restaurant in Chicago, a vegetable stew composed of zucchini, onions, peppers, potatoes, eggplant, and tomatoes.[19] Larger vegetables were used as meat substitutes, layered with hard-boiled eggs and cheese in casseroles or hollowed out and stuffed with bread crumb mixtures. Legumes were used in soups or molded (*sformato*) to resemble meat pastes. Corn meal was also a versatile ingredient, shaped into croquettes or fritters. Recipes for meat extended a rather small portion of meat to be used, either by mixing a meat-based stew with pasta or preparing it *cacciatora* style, stewed with tomato sauce and vegetables. Recipes for meat stews not only extended meat with pasta and vegetables, but the practice of stewing made tougher cuts of meat more palatable.

Cuniberti's book was unusual. It stands as an artifact of wartime cookery that promotes foreign dishes as wholesome, economical, and flavorful. Yet the book organizes and promotes Italian cooking through a careful selection of recipes. Thus, readers understood that Italian cuisine was based on carbohydrates like pasta, polenta, and bread, supplemented with ample fresh vegetables and fruits. Animal products such as dairy products, eggs, and meat were featured in recipes but not in abundance. Rather, meat was frequently treated as more of a flavoring (in sauces) or as a minor ingredient (in stews). Limited meat consumption and meat substitutions were necessary during wartime, when meat supplies were reserved for soldiers, not civilians. Yet the relative scarcity of meat recipes in Cuniberti's book underscored Italy's recent culinary history and anticipated Italian nationalist pride in a diet based primarily on carbohydrates and fresh fruits and vegetables.

From Wartime Adversity to Postwar Autarky

Italian nationalist pride in a simple, economical diet would take several years to develop. Immediately after World War I, Italians were thrown into a spiral of inflation as a result of wartime demobilization and the cessation of allied loans. Postwar Italian governments rose and fell on the price of food and in particular, Italian politicians were reluctant to pull the popular bread subsidy. Italian consumers protested the high price of food and rioted (in 1919) when they could no longer afford foods like cheese, olive oil, wine, dried pasta and canned goods. By the time Mussolini assumed power in 1922, popular consumption levels stabilized and, while few Italians were starving, most Italians lived on a subsistence diet. After the mid-1920s, popular consumption, including food habits, had to adjust to fascist economic policies and foreign policy decisions. Fascist propaganda advised citizens not to waste food, not to purchase foods from foreign countries, and to restrict food intake whenever it interfered with national economic health. Officially, this policy was known as autarky and restrictions grew more severe as Italy inched closer to war. [Editor's note—this concept of food autarky is also discussed in Jing Sun's chapter

"Hungry Empire" in this anthology.] Domestically produced foods were highlighted in fascist propaganda (film, posters, newspapers, women's magazines, cookbooks) and officially sponsored food holidays reminded citizens that their dietary choices had national significance. Not surprisingly, many of the foods touted by the fascist regime were similar to those promoted by Cuniberti's wartime cookbook: simple peasant dishes like polenta or pasta, supplemented by fresh fruits and vegetables. The contours of culinary nationalism as outlined in wartime cookbooks came into sharp relief under fascism, given the regime's desire to control consumption for political benefit.

Whereas wartime cookbooks published in the United States elevated simple dishes for the sake of a temporary wartime economy, cookbooks published in fascist Italy elevated the same dishes as a permanent solution to Italian economic woes. Mussolini's revaluation of the lire and his efforts to promote agricultural self-sufficiency (through the Battle for Grain and the promotion of domestic crops like grapes and olives) squeezed household incomes and challenged Italian women to become more inventive in order to feed their families. A publication boom in cookbooks and domestic economy manuals during the fascist decades reinforced the regime's support for simple and wholesome dishes that did not rely on imported ingredients. And cookbooks became increasingly strident in their calls for women to economize during and after the Ethiopian invasion and the subsequent economic sanctions against Italy. Calls to limit consumption were commonplace in nutritional literature as well. Italians were advised to eat less and to substitute eggs, milk, and honey for meat, to eat slowly, and not to waste anything.[20]

By instructing women to purchase and cook only foods produced in Italy, cookbook authors supported the fascist regime's policies while also promoting the Italian-ness of popular diet. Adhering to a diet comprised mainly of rice, bread, citrus, and native fruits and vegetables became a patriotic obligation. Cookbooks and pamphlets were more than helpful advice literature; they made one's allegiance to fascism possible through reading and thinking about food choices and practices in the kitchen. The act of saving became an activity measured in the smallest gestures performed to secure the family's health and economic security. *Economia* was the "fruit of patient activity, of vigilance, or renunciation." No scrap of food was so small that one should not waste it.[21] The ideal meal promoted in cookbooks was the *minestra*, a dish built on rice or pasta, served either in broth or dry. Easy to prepare out of what was on hand, minestra was usually based on a seasonal variety of foods, "a dish that keeps the population healthy and strong and that demonstrates our fairly simple way of life."[22] Readers were also instructed how to save food by giving bread out after the first course, chewing slowly, skipping meat for the evening meal, and finding substitutes for coffee, tea, and wine.[23] Lenten dishes were common in cookbooks, dishes such as dried cod, rice croquettes, frittata, and pasta with sardines were recommended as healthy and filling dishes for families. Readers were also instructed on the art of using leftovers. "Little things that one must never throw away" included such items as celery tops, which could be added to soups, eaten in salad, or fried in butter; cheese crusts to be boiled with meat bones for broth; and potato peels, burned and pulverized to serve as cockroach deterrents.[24]

Fascist calls for consumers to economize in the kitchen assumed panicked tones at the start of World War II. The war was a complete disaster for Italy. Mussolini shipped soldiers to the eastern front, Italian workers and agricultural products to Germany. Cookbooks published at this time suggested housewives shift from economizing to "cooking with nothing" during the war. In *Che si mangia domani?*, a 1941 cookbook, substitutions and extensions were popular: "wartime mayonnaise" made with flour and butter instead of eggs; "pastina in broth without pastina" substituted grated potato and cheese for pasta; and "meatballs made of nothing" used only fifty grams of chicken to make six servings of meatballs.[25] Conditions for Italians worsened as the war dragged on, with citizens resorting to the black market or foraging in the wilderness in order to feed their families. Food scarcity turned citizens against a regime that so desperately tried to control their everyday habits. When the allied forces landed in Italy in 1943, they found an exhausted and hungry population that offered little resistance to allied occupation. Instead, Italians begged for food and the allied advance through the peninsula was hampered by provisioning shortages. American and British soldiers were shocked by the grim conditions throughout Italy and did what they could with chocolate bars and impromptu soup kitchens in order to forge new alliances through food.[26]

Conclusion

World War I provided a unique opportunity for American consumers to learn about the recipes and habits of European populations fighting on the same side as the United States. Cookbook authors who promoted the cuisines of Belgium, Russia, Serbia, France, and Italy emphasized sim-plicity and thrift when it came to ingredients and preparation. Although some cookbooks featured refined and complex dishes, most of the recipes promoted for wartime were for types of dishes that European workers and peasants might consume with their families. This elevation of rustic cooking must have stood in sharp contrast to the vast amount of pre-scriptive literature published for the middle and upper classes before the war. While not a unified vision of wartime economy through cooking, this small collection of ethnic cookbooks emphasized what we might today call a healthy diet: an abundance of fruits, vegetables, legumes, and dairy products with a minimum of fats, sugar, and alcohol. This simple diet was promoted by only a few Americans before the war, but the war changed the context for thinking about what was good to eat and why. Allied nations were not unique in experimenting with natural and vege-tarian diets for political purposes. In the early twentieth century, raw and vegetarian diets were considered by German naturists as ways to feed Germany's burgeoning population with limited land resources.[27] Indeed, Germany's quest for a greater empire in both World Wars was motivated in part by a desire for *lebensraum*. Living space presumably included eat-ing space and thus the ultimate goal of war was to obtain enough land so that all Germans could eat their fill.

And in Italy, World War I brought a slight improvement in popu-lar consumption habits; allied loans of money and food plus the gov-ernment's willingness to subsidize the price of bread meant that most Italians could afford a few additional food items outside their staples of pasta, corn, and bread. Such improvements were short-lived, as the post-war years once again cast Italian consumers back to subsistence levels of food consumption. Whereas consumers in the United States and parts of Europe were interested in diversifying tastes through sampling for-eign cuisines, Italians were advised against doing so. After 1922, the fascist regime vigorously promoted a type of culinary nationalism, a vision of cuisine very similar to the simple diet of the Italian peasantry. Ironically, perhaps, the same types of dishes promoted in American wartime cook-books were highlighted in cookbooks published in fascist Italy: simple dishes with little or no meat, created with an abundance of fresh fruits and vegetables. While the dishes and menu suggestions were similar, the purpose behind such suggestions differed dramatically. In the United States, ethnic cookbooks familiarized American consumers with new ingredients, preparation techniques, and tastes, in an attempt to acquaint them with the habits and traditions of their allies. In the process of doing so, cookbook authors also raised the culinary status of immigrant populations within the United States, in declaring their diets thrifty, healthy, and wholesome. While the promotion of international or ethnic cuisine in these cookbooks lasted only the duration of the war, it was nonetheless a significant moment in American culinary history. This collection of books and pamphlets defined national cuisines outside the boundaries of those nations, solidifying what was to become Italian American or Franco-American cuisine, selections of national dishes preferred by immigrants and non-immigrants in the United States. And, given their uniquely early status as ethnic cookbooks, these published works began a much longer conversation about the value of diversifying American cuisine.

While the conversation about the value of diversifying American cuisine would stretch across several more decades, culinary nationalism took root in several countries in Europe, in particular, the new fascist regimes of Italy and Germany. In fascist Italy, the simple economical fare of the peasantry was not only elevated, but Italian consumers were actively discouraged from eating other cuisines, especially American dishes. Culinary nationalism, as defined and promoted in cookbooks during and after World War I, was politically ambiguous, able to fit the circumstances of democratic wartime shortage as well as fascist biopolitical mandates.

NOTES

1. Donna Gabaccia, *We Are What We Eat: Ethnic Food and the Making of Americans* (Cambridge, MA: Harvard University Press, 1998); Rachel Laudan, *Cuisine and Empire: Cooking in World History* (Berkeley: University of California Press, 2015); Havey Levenstein, *Paradox of Plenty: A Social History of Eating in Modern America* (New York: Oxford University Press, 1993); Laresh Jayasanker, *Sameness in Diversity. Food and Globalization in the United States* (Berkeley: University of California Press, forthcoming); Richard Pillsbury, *No Foreign Food: The American Diet in Time and Place* (New York: Routledge, 2019).
2. Lizzie Collingham, *The Taste of War and the Battle for Food* (New York: Penguin, 2012); Laudan, *Cuisine and Empire.*
3. Rachel Duffet, *The Stomach for Fighting: Food and Soldiers of the Great War* (Manchester: Manchester University Press, 2011).
4. Belinda Davis, *Home Fires Burning: Food, Politics and Everyday Life in World War I Berlin* (Chapel Hill: University of North Carolina Press, 2000).
5. Belinda Davis, *Home Fires Burning.* See also: Avner Offer, *The First World War. An Agrarian Interpretation* (Oxford: Clarendon Press, 1991); Corinna Treitel,

Eating Nature in Modern Germany: Food, Agriculture and Environment, c. 1870 to 2000 (Cambridge: Cambridge University Press, 2017).

6. Advertisements in Otto Carqué, *The Folly of Meat Eating: How to Conserve our Food Supply: A Plea for Saner Living* (Chicago: Kosmos Publishing Company, 1918).

7. Carqué, *The Folly of Meat Eating*, 8.

8. Anna Lindlahr and Henry Lindlahr, *The Lindlahr Vegetarian Cook Book and ABC of Natural Dietetics* (Chicago: Lindlahr Publishing Company, 1922): 24–5.

9. Jeffrey Miller, *WWI Crusaders* (Denver: Milbrown Press, 2018).

10. Mrs. Brian Luck, *Belgian Cookbook* (New York: E. P. Dutton and Company, 1915).

11. Luck, *Belgian Cookbook*, 33.

12. Grace Clergue Harrison and Gertrude Clergue, *Allied Cookery: British, French, Italian, Belgian, Russian* (New York: G. P. Putnam's Sons, 1916).

13. Donna Gabaccia, *We Are What We Eat*.

14. Antonia Isola (Mabel Earl McGinnis), *Simple Italian Cookery* (New York: Harper and Brothers, 1912).

15. Carol Helstosky, "State of Meatlessness: Voluntary and Involuntary Vegetarianism in Early Twentieth Century Italy," in Cristina Haganu-Bresch and Kristin Kondrlik, eds., *Veg(etari)an Arguments in Culture, History and Practice: The V Word* (New York: Palgrave, 2021): 3–24.

16. Lindlahr and Lindlahr, *The Lindlahr Vegetarian Cookbook*, 223.

17. Alberto Capatti and Massimo Montanari, *Italian Cuisine: A Cultural History* (New York: Columbia University Press, 2003); Gabaccia, *We Are What We Eat*; Carol Helstosky, *Garlic and Oil: Politics and Food in Italy* (Oxford: Berg, 2006); Fabio Parasecoli, *Al Dente: A History of Food in Italy* (London: Reaktion, 2014); Emanuela Scarpellini, *Food and Foodways in Italy from 1861 to the Present* (New York: Palgrave Macmillan, 2015).

18. Julia Lovejoy Cuniberti, *Practical Italian Recipes for American Kitchens* (Janesville, WI: Gazette Printing Company, 1918): 3.

19. Cuniberti, *Practical Italian Recipes*, 14.

20. See for example: Vezio Manci, *Nutrizione ed Assicurazioni (Appunti)* (Castelplanio: Prem. Tip. Romagnoli, 1931); and Ettore Piccoli, *L'alimentazione dell'uomo* (Milan: R. Quintieri, 1921).

21. Chiara Bellati, *La nostra casa* (Milan: Soc. Ed. 'Vita e Pensiero,' 1937): 70.

22. Ines and Mimy Bergamo, *A tavola! Menus stagionali relative ricette* (Milan: U. Hoepli, 1936): xiii.

23. Dott Maria Diaz Gasca, *Cucine di ieri e cucine di domani* (Rome: Tip. delle Terre, 1928).

24. Lidia Morelli, *Nuovo ricettario domestico* (Milan: U. Hoepli, 1941): 435–37

25. *Che si mangia domani?* (Rome: Tip. V. Ferri, 1941).

26. See for example: Norman Lewis, *Naples '44: A World War II Diary of Occupied Italy* (New York: Da Capo, 2005).

27. Treitel, *Eating Nature in Modern Germany*.

CHAPTER 12

Still Poor, Still Little, Still Hungry?

*The Diet and Health of Belgian Children
after World War I*

NEL DE MÛELENAERE

World War I brought misery, illness and hunger to many Belgian door-steps.[1] For four long years, "poor little Belgium" was partly battlefield and partly occupied by Germany.[2] Cut off from crucial imports and squeezed dry by an insatiable demand for materials and food by the German army, the country's food supplies started to dry out as early as December of 1914.[3] The Belgians were saved from full-on famine by private philanthropy: the much-praised work of Herbert Hoover's Commission for Relief in Belgium (CRB), and tens of thousands of Belgians volunteering for the *Comité National de Secours et d'Alimentation* (National Aid and Food Committee).[4] Money and food poured in from all over the world, and the beaten nation became a testing ground for international food relief.

Children, the poorest and littlest of all Belgians, were central in the relief work and propaganda of the CRB and the *Comité National*.[5] Canteens catered lunch, the Babies' Milk Fund provided milk to infants in every Belgian town, and the CRB founded a national organization for Belgian war orphans.[6] The child welfare work of the CRB and Herbert Hoover received worldwide praise. In 1920, Sally Lucas Jean, staff director of the Child Health Organization, wrote to him in 1920: "you have . . . put children on the map of the world."[7]

This chapter examines how the iconic war-children of Belgium fared after the period between 1914 and 1918. It reconstructs what they ate, how healthy they were, and which agencies concerned themselves with their food consumption and health. The unique material providing this information recently resurfaced in the archives of Cornell University. In 1923, the nutritionist and Cornell professor Flora Rose did a large-scale study on the food and health practices of Belgian children. She conducted an intensive diet history survey of 4,619 school children, whose parents, teachers, and doctors filled in elaborate questionnaires. The survey was part of a disbanded and largely forgotten experiment in child health prevention by the Commission for Relief in Belgium Educational Foundation (CRBEF), the successor of the CRB.

Rose's survey provides a unique window into Belgian living conditions right after the war, and this chapter examines these documents for the very first time. The first section explores the reasons and methods behind the survey, which was part of a broader American preoccupation with child-centered aid in postwar Europe. After that, I look into what the survey unveils about the diet and health of the younger generations in 1923. In the third section, I make the link between the war and the children's physical condition, which was strangely absent in Rose's work.

Flora Rose's Study of the Nutritional Status of Five Thousand School Children

In 1923, Jeanne Poriau was a twelve-year-old schoolgirl from the Marolles, one of the poorest neighborhoods of Brussels. She was 4.36 feet tall and weighed 68.34 pounds. Jeanne and her three older brothers lived with her fifty-year-old mother in a little workmen's house with three rooms. All five of them shared one bedroom. Her mother had a small shop, and earned about a hundred francs per week, but often less. Jeanne was sickly, her teeth were in bad condition (she never brushed them), she was near-sighted, her tonsils were swollen, and she was not breathing well. She did not have much energy or a good appetite. Jeanne breakfasted with bread and margarine at home and a *soupe scolaire* (free vegetable soup) at school. For lunch, she alternated between two or three potatoes with vegetables and potatoes with meat. In the evening, the girl ate more bread with margarine or jam. She had rice once a week and, three times per week, one egg. Jeanne never consumed fish, fruit, or butter. She drank five mugs of coffee and one glass of beer every day and had done so since she was three years old.[8]

Jeanne is one the many school children whose questionnaires are kept in heavy archival boxes in the underground Karl A. Kroch library at Cornell University. Before diving deeper into the diet and health patterns of Jeanne and the other school children, I want to expand on how their personal information ended up in the Cornell archives. The survey was the work of the Child Health Section, a division of the CRBEF that wanted to set up a nationwide health education program in Belgian primary schools. After the war, the CRB was shaped into two organizations, the Belgian University Foundation and the American CRBEF that used the considerable funds left over from wartime contributions to help revitalize Belgian higher education and facilitate academic exchange between the two countries.[9] A small portion of the budget, however, was reserved for the improvement of children's welfare.

So, the CRB went from organizing emergency food relief for destitute children during the war to organizing a nationwide health education program for non-destitute children. The fact that an American philanthropic organization would feel inclined to introduce health education in the school program of a foreign country is a testament to the increasing international—and specifically U.S.—interest in worldwide child welfare after the war. For the American Red Cross, the American Relief Administration, and the CRBEF, investing in long term children's health, creating strong and "normal" citizens, and, as Flora Rose puts it, "build[ing] vigor and resistance in the human race" was a way to fundamentally transform Europe's future.[10] Deeply rooted in the social ideals and belief in scientific methods of the Progressive Era, U.S. relief workers were convinced that the best way to improve the old world was to introduce the new world's child care and health practices in European nations.[11] These nations, however, did not necessarily share the belief in American solutions for European social problems. In Belgium, the Child Health Section was met with resistance by l'Oeuvre National de l'Enfance (ONE), founded in 1919 by the Belgian government to continue the private child welfare work of the war. The continuous opposition of the ONE eventually led to the termination of the Child Health Section in 1924.

Before its disbandment, the Child Health Section did succeed in introducing a health education program in 1,221 primary schools. Part of that program was based on the observations of Cornell nutritionist Flora Rose. Rose, who had worked with Herbert Hoover in the Food Administration during the war, travelled to Europe in March of 1923 to study the health and diet of Belgian school children and identify any deficiencies. In collaboration with the Belgian inspector-generals of education, Rose selected fifty schools for study.[12] The sample of 4,619 children was quite large, much to the chagrin of Rose, who would have preferred to do an intensive, more controlled study in four prototypical Belgian centers. Instead, the Belgian partners of the Ministry of Arts and Science (which had jurisdiction over education) insisted on a larger representation, claiming that Belgium was too diverse to be confined in four categories.[13] In comparison: two years before, in 1921, an inquiry in laborer's household expenses by the Belgian Ministry of Labor sampled 848 families.[14] Together, the children were meant to represent all groups of children, both Flemish and Walloon, Catholic and public schools, and the wealthiest and poorest families. They were between five and thirteen years old in 1923, thus born right before, during, and just after the war years of 1914–18. The survey questionnaires were eight pages long and contained a little over two hundred questions to be filled in by the school doctors, teachers, and the children themselves, providing a full picture of the children's daily lives.

The teachers visited each child at home, and asked about personal information on family living conditions, finances, schedules, hygiene, and food habits. These quantitative and qualitative surveys were conducted in the spring of 1923, and ordered teachers, parents, and children to reconstruct a typical daily menu in summer and winter, asking what they ate the last three days, and requesting that they weigh the food the family consumed in one week. In total, at least 12 school inspectors, 50 school directors, 41 physicians, 139 schoolteachers, 3 statisticians, and a translator collaborated in the survey.

The questionnaires were completed by the Belgian partners after Flora Rose travelled back to the U.S. in September of 1923 and they remained property of the CRBEF. In 1926, however, Rose asked the foundation to ship the questionnaires from Brussels to Ithaca, NY for further research.[15] She eventually wrote a doctoral dissertation for Columbia University entitled "A Study of the Nutritional Status of Five Thousand Belgian School Children as Basic Material for Program in Health Education" (1932), which was never published.[16]

What Belgian Children Ate in 1923

Most Belgian children followed a predicable menu. Breakfast at 8:00 a.m. with bread and butter and café au lait, and sometimes jam, followed by midmorning lunch at 10:00 a.m. with bread and butter and coffee, and sometimes cheese or meat. Thick slices of white bread, often unbuttered, were dipped in coffee that had one fourth to three fourths of chicory and skimmed milk.[17] The children had a hot lunch with soup, bread, meat, potatoes, and vegetables at noon. Wealthy families added a dessert, poorer families often omitted the meat.

Many of the children had a midafternoon snack with bread, butter, coffee, or small beer. Wealthy families might have had cake, some chocolate or fruit. And supper consisted of bread, butter, coffee or beer, salad, some beef, ham, or an egg. Rose calculated that in total, the average ten-year-old Belgian child consumed daily eight to ten slices of bread; one and two-thirds cups of milk; four or five potatoes of medium size; two-thirds of a cup of a cooked green-leafed vegetable; the equivalent of half of an orange; two to three tablespoons of fat; a slice of meat one eighth of an inch thick, two inches wide, and three inches long; a half inch cube of cheese; and one-seventh of an egg.[18]

The average diet might seem sufficient, but Rose still found that 36 percent of the children in the survey were at least seven percent underweight and 28 percent were ten percent or more underweight. Rose concluded that undernutrition as measured by underweight (relative to the height) was similar in the United States—although she did not account for the undernourished children staying in the Belgian ONE colonies, who would certainly increase the average of underweight children.[19] In a comparison between a 1923 weight and height study of 10,560 Iowa children, Belgian children came out skinnier and shorter.[20] Nonetheless, Rose found many Belgian children to be "of the stocky type." She pondered if this was because of a traditional fondness for a robust physique. Apparently, Belgians experienced distress over skinniness—even in adults. This might have been a remnant of traumatizing wartime food scarcity and resulting scrawniness during the war. The robustness also came from a diet that was high in calories but still lacked vital nutrients.[21] The Belgians ate a lot of soup, a lot of wheaten bread, and a lot of potatoes.

There were troubling absences in the Belgian children's diet, according to Rose. The families of most did not have the money for them to consume many high-quality proteins such as meat, milk, cheese, and eggs. The average child ate just three ounces of meat, 0.3 ounces of eggs, 0.45 ounces of cheese, 1.2 ounces of butter, and twelve ounces of milk each day. Thirty-five percent never had cheese. Rose calculated that the children consumed 77 grams of proteins and 2046 kilocalories—which was more or less the standard for children that age.[22] The children ate 3.9 times more wheat than meat, and 7.9 times more potatoes and wheat than meat.[23] This demonstrates the decline of wheat consumption and an increase of meat consumption described by Peter Scholliers. He found that in 1890, the average Belgian was eating 11.2 times more wheat than meat.[24] Fifty years later, Belgians ate only 3.9 times more wheat than meat—Belgian children apparently reached that ratio even earlier.

The largest gap in the children's diet was fruit. In Belgium as a whole, eating fruit was increasingly common, evidenced by rising imports (which increased 27 percent between 1908 and 1921) and consumption (almost five times as much between 1920 and 1924 as compared to 1890–94). Yet these trends did not materialize in Rose's study, where 14 percent of the children reported never eating fruit, and the majority of the children ate very little.[25] The resulting lack of vitamin C was not compensated with raw vegetables, and Rose speculated that the use of human excreta as fertilizers might be the cause. Many of the children had inflamed and spongy-looking gums, and showed symptoms of scurvy.[26] By thirteen years old, almost one-third of the children in the survey had decayed teeth.[27] Almost one in ten school children had poor skeletal development, and 14 percent showed poor posture.[28] The physicians found that a lot of children were suffering colds, about 14 percent had obstructed noses, seven percent had weak lungs, and 19 percent had enlarged tonsils.[29] Although they paint a rather bleak picture, the figures might still overestimate the children's healthiness: Rose found that the medical examinations were often not thorough, and the weakest and most undernourished children were staying in sanatoria run by the Belgian ONE.[30]

The Impact of the War

The rather weak health of the children was probably linked to chronic food deprivation in their younger years. Surprisingly though, Rose makes no mention of the negative effect of the war on the health of the children in her dissertation, and not one question in the survey asked about living conditions during the war. On the contrary, she painted quite a rosy picture of children's health and nutrition during the war—repeating the idea that the U.S. saved the Belgians from hunger. She stated boldly that although some malnutrition existed, it was minimized "particularly among the children." The approximately 2,250,000 children under sixteen years of age "survived its hardships in reasonably good condition and that of this number there were many who probably fared better than in normal times. Certainly no children in the warring countries in Europe were more scrupulously protected against the ill effect of poor nutrition than were the children of Belgium."[31] She was not the only researcher presuming that the Belgians were spared from the worst of war, and just might have been better off than before the war, all thanks to foreign philanthropy. In 1919, John Maynard Keynes wrote that "Belgium has made the least relative sacrifice of all the belligerents except the United States."[32] That idea still persists today. In his 2016 biography of Herbert Hoover, Glen Jeansonne proclaimed that during World War I, "the child mortality rate dipped below the ratio for normal times, and child health improved overall" in Belgium.[33]

The idea that (American) philanthropy spared Belgian children from going hungry is blatantly untrue. Rose was right that a majority, if not all, of the children had benefitted from free meals during the war. In fact, by 1917, the food scarcity and inflation had become so bad that the entire population was eligible for social security, unparalleled in Belgian history.[34] However, the food imports of the CRB (distributed by the *Comité National*) stayed well under the prewar food supply. Peter Scholliers estimated in 1982 that it covered one-fourth of the population's needs and supplied no more than 950 kilocalories a day—barely enough to survive.[35] Initially, the *Comité* provided bread and soup for lunch and meat and vegetables in the evening, but as the war continued and the import staggered, only the soup remained. Many citizens lived on poor quality bread made of potato starch, spelt, and cattle fodder, and soup with small, black potatoes that delivered at maximum 300 kilocalories.

Private philanthropy tried to protect children from starvation. By the end of the war, there were 769 milk stations for infants, 435 canteens for underfed children, and 474 centers for young mothers. Rose was right that in 1914 and 1915 the increase in infant care seemed to have had a positive effect on the health of infants. In the first years of the war, the mortality for infants fell from 139 per 1000 births in 1913 to 116 per 1000 births in 1916, although the declining trend in infant mortality had started around the turn of the century.[36] When the food situation worsened, however, infant mortality started to rise in the areas where the care provisions were lacking, tragically surpassing the prewar rate with 24 to 28 percent. In urban centers, where (expectant) mothers were getting free supplementary meals, newborns weighed an average of 2.2 pounds less than in 1913 and failed to gain weight in the first weeks (gaining just 1.8 ounces/week instead of the prewar 6.3 ounces/week).[37]

For older children, a lack of statistics blurs the picture, which was no doubt even more tragic, because there were fewer provisions for them. In

Ghent, police registered an increase of 320 percent in children begging in 1916 as compared to 1913.[38] Many children physically carried the legacy of the war the rest of their lives. They had tuberculosis, rickets, and scrofula, an infection of the lymph nodes caused by diluted and infected milk.[39] Their mothers organized food protests and strikes that grew more desperate as the food shortages grew worse.[40] By 1919, medical reports estimated that 65 percent of the population was chronically undernourished and very weak.

After the war, the ONE partly continued the private, nationwide child welfare work during the war. The ONE particularly focused on infants and the most vulnerable, sick, and severely undernourished children. The survey also shows that many schools in poor districts kept the system of free vegetable *soupe scolaire*. Meanwhile, the new Belgian government (1919–21) tried to curb rising social unrest with a range of social and political measures (universal suffrage for men above 21years old being the most notable). Getting food on Belgian plates played an important role in that, and the employees, employers, and cooperatives carried forward their wartime collaborations. The socialist Minister of Industry, Labor and Food Supplies, Joseph Wauters, introduced a range of measures to secure food distribution for reasonable prices. He centralized the organization of food supplies of bread, sugar, butter, and meat; put price caps on necessities; and bought large bulks of foods to put on the Belgian market for lower prices. Meanwhile, his colleagues did their share in increasing individual purchasing power with efforts such as controlling the rental housing prices and investing in large reconstruction projects.

These unparalleled, expensive, and much-criticized public interventions towards the betterment of living standards were efficient. By 1920, the Belgian government had reversed the downward economic trend, and the living conditions of its citizens increased sharply.[41] The average Belgian started to eat better and more diversely—with meat and fruit replacing wheat and potatoes. Poor workers' families benefitted the most from the improvement in diet. Peter Scholliers found that their food consumption reached that of the average Belgian by 1935.[42]

Rose's survey largely confirms the findings of Scholliers—as is evident in the wheat/meat balance in the children's diet and the average kilocalories—but nuances the implications he made about the quickly rising standard of living in the early 1920s. Part of that nuance comes from the change of perspective and does not alter his main argument. Scholliers looks at the long-term transformation based on import statistics and workers' family budgets in 1910, 1921, and 1928–29 from a bird's-eye view.

Rose provided an eye-level angle of what the poorest citizens actually ate and did not eat in 1923. In that period, prices of food were still many times higher than before the war. In 1923, Belgian families had to pay three times as much for beef, four times as much for bread and coffee, and six times as much for eggs as compared to 1913. Wages had grown some, but not much.[43] Rose's study unveils the troubling physical effects of inequality and shocking living conditions of the very poor, who in 1923 might not take much notice of or solace in the long-term trend towards better living conditions.

But Rose's work also corrects the existing data, because the nutritionist included parts of the poorest population not previously included in the statistics on food consumption. Laborer's budget surveys polled traditional working families and ignored poor families with unemployed and imprisoned fathers or with single mothers and working mothers—like Jeanne Poriau's. From Rose's calculations, it appears that the extreme gap in food consumption between rich and poor diets during the war lingered longer than scholars have assumed. Previous calculations based on the workers' and average family budgets showed that from 1924 laborers ate as much wheat bread and potatoes as before the war, but that their meat consumption had risen as well, even surpassing the meat consumption of the average Belgian. This has been taken as proof that working families' food consumption quickly improved after the war. The data from the workers' family budget surveys is contradicted by Rose's survey, which shows that the poorest children did eat slightly more bread and potatoes than the average, but also ate considerably less meat.

Comparing the 155 poorest children and the 231 richest children in Rose's data provides a tangible demonstration of the food inequality that still ruled Belgian society after the war. An average poor six-year-old was 3.4 feet tall and weighed 37.7 pounds; a rich six-year-old had a height of 3.9 feet and weighed 45.5 pounds.[44] The differences in height and weight do not come as a surprise. Rich six-year-old children ate almost double the amount of meat and vegetables, three times as much butter and eggs, and almost four times as much fruit as poor children ate. They did consume about the same amount of cheese, and about 50 percent more bread and potatoes. Despite the high calorie content of bread and potatoes, the wealthier children still consumed 300 more kilocalories per day. Many of the poor of all age groups claimed to never consume certain food types. About half of them never ate fruit or cheese, one-third never consumed butter, and one-fourth allegedly never had milk or vegetables.[45] The health of the children reflected these differences in diet. Of the poorest children, half had decayed teeth and bad gums, one in three had poor development, and one in five suffered from weak lungs. The health of the wealthy children stood in stark contrast: only one in sixteen had dental problems, one in fourteen had poor development, and one in eleven suffered from weak lungs.

Conclusion

Scientists are still unraveling the precise long-term impact of wartime trauma and starvation on the health of the younger generations and the generations that follow them. This line of research originated in the era of World War I, with American philanthropy sending scientists and experts to measure the suffering of European children. The Great War, in the words of Flora Rose, "called the world's attention to the status of human affairs and aroused its conscience regarding the welfare of children."

The work of the Child Health Section and Rose's survey are early examples of the many American postwar child welfare programs that would emerge in the course of the twentieth century. But the survey is not only part of the international history of Americanization and humanitarian aid. It is also an exceptional source on the daily living of Belgium children after the war. While historians possess solid knowledge on general food intake, what people were advised to cook, and how food distribution was organized in postwar Belgium, the literature has been surprisingly silent on what children actually ate following the war and how that related to their health.

The lack of knowledge about the daily diet of children has to do with a scarcity in sources. Archives of hospitals, armies, prisons, and social services are an accessible source for food historians. Unfortunately, that leaves out the bulk of the population that was fortunate enough not to be imprisoned, hospitalized, or in any way dependent on external care. Firsthand accounts and recipes show what was on the menu in homes, but primary sources of eating habits that are both qualitative and quantitative are rare. Flora Rose's diet history survey was pioneering, and strikingly similar to the diet history survey conducted by Burke several years later in 1947, which is generally considered the first.

So, were the little Belgians still poor and still hungry? Children who had grown up in the years 1914–18 had probably been chronically under-nourished for at least two years, and Rose's research suggest that five years later, many of them—and especially the poorer children born in 1916 and 1917—still had serious deficiencies in their diet and many health problems. It is hard to make direct comparisons with the prewar child welfare because of the lack of statistics on children's diet and health, which was probably far from ideal in an industrial, urban nation with a minimum of social welfare. Nonetheless, this contribution suggests that the road to progress in diet and living conditions was a lot bumpier than previously thought, and that many poor Belgian families had not yet shaken off the war legacy of inequality, food deprivation and illness by 1923.

NOTES

1. This chapter benefited from the kind suggestions of Justin Nordstrom, Peter Scholliers, and the anonymous reviewers and the editing of Molly Rector and Janet Foxman at the University of Arkansas Press. My research was financed by the Cabeaux-Jacobs postdoctoral fellowship of the Belgian American Educational Foundation and the Dean's Fellowship for the History in Home Economics (College of Human Ecology, Cornell University).

2. Luis Angel Bernardo y Garcia, *Le Ventre des Belges: Une Histoire Alimentaire des Temps d'Occupation et de Sortie de Guerre (1914–1921 & 1939–1948)* (Bruxelles: Archives Générales du Royaume): 91–121; Peter Scholliers and Frank Daelemans, "Standards of Living and Health in Wartime Belgium," in *The Upheaval of War: Family, Work and Welfare in Europe, 1914–1918*, Richard Wall and Jay Winter, eds (Cambridge: Cambridge University Press, 1988): 139–58.

3. Scholliers and Daelemans, "Standards," 140.

4. Branden Little, "The Commission for Relief in Belgium," *1914–1918-Online, International Encyclopedia of the First World War* (Updated October 8, 2014), https://encyclopedia.1914-1918-online.net/article/commission_for_relief_in _belgium_crb; Liesbet Nys, Kenneth Bertrams and Kaat Wils, *The Belgian American Educational Foundation 1920–2020: A Century of Transatlantic Scientific Exchange* (Leuven: Leuven University Press, 2021).

5. Dominique Marshal, "Children's Rights and Children's Action in International Relief and Domestic Welfare: The Work of Herbert Hoover between 1914 and 1950," *Journal of the History of Childhood and Youth*, no. 3 (2008): 351–88.

6. Glen Jeansonne, *Herbert Hoover: A Life* (New York: New American Library, 2016): 98.

7. James N. Giglio, "Voluntarism and Public Policy between World War I and the New Deal: Herbert Hoover and the American Child Health Association," *Presidential Studies Quarterly* 13, no. 3 (1983): 431.

8. Cornell University Library's Division of Rare and Manuscript Collections, New

York State College of Home Economics Records, 1875–1979 (23-2-749), Box 116, Jeanne Poriau.

9. Kenneth Bertrams, "The Domestic Uses of Belgian–American 'Mutual Understanding': The Commission for Relief in Belgium Educational Foundation, 1920–1940," *Journal of Transatlantic Studies* 13, no. 4 (2015): 331.

10. Rose, *A Study*, 199; Joseph L. Barona, "Nutrition and Health: The International Context during the Inter-War Crisis," *Social History of Medicine* 21, no. 1 (2008): 90.

11. Julia Irwin, "Sauvons Les Bébés: Child Health and U.S. Humanitarian Aid in the First World War Era," *Bulletin of the History of Medicine* 86, no. 1 (2012): 41–42; Tammy M. Proctor, *Civilians in a World at War, 1914–1918* (New York: New York University Press, 2010): 201.

12. This included 4,619 children in total, of whom 2,251 were French-speaking and 2,368 Flemish-speaking; 1,996 were boys and 2,623 girls. The survey covered 62 schools, 38 communal and 24 Catholic. The children were between the ages five and fifteen, and from Antwerp (715), Assenois (26), Brugge (209), Brussels (1224), Ebly (65) Fiebecq (186), Gent (103), Geraardsbergen (185), Heyst (281), Herstal (320), Ieper (259), Jumeret (41), Jumet (249), Kasterlee (332), Longlier (44), Massul (48), Turnhout (284), Wittemont (48).

13. Cornell University Library's Division of Rare and Manuscript Collections, New York State College of Home Economics Records, 1875–1979 (23-2-749), Box 52, Folder 1, Flora Rose, Draft report, undated, 3.

14. On the methods of sample taking and the question of representativeness in social surveys, see: Patricia Van den Eeckhout, "Statistics and Social Policy in Inter-War Belgium," *Histoire & Mesure* 19, no. 1–2 (2004): 102–6.

15. Hoover Presidential Library, Belgian American Educational Foundation Records, Box 254, Belgian Child Health Program, Letter from Flora Rose to Perrin C. Galpin, 20 March 1926.

16. Cornell University Library's Division of Rare and Manuscript Collections, New York State College of Home Economics Records, 1875–1979 (23-2-749), Box 34, map 44, Flora Rose, *A Study of the Nutritional Status of Five Thousand Belgian School Children as Basic Material for Program in Health Education*, 1932.

17. Rose, *A Study*, 207.

18. Rose, *A Study*, 394.

19. Rose, *A Study*, 400–401.

20. Rose, *A Study*, 131.

21. Cornell University Library's Division of Rare and Manuscript Collections, New York State College of Home Economics Records, 1875–1979 (23-2-749), Box 35, Folder 24, F. Rose, Untitled report, 1923, 1–2.

22. Rose, *A Study*, 296.

23. Rose, *A Study*, 248, 306, 374.

24. Peter Scholliers, "Oorlog en Voeding: de Invloed van de Eerste Wereldoorlog op het Belgische Voedingspatroon, 1890–1940," *Tijdschrift voor Sociale Geschiedenis*, no. 1 (1985): 42.

25. Scholliers, "Oorlog," 41; Rose, *A Study*, 307.

26. Rose, *Report*, 4.

27. Rose, *A Study*, 195.

28. Rose, *A Study*, 196.

29. Rose, *A Study*, 197.

30. Claudine Marissal, *Protéger le Jeune Enfant: Enjeux Sociaux, Politiques et Sexués (Belgique, 1890–1940)* (Bruxelles: Editions de l'Université de Bruxelles, 2014): 54.

31. Cornell University Library's Division of Rare and Manuscript Collections, New York State College of Home Economics Records, 1875–1979 (23-2-749), Box 52, Folder 2, Flora Rose, Draft chapter dissertation, undated, 9.

32. Cited in Scholliers and Daeleman, "Standards," 140.

33. Jeansonne, *A Life*, 98.

34. Scholliers, "Oorlog," 38.

35. Scholliers, "Oorlog," 32.

36. Marc Debuisson, "The Decline of Infant Mortality in the Belgian Districts at the Turn of the 20th Century," *BTNG-RBHC* 31, no. 3–4 (2001): 522–23.

37. Scholliers and Daelemans, "Standards," 152–53.

38. Giselle Nath, *Brood Willen we Hebben! Honger, Sociale Politiek en Protest tijdens de Eerste Wereldoorlog in België* (Antwerpen: Manteau): 223.

39. Nath, *Brood,* 243.

40. Vrints, "Beyond Victimization," 100.

41. Bernardo y Garcia, *Le Ventre*, 93–121.

42. Scholliers, "Oorlog," 44.

43. Peter Scholliers, "Koopkracht en Indexkoppeling. De Brusselse Levensstandaard tijdens en na de Eerste Wereldoorlog, 1914–1925," *BTNG-RBHC* 9, no. 3–4 (1978): 334, 375.

44. Cornell University Library's Division of Rare and Manuscript Collections, New York State College of Home Economics Records, 1875–1979 (23-2-749), Box 34, map 42, Flora Rose, *Condensed report of a survey of the nutritional status of 5000 Belgian School Children in 1923*, Ithaca, 1931,12.

45. Rose, *Condensed report*, 16.

CHAPTER 13

Planting Pan-Americanism

*The Good Neighbor Policy and
the Visual Culture of Corn, 1933–45*

BREANNE ROBERTSON

In the years leading up to and including World War II, the U.S. govern-ment worked to build a strategic alliance with Latin American nations to prevent Nazism from entering the New World. Weaker than the United States both militarily and economically, Latin American nations ostensibly offered Germany, Italy, and Japan easy entry to the hemisphere and a stag-ing ground for attacks against the United States. Secretary of War Henry L. Stimson predicted that Latin American political allegiance would follow trade routes, while President Franklin Delano Roosevelt's economic advi-sor Bernard Baruch warned that "German economic penetration could bring [Latin America] under her control without firing a shot."[1]

Pan-American solidarity formed a significant component of the U.S. government's plan for national defense. In his inaugural address on March 4, 1933, President Roosevelt launched the Good Neighbor Policy, hoping to rehabilitate imperialist images of the United States to facilitate its economic recovery from the Great Depression and to preserve peace. The history of U.S. relations with Latin American nations is tumultuous and complex. Under the 1823 Monroe Doctrine, the United States enacted and justified military interventions in Central and South America, breed-ing resentment among citizens of Latin American countries. Three major incidents—the U.S.–Mexico War (1846–1848), the Spanish–American War (1898) and Panama's independence (1903)—deepened antagonism between the United States and Latin America as the U.S. government showed far more interest in enlarging its territory and trade than in preserving democracy. Roosevelt's Good Neighbor Policy sought to reverse Latin American views of the United States by presenting the country less as a threat and more as a partner. By implementing policies of nonintervention, cultural respect, and free trade, the U.S. government aimed to repair relations with Latin American nations and secure their cooperation in forging a hemispheric alliance against Axis aggression.

This chapter examines one strain of this diplomatic discourse: the visual culture of corn. Considering U.S. artists' portrayal of the crop within the political context of the Good Neighbor era, this essay argues that the visual pairing of Latin American subjects and corn in American books, murals, and animated films represents a concerted effort to overturn prevailing racial stereotypes, engender a sense of collective identity, and strengthen hemispheric defense.

National Identity as the Basis of Pan-Americanism

By calling upon traits that could be considered both American and Latin American, U.S. foreign policy initiatives strove to establish a sense of cultural nationalism throughout the hemisphere. For example, Muna Lee's 1944 book *Pioneers of Puerto Rico* recounts a dramatic wartime encounter during the American Revolution to demonstrate the innate patriotism of Latin Americans in this future U.S. territory. In doing so, the textbook imparts a historical lesson about inter-American unity against the backdrop of World War II, a global conflict in which the allegiance of neighboring territories and nations carried significant import.[2] The protagonist in Lee's book is a young boy named Paquito, who travels to San Juan from the mountains to sell yucca and corn. While he is in the city, an American ship arrives under British threat. The Puerto Rican colonists eagerly provide refuge to the rebel soldiers, and the colonial governor sends Paquito to fetch a Spanish flag. With little time to spare, the boy rides away after the fashion of Paul Revere to retrieve it. The colonists mount the flag on the American ship and thus foil any British plan of attack. As the clever governor explains, English aggression against the privateer would be considered an act of war against Spain, not the colonial United States.[3]

As this story demonstrates, U.S. efforts to generate Pan-American solidarity typically began with established symbols or events tied to national identity and then extended these tropes to apply to Latin Americans as well. Previously, American Indians and Latin Americans had fulfilled the role of the exotic "other" against which the United States defined its people and culture. As Helen Delpar and James Oles have demonstrated in their surveys of U.S.–Mexico cultural exchange, American artists and intellectuals of the 1920s and early 1930s generally interpreted Mexican culture with an evolutionary bias resulting in romantic speculation and disdainful condescension, often at the same time.[4] By contrast, the people of San Juan—and Paquito, especially—demonstrate a commitment to democracy that aligns them with their New England counterparts.

Paquito's rural background further assimilates his Latin American ethnicity to U.S. definitions of Americanness. In addition to his love of freedom, Paquito is a farmer, who comes to San Juan to sell "plump ears of corn."[5] In the United States, corn has long been associated with national identity and American values, both for its New-World origins and for its prevalence in U.S. history and culture. Corn plays a major role in meals and holiday decorations; corn-based words like "shucks," "corny," and "corn-fed" pepper the English language; and the Corn Belt, an agricultural region spanning a large swath of the Midwest, evokes notions of rural self-sufficiency, wholesomeness, and tradition. To this day, the story of the first Thanksgiving looms large in the cultural memory of the United States. According to tradition, the Pilgrims held their first harvest celebration in gratitude to the Wampanoag Indians, who saved the Plymouth settlement from starvation by providing them with corn and teaching them how to grow it from seed. This origin myth highlights the antiquity of corn, which flourished on the American continents before the arrival of European settlers. Remarking on the national character of corn in 1893, textile designer Candace Wheeler wrote: "No other plant is so typical of our greatness and prosperity as a nation; no other has such artistic meanings and possibilities; no other is so wholly and nobly and historically American."[6]

Paquito's corn culture provides both the impetus and the equine transportation that allows him to perform his heroic task. Illustrator Katharine Sturges Knight underscores this agricultural premise in her cover illustration. The two-tone illustration features two uniformed American soldiers amid a cheering crowd of sympathetic Puerto Rican colonists. The central figure tilts his face upward and raises his arm in a salutary gesture; a hint of a smile suggests a kind demeanor that subdues his martial appearance. The second soldier, seen from behind, directs the viewer's gaze to a distant figure on horseback. Dressed in a simple white tunic and sporting the ponytail typical of colonial coiffures, Paquito rides confidently on his small steed, whose extended hooves and whipping tail suggest the great speed at which he travels. A bulging saddlebag overflows with yucca, corn, and other local vegetables as the young Puerto Rican colonist makes his historic ride for U.S. freedom. Only palm trees and a sliver of coastline reveal that this bustling urban scene takes place in a tropical climate, far from the continental United States.

Following the rhetorical strategies of the U.S. government during World War II, the storyline and images in the elementary school reader aimed to establish a spirit of hemispheric unity and goodwill among Americans of the United States and their neighbors to the south. The Roosevelt administration needed to convince not only foreign audiences of the benefits of inter-American unity but domestic citizens as well. Corn was a familiar crop to North American schoolchildren. Not only was it a primary source of food in U.S. diets, but it was also a major agricultural industry at a time when roughly one in four Americans earned their living from the land. Paquito and his fellow Puerto Ricans therefore appear as virtuous, hardworking people whose agricultural endeavors and republican spirit reveal them to be true "Americans"—that is, just like citizens in the United States. This discursive reconfiguration of American identity ruptured negative stereotypes of Latin Americans by presenting them to wartime audiences as willing and capable allies in the fight against European fascism.

Corn in Hemispheric Visual Culture

The widespread acceptance of corn as a marker of American culture made it an attractive theme for inter-American foreign policy efforts, especially those rendered in visual form. American artists of the 1930s and 1940s had a robust visual tradition upon which to grow their hemispheric garden of corn. For example, sculptor Benjamin Latrobe designed and executed six corn cob columns for the U.S. Capitol Building in 1809. The finely carved stalks, husks, cobs, and kernels represent Latrobe's attempt to establish a uniquely American iconography. In the latter part of the nineteenth century, corn imagery celebrated the fecundity of American soil. The corn palace in Mitchell, South Dakota, exemplifies the cereal architecture and monumental sculptures that routinely appeared at world's fairs and agricultural festivals at this time, while photomontage tall tale postcards proliferated in the nation's correspondence well into the first decades of the twentieth century. As Pamela Simpson has observed, these theatrical visual depictions present an idealized narrative of national agricultural

Katharine Sturges Knight, illustration for Muna Lee's
Pioneers of Puerto Rico, New World Neighbor series
(Boston: D. C. Heath and Company, 1944).

abundance; the United States touted itself as "the world's breadbasket," and corn was its highest yielding crop.[7]

Several factors strengthened this cultural resonance, making the plant even more powerful as a container of political thought under the Good Neighbor Policy. First, the emergence of corn husking competitions brought corn culture to the forefront of American consciousness during the interwar period. Initiated by agricultural leader Henry A. Wallace in 1922 as a way to increase farm efficiency, harvesting contests became wildly popular all across the country. Heats lasted eighty minutes, during which time individual farmers would compete to see who could harvest the most bushels of corn by hand. These events attracted huge crowds and received nationwide media coverage in *Time, Life,* and *Newsweek.* Champions became instant celebrities, giving interviews, endorsing products, and even fielding marriage proposals from female fans. At its peak popularity, the National Corn Husking Competition boasted the second largest attendance for any single-day athletic event. With crowd estimates near 160,000 people, the audience for the 1940 harvesting contest was second only to the Indianapolis 500 auto race, held the year before.[8]

Second, commercial advertisements frequently evoked the uniquely American nature of corn to appeal to patriotic consumers. Norman Rockwell's illustration for Green Giant niblets depicts an innocuous dinnertime scuffle over the last ear of corn. Details throughout the scene—the napkin bibs, the boy's stubborn cowlick—lend an air of intimacy that encourages viewers to identify with this White, middle-class family as being typically American. Corn, which is beloved by everyone in the scene, also seems quintessentially American. In fact, we are told nothing could be *more* American than eating corn, since this culinary joy is as old as the nation itself. As the accompanying text explains, Green Giant's canned niblets are a "modern version" of the "old-as-America" thrill of eating corn on the cob. While such claims maintained their attachment to national identity and lore, the conception of American antiquity and indigeneity enlarged during this period as scientific studies furnished evidence that the earliest strains of maize originated south of the U.S. border, in southeastern Mexico. Numerous books published in the 1930s and the early 1940s highlighted this international discovery. With titles like *Foods America Gave the World* (1937) and *Corn in the Development of the Civilization of the Americas* (1940), these publications provided a factual basis for expanding the geographic boundaries of cultural nationalism to include Latin American countries as well.[9]

Finally, the immense popularity of Mexican mural art permitted U.S. citizens greater exposure to Latin American conceptions of their own cultural identity through museum exhibitions and magazine reproductions of their work. Diego Rivera's murals in the National Agricultural School in Chapingo exemplify Mexico's postrevolutionary attachment to corn as an expression of indigenous peasant culture. In the section entitled *Blood of the Martyrs Fertilizing the Earth* (1927), Rivera imagined agrarian reform

Norman Rockwell, *"Gee Whiz There Goes the Last One" (The Last Ear of Corn)*, Green Giant advertisement in *Life* (December 3, 1945), 146.

through a process in which the landscape serves as a womb housing the buried bodies of revolutionary heroes, who in turn nourish the soil with their blood. A dedicatory inscription reads: "To those who fell, and to the thousands who will yet fall, in the fight for the land and to all those who make it fruitful by the labor of their hands. Earth manured with blood, bones, and flesh!"[10] When combined with U.S. government pronouncements of

inter-American friendship, these developments gave writers and artists greater license to posit a single agricultural tradition that belonged to all Americans, North and South. Prior to the outbreak of World War II, such assertions of Pan-American identity helped cultivate the notion of a peaceful and self-sustaining hemisphere, insulated from the mounting political and economic insecurities of Europe. In 1938, Iowa artist Lowell Houser designed a mural for the Ames Post Office that did just that.

Corn Cultivation as Shared Tradition and Practice

Measuring roughly eighteen by six feet, *The Evolution of Corn* presents an epic historical narrative of corn cultivation from its first practitioners in ancient Mexico to those in the modern United States. The left section of the mural shows a tawny, muscular Maya with an obsidian-tipped staff planting seeds of corn. Lush green cornstalks attest to his agricultural skill, while a stone Maize God effigy alludes to the Maya belief that the first humans were made from corn. In the right panel of the composition, a Midwestern farmer in denim overalls, work gloves, boots, and a denim cap manually harvests ripe ears of corn. Cascading strips of tickertape and a microscope stress the importance of science and commerce to modern farming. The central panel depicts a monumental ear of corn, a

Lowell Houser, *The Evolution of Corn*, 1938. Oil on canvas, 18' × 6' Ames Post Office, Ames, Iowa. *Courtesy of Ames History Museum.*

transparent kernel sprouting roots, and a superimposed cornstalk. These overlapping elements encapsulate the full growth cycle of corn, from seed embryo to ripened ear, against a vibrant red background.

As a mechanism of hemispheric identity formation, Houser's mural compositionally and thematically constructs a visual argument claiming a seamless historical lineage in which the Iowa farmer descended, culturally at least, from the ancient Maya. To convey this point, Houser employs an explicit one-to-one correlation that underscores the similarities of the two men. Facing one another in identical bent postures, the Maya and the Iowan exhibit shared agricultural interests and equal standing—both literally in the picture frame and figuratively in their respective societies. Houser even modeled both figures on the same individual: Frank J. Linn, a student at Iowa State College.[11]

For Houser, corn stands as irrefutable evidence of a distinct Pan-American tradition rooted in the mythic pre-Columbian past. Residing in the north-central region of the Midwest known as the "Corn Belt," Iowans had long associated the crop with local and regional identity. In 1912, George Hamilton of the Des Moines Chamber of Commerce composed the "Iowa Corn Song" to advertise the state's chief product; the rousing chorus proclaims: "We're from I-O-way, I-O-way. / That's where the tall corn grows."[12] Throughout the 1930s, corn production formed a major base of the state economy; Iowa cultivated over nine million acres of corn in 1935. Although the methods of farming had advanced, as the word "evolution" in Houser's title suggests, the symmetrical scenes stress continuity of tradition and equivalent results. The ancient farmer prefigures the modern Iowan, and both maintain a peaceful, agrarian lifestyle. The central motif of the growth cycle forms an ideological hinge upon which the mural's message turns. Fixed permanently in the post office mural, the crop continually evolves from seed to mature plant to harvest; the growth cycle renews and advances, forever carrying forward the culture of corn.

Amid the economic uncertainties of the Great Depression and the looming threat of war, Houser's composition envisioned a peaceful and prosperous future for both North and South Americans. This reassuring agricultural message echoed U.S. foreign policy initiatives, which promoted Pan-Americanism as a cooperative promise for peace. Houser's decision to feature a hybrid seed kernel imbued his mural with further political meaning by recalling the career of Henry A. Wallace. In addition to his role as the father of corn husking competitions, Wallace was an Iowan entrepreneur who established the first hybrid seed corn company. As a committed New Dealer and prominent member of Roosevelt's administration, Wallace also provided a formal linkage between American corn culture and the Good Neighbor Policy.

Nonetheless, the mirrored figuration in Houser's mural also serves to underscore discrepancies in the physiognomy and attire of the two men. Made by an artist with firsthand knowledge of pre-Hispanic art, the racialized physiognomy and near-nudity of the Maya figure is telling. The pendant portrayal operates on a secondary level as a study in contrasts: Native vs. Anglo, superstition vs. science, and past vs. present.[13] Despite the well-meaning intentions behind such murals as Houser's *Evolution of Corn* or Kenneth Adams's 1939 *Three Peoples*, described below, U.S.-led Pan-Americanism never fully supplanted antiquarian and primitivist understandings of pre-Columbian and modern Latin American cultures, but rather maintained these earlier discourses in tension with the egalitarian rhetoric and revisionary cultural narratives of hemispheric defense.

Corn as a Cultural Gift

While Houser's mural received a welcome reception in the predominantly white community of Ames, Iowa, the Good Neighbor Policy and its hemispheric configuration of American identity encountered greater resistance in regions with large populations of indigenous and Latin American descent. To be sure, one of the primary advantages for Houser in turning to ancient Maya civilization in this diplomatic context was its geographic and temporal distance from both modern Latin American nations and the United States. The domestic limitations of Pan-American equality and fraternity were nowhere more apparent than in the Southwest, where local border politics came into direct conflict with the global aims of the Good Neighbor Policy. Discrimination remained a daily reality for Mexican Americans and other non-white peoples in the United States.[14] The obvious discrepancy between U.S. narratives of Pan-Americanism and the reality of domestic social injustices threatened to damage U.S. relations with other nations, especially in Latin America. Furthermore, the Roosevelt administration worried that Nazi messages of anti-Americanism would appeal to disenfranchised minorities, thereby creating ideological inroads for enemy subterfuge.[15]

Kenneth Adams's four-panel mural for the University of New Mexico attempted to assuage these anxieties by presenting an idealized vision of multiethnic domestic harmony and peace in the present day. The primary diplomatic aim, in this instance, was to bolster a sense of patriotism among Spanish-speaking populations of the American Southwest. Completed in 1939, Adams's design followed the thematic guidelines set forth by the university's president, James Fulton Zimmerman. Seeking to enhance interethnic relations on campus, Zimmerman conceived of the artwork as a platform for social equality, and he instructed Adams to paint the unique cultural contributions of Native Americans, Spanish Americans, and Anglos to the Southwest.[16]

The assigned theme borrows language from the Cultural Gifts movement, an antiprejudice campaign that promoted tolerance by calling attention to the contributions of immigrant and minority groups to American life. Distressed by the virulent nativism and restrictive immigration laws of the 1920s, liberal thinkers and educators seized upon the idea that prejudice was a learned behavior and, hence, could be unlearned through proper instruction. The movement further decreed that its cultivation of "world friendship" would strengthen American democracy and advocate for international peace.[17] By highlighting the cultural achievements and contributions of various ethnic groups in his description of *Three Peoples*, Zimmerman likewise expressed faith that progressive education through public art was an essential component of the university's wartime preparation.

Kenneth Adams, *Three Peoples*, 1939. Oil on canvas, 7 1/3' × 42'. Zimmerman Library, University of New Mexico. *Courtesy of Center for Southwest Research, University Libraries, University of New Mexico.*

Such sociological and cultural aspirations flourished in the New Deal era, when the rhetoric of democracy in government programs aligned with the antiprejudice cause. The Bureau of Indian Affairs, under the directorship of longtime activist and antiassimilationist John Collier, adopted reformist policies to protect and preserve Native American community identity and traditions, while the Department of the Interior promoted Hispanic small-scale farming and traditional arts and crafts as a means to secure minority self-sufficiency. Federal art programs further enunciated a democratic nationalism through the explicit embrace of diverse regional histories and folk traditions.[18]

Adams, who had recently completed a post office mural under the Treasury Department's fine arts program, was well-versed in New Deal administrators' liberal ideology and so would have understood Zimmerman's reformist agenda for the library mural. Painted in a flat, static style and soft, low-key tones, Adams developed a sequence of multifigure compositions illustrating the various activities and industries of New Mexico's principle ethnic groups. The first panel features Native Americans engaged in traditional arts and crafts. Seated before a loom with a patterned bowl near her feet, a Navajo woman wears silver and turquoise jewelry. A Taos couple, set against a tall, stylized cornstalk and a distant Pueblo, demonstrates the artistry of fine-line pottery, while opposite them, an Apache couple weave basketry before a desert landscape of grazing sheep and a Plains Indian teepee. The second panel highlights the distinctive architecture and strong faith of Hispanic populations in New Mexico. Two women, both wearing traditional rebozos, apply plaster to an adobe home, while a third figure, a man, leads a plow through patchwork fields. Significantly, this figure's agricultural achievements include distinctly American produce: a sheaf of wheat, an apple, and a golden ear of corn. In the third panel, a trio of Anglo scientists diligently pursue medical and scientific research. A masked physician, wearing a pristine white coat, lifts a blond infant to an examination table, while fair-haired laboratory technicians peer into scientific instruments and note their findings. The final panel announces a new era of equality. Three men, dressed in nearly identical attire and distinguishable only by their physical coloring, join hands in a fraternal clasp of multiethnic unity and cooperation. Behind them, Adams imagines a blended cultural landscape of Pan-American promise. The cultural trinity stands surrounded by scenes of New Mexico's bountiful resources and natural scenery, whose plowed fields and flowing river promise growth and prosperity in a culturally united future.

In recognizing the cultural contributions of Spanish Americans, Native Americans, and Anglos to the American Southwest, *Three Peoples* seeks to cultivate ethnic tolerance and support for the Good Neighbor Policy and, subsequently, the U.S. war effort through its resonance with the Cultural Gifts antiprejudice campaign and New Deal social reform; and yet, like these broader efforts, it falls short. The iconography of Native and Hispanic figures wearing colorful garb and engaged in farming and handicraft not only conforms to stereotype but contrasts sharply with the scientific modernity of the Anglo figures, whose apparent leadership in the fourth panel underscores the unequal status of each culture.[19] In these and other Pan-American-themed murals, conceptions of race posed a particularly thorny challenge for artists in depicting transnational identity. Although American artists and culture leaders consciously attempted to overturn discriminatory attitudes, their efforts remained grounded in ethnocentric assumptions about white superiority. Accordingly, Adams's mural—despite its hemispheric vision of agricultural harmony—employs an essentializing language that reproduces the rhetorical missteps of government officials and university administrators alike, who put forward a language of equal transnational cooperation in a transparently unequal hemisphere.

Zimmerman nevertheless praised *Three Peoples* for its perceived social benefits to the campus community, as did local newspapers. Following U.S. entry in World War II, the university continued to understand the mural as helping to strengthen national defense. In August 1942, the administration identified its "continuing and expanding . . . emphasis on friendly understanding between the United States and the Latin American countries" as key to students' wartime preparedness.[20]

Corn as a Weapon of War

After the United States declared war on Germany, Italy, and Japan in December of 1941, the unifying discourse of Pan-Americanism turned more explicitly toward themes of military combat and the manufacture of war supplies. The visual culture of corn followed suit. The marked shift owed much to concurrent changes in U.S. foreign policy regarding Latin American nations. Prior to the Japanese attack on Pearl Harbor, the United States government remained hopeful that isolationism and neutrality would safeguard the nation from the mounting political crises in Europe and Asia. Yet by the spring of 1942, American military forces were stationed in Britain and performing airstrikes on the European continent. A foreign policy of isolationism was not enough to preserve the physical security of the United States. Whereas the primary diplomatic aim of Pan-Americanism previously had focused on the maintenance of peace, U.S. entry in the war meant that idealized depictions of corn as a symbol for cultural unity were no longer sufficient—the U.S. also needed to convince Latin American countries to join the winning side.[21]

The 1943 Walt Disney Studio film *The Grain that Built a Hemisphere* exemplifies this modified rhetorical approach. Produced in cooperation with the newly formed U.S. Office of Inter-American Affairs, the animated documentary promotes hemispheric unity through its presentation of a seamless agricultural tradition from the Maya, Aztec, and Inca civilizations to the modern United States. In a manner similar to Houser's Ames Post Office mural, viewers learn that corn holds important meaning for the world conflict. Bound not only by proximity but also by a shared culture of corn, Latin America and the United States form natural allies in defeating the Axis threat. The narrator explains that "Corn is the symbol of a spirit that links the Americas in a common bond of union and solidarity."[22] But this is not all. The international transfer of native materials, whether agricultural, mineral, or animal, ostensibly strengthened inter-American relations, enhanced hemispheric self-sufficiency, and supplied the United States with materials for ammunition and military equipment. Although this conceptual leap may seem farfetched to modern readers, the public discourse of the Good Neighbor Policy frequently linked U.S.–Latin American trade to Pan-Americanism and transnational security.[23] Indeed, viewers learn in the final sequence of the film that corn, more than a mere foodstuff, has practical applications in the manufacture of explosives, parachute fabrics, tanks, and other essential war materials.

A relatively new development that originated in the scientific approach to farming in the 1920s, hybrid corn seeds produced plants that were more productive and robust than either of the parental strains. The United States enjoyed more corn to feed livestock, process into starch and oil, and ferment into ethanol for fuel and industry. As a starch, corn served as an ingredient in the manufacture of an explosive similar to dynamite, while in the form of ethanol, the crop could be converted to butadiene for the synthesis of rubber. Non-edible components of the plant contributed to the war industry as well. Corn silk offered an alternative fabric for parachutes, and cornstalks entered in the production of fiberboard and plastics.[24] Edmond C. Foust, editor of the Indiana Farm Bureau's monthly newspaper the *Hoosier Farmer*, advertised these various wartime applications of the surplus grain and petitioned the U.S. government to establish manufacturing plants directed to this purpose in the 1942 pamphlet *Corn Fields Can Lick 'Em*.[25]

Corn as a weapon of war became a prevalent motif in U.S. propaganda. As it had earlier during World War I, the United States commissioned artists to create posters, pamphlets, films, and cartoons reminding viewers that "food is a weapon."[26] Posters carrying slogans such as "Corn Goes to War" and "War Plants Need Corn!" exhorted farmers to adapt to wartime demands by increasing their harvests and moving their corn yields to market. As a valuable ally and trading partner, Latin America contributed to U.S. national security as well. One such poster, *Resources of the Americas for War and Peace*, circulated between 1942 and 1945, underscores this point by visualizing the myriad natural resources needed for victory on a map of Central and South America. Responding to agricultural labor shortages nationwide, the U.S. government established farm worker programs, including the Women's Land Army and the Bracero Program, to mobilize civilian women and Mexican guest workers to alleviate U.S. labor shortages during the war.[27]

U.S. Government Printing Office, *Resources of the Americas in Peace and War*, 1942–45. Color lithograph, 19 ¾" × 26". *The University of Montana Mansfield Library Collection. Courtesy of the Historical Museum at Fort Missoula Collections.*

With the arrival of Mexican braceros to the United States starting in 1942, corn moved beyond its role as a symbol denoting Pan-American culture and identity to a shared agricultural endeavor in support of the war effort. Despite aggressive rhetorical claims of inter-American equality, Roosevelt unabashedly framed his foreign policy initiatives to achieve

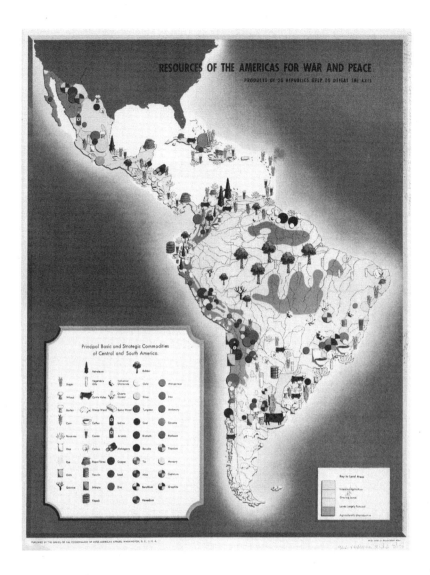

national gains. That same year, another Disney film entitled *Food Will Win the War* (1942) proudly announced that U.S. farmers had grown nearly three billion bushels of corn more than in the previous year. The animated feature imagines this volume in the form of giant golden ear of corn spanning the length of Europe as the narrator warns that it "hangs right over your head, Adolf."[28] While not always so explicitly stated as this, the visual culture of corn had already served several years as an ideological weapon against European fascism. Under the Good Neighbor Policy, the crop functioned as a symbol of Pan-American cultural unity and as a diplomatic lubricant for U.S. economic expansion and hemispheric defense. In this way, corn worked as a visual shorthand, assuring viewers that American life would continue much as it always had, not only in the United States, but throughout the Western hemisphere. Once wartime industry occasioned a rebound in the U.S. economy and Latin American nations joined the United States in defeating Nazi Germany, the U.S. government determined that Pan-Americanism was no longer necessary for national security or prosperity and began dismantling federal agencies devoted to that cause.

NOTES

1. Max Paul Friedman, *Nazis and Good Neighbors: The United States Campaign against the Germans of Latin America in World War II* (Cambridge: Cambridge University Press, 2003): 4. I wish to extend my sincere thanks to Renée Ater, Sally M. Promey, Lauren Kroiz, Erika Doss, Jordan Malfoy, Justin Nordstrom, and the anonymous reviewers of this volume for their valuable feedback on earlier drafts. My research also benefited from the support of the State Historical Society of Iowa and the University of New Mexico's Latin American and Iberian Institute and University Libraries. The views expressed in this chapter are those of the author and do not necessarily reflect the official policy of any U.S. Government organization.

2. Muna Lee was the Puerto Rican founder of the Inter-American Commission of Women and inter-American cultural affairs specialist for the U.S. State Department. Such contributors to *The New World Neighbors* series reflect U.S. scholars' and government officials' belief that textbooks could build popular consensus for Roosevelt's foreign policy. See: Breanne Robertson, "Textbook Diplomacy: The New World Neighbors Series and Inter-American Education During World War II," *Hemisphere: Visual Cultures of the Americas* (2011): 67–93.

3. Muna Lee, *Pioneers of Puerto Rico*, The New World Neighbors (Boston: D. C. Heath and Company, 1944): 41–44.

4. Such verbal and visual representations adhered to a prevailing orientalizing discourse that Delpar has termed "romantic primitivism." See: James Oles, *South of the Border: Mexico in the American Imagination, 1914–1947* (Washington, DC: Smithsonian American Art Museum, 1991); Helen Delpar, *The Enormous Vogue of Things Mexican: Cultural Relations between the United States and Mexico, 1920–1935* (Tuscaloosa: University of Alabama Press, 1992).

5. Lee, *Pioneers of Puerto Rico*, 41–44.

6. Candace Wheeler, *Columbia's Emblem, Indian Corn: A Garland of Tributes in Prose and Verse* (Houghton Mifflin, 1893). See also: Mary W. Blanchard, "Anglo-American Aesthetes and Native American Corn: Candace Wheeler and the

Revision of American Nationalism," *Journal of American Studies* 27 (1993): 377–97.

7. Pamela H. Simpson, *Corn Palaces and Butter Queens: A History of Crop Art and Dairy Sculpture* (Minneapolis: University of Minnesota Press, 2012).

8. Richard S. Kirkendall, "Corn Huskers and Master Farmers: Henry A. Wallace and the Merchandising of Iowa Agriculture," *Palimpsest* 65 (1984): 82–93; Denise Lorraine Dial, "The Organized Corn Husking Contests: Conduits of Industrial Culture in the Rural Midwest, 1922–1941" (unpublished dissertation, Iowa State University, 1998).

9. A. Hyatt Verrill, *Foods America Gave the World* (Boston: L. C. Page and Company, 1937); Louise O. Bercaw, Annie M. Hannay, and Nellie G. Larson, *Corn in the Development of the Civilization of the Americas* (Washington, DC: U.S. Department of Agriculture, 1940).

10. David Craven, *Diego Rivera: As Epic Modernist* (New York: G. K. Hall, 1997): 104.

11. Carol Phelps, "From ISU Halls to Post Office Walls," *Ames (IA) Daily Tribune*, May 11, 1985.

12. *The WPA Guide to 1930s Iowa* also noted the prominence of corn in Iowa culture by listing the giant corn palaces of Sioux City as state landmarks. Federal Writers Project, *The WPA Guide to 1930s Iowa* (1938, repr., Iowa City: University of Iowa Press, 1986): 299–312.

13. See: Elazar Barkan, *The Retreat of Scientific Racism: Changing Concepts of Race in Britain and the United States between the World Wars* (Cambridge: Cambridge University Press, 1992).

14. Throughout the 1930s, the perceived problem of "illegal" residents from Mexico precipitated a series of New Deal programs that attempted to provide a path to "worthy citizenship," which effectively meant assimilation to mainstream white culture. See: Stephanie Lewthwaite, *Race, Place, and Reform in Mexican Los Angeles: A Transnational Perspective, 1890–1940* (Tucson: University of Arizona Press, 2009).

15. By casting into sharper relief the discrepancy between U.S. claims of democracy and the reality of domestic social injustices, official narratives of Pan-Americanism spurred activism among disenfranchised non-white populations in the United States. See: Breanne Robertson, "Pan-Americanism, Patriotism, and Race Pride in Charles White's Hampton Mural," *American Art* 30, no. 1 (Spring 2016): 52–71.

16. James F. Zimmerman to F. P. Keppel, 27 October 1939, Kenneth Adams Vertical Files, Center for Southwest Research, University of New Mexico.

17. For more on the Cultural Gifts movement, see: Diana Selig, *Americans All: The Cultural Gifts Movement* (Cambridge, MA: Harvard University Press, 2008).

18. See: Jennifer McLerran, *A New Deal for Native Art: Indian Arts and Federal Policy, 1933–1943* (Tucson: University of Arizona Press, 2009); Stephanie Lewthwaite, *A Contested Art: Modernism and Mestizaje in New Mexico* (Norman: University of Oklahoma Press, 2015).

19. In the last fifty years, Adams's mural emerged as a site of controversy for its perceived sexism and racism. A detailed discussion of the historical motivations underlying its imagery and the ongoing campus debate surrounding its fate can be found in Breanne Robertson, "An Old Solution for an

Old Problem? Kenneth Adams, Jesús Guerrero Galván, and the Failure of Recontextualization," *Public Art Dialogue* 10, no. 2 (Fall 2020): 131–59.

20. James Fulton Zimmerman Papers and Kenneth Adams Vertical Files, Center for Southwest Research, University of New Mexico.

21. Monica A. Rankin, *México, la Patria! Propaganda and Production during World War II* (Lincoln: University of Nebraska Press, 2009).

22. Steven Watts, *The Magic Kingdom: Walt Disney and the American Way of Life* (Columbia, MO: University of Missouri, 1997): 230. This animated film formed part of a series the studio produced in collaboration with the OIAA to promote hemispheric goodwill. See also: Julianne Burton, "Don (Juanito) Duck and the Imperial-Patriarchal Unconscious: Disney Studios, the Good Neighbor Policy, and the Packaging of Latin America," in Andrew Parker et al., eds., *Nationalism and Sexualities* (New York and London: Routledge, 1992): 21–41; J. B. Kaufman, *South of the Border with Disney: Walt Disney and the Good Neighbor Program, 1941–1948* (New York: The Walt Disney Family Foundation Press, 2009).

23. Prior to the U.S. declaration of war in 1941, the Roosevelt administration hoped that increased trade would enhance inter-American relations and create a self-sustaining hemisphere, thereby insulating the Americas from foreign instability and aggression.

24. Judith Sumner, *Plants Go to War: A Botanical History of World War II* (Jefferson, NC: McFarland, 2019): 129–35.

25. Edmond C. Foust, *Corn Fields Can Lick 'Em* (Indianapolis: Indiana Farm Bureau, 1942). See also: Sumner, *Plants Go to War*, 133–35.

26. Despite the myriad applications of corn in making munitions and supplies, the U.S. government struggled to convince Midwestern farmers to send their crops to market rather than selling them as feed to cattle and pig farmers.

27. See: Judy Barrett Litoff and David C. Smith, "'To the Rescue of the Crops': The Women's Land Army during World War II," *Prologue* 25, no. 4 (Winter 1993): 347–62; Deborah Cohen, *Braceros: Migrant Citizens and Transnational Subjects in the Postwar United States* (Chapel Hill: University of North Carolina Press, 2011).

28. This impressive harvest represented a substantial increase from a prewar average of eight hundred million bushels. For further analysis of this film, see: Tracey Louise Mollet, *Cartoons in Hard Times: The Animated Shorts of Disney and Warner Brothers in Depression and War, 1932–1945* (New York: Bloomsbury Academic, 2017): 136.

CHAPTER 14

"Six Taels and Four Maces (*Luk-Leung-Sei*)"

Food and Wartime Hong Kong, 1938–46

KWONG CHI MAN

The Japanese occupation of Hong Kong from December 25, 1941, to August 30, 1945, known by the locals as the "Three Years and Eight Months," has been remembered by the survivors and portrayed by historians as one of the darkest pages of the modern history of Hong Kong.[1] The experience of Hong Kong under the Japanese was marked by constant hunger. Oral histories of the period invariably mentioned hunger and the very phrase "six taels and four maces (*luk-leung-sei*)" (the amount of rationed rice that each resident could buy every day during the occupation) persisted in the mind of Hong Kong residents who experienced the period and captured the imagination of those who did not. Another recurring theme about the Japanese occupation was the mass exodus of Hong Kong residents to South China and beyond. After the war, Lt. Gen. Isogai Rensuke, the Japanese governor of Hong Kong from March of 1942 to December of 1944, was tried for war crimes allegedly committed in Hong Kong. He was charged not for mismanagement of food but for forcibly removing residents from Hong Kong, which caused death due to exposure and starvation in outlying islands.[2]

Previous historians have viewed Hong Kong's deprivations under Japanese occupation as indications of the cruelties of Japanese imperialism but have not discussed the issues of hunger and starvation in detail. Using archival sources from Hong Kong, Japan, the United Kingdom, and the United States, this chapter argues that the wartime experience of Hong Kong provides insights into the complexities of food in World War II. Hong Kong, a British colony with a population of around 1.6 million by December of 1941, was one of the most vulnerable places in Asia in terms of food security during World War II. The port city could not produce enough food for the large population, many of whom were refugees from China as the result of the Second Sino–Japanese War (1937–45). The colonial government took pains to feed its ever-increasing population and store enough food for a possible Japanese attack, which took place in December 1941. When Japanese forces took the city, food storage was thoroughly looted. To prevent starvation, the Japanese authorities introduced the policies of forced migration and food rationing that led to the displacement of more than a million people

By evicting a large number of residents from Hong Kong, the Japanese authorities also weaponized hunger by forcing the Chinese and British to take care of the refugees. Because of Tokyo's failure to coordinate various areas under its control and the wartime disruption of shipping, the food situation in Hong Kong steadily worsened despite efforts to send away residents. The result of the combination of incompetence on part of the Japanese authorities and the Allied counterattack against Japanese shipping was the famine of 1945, during which many died because of starvation and malnutrition. The situation was not relieved until August of 1945 with the return of the British, who recognized the importance of food to Hong Kong and were able to organize a large-scale relief operation that lasted until 1946. Thus, this chapter addresses the overlapping issues of wartime refugees, food policy, and military occupation, all of which had a dramatic impact on the starvation and dislocation of Hong Kong residents in the 1940s.

This chapter shows the crucial role of food in the wartime experience of Hong Kong. It also shows how globalization made port cities especially vulnerable, particularly in terms of their reliance on maritime trade for daily necessities and resources. Moreover, this chapter illustrates one of the often-overlooked factors in Japan's defeat during the Asia-Pacific War, namely the failure of the Japanese government to coordinate areas under its control. While the Japanese planners in Tokyo did try to coordinate the production and logistics within the vast swath of Asia under control of Japanese forces, it paid little attention to the needs of the people in these areas. The drastic measures taken by the Japanese occupation authority led to much suffering for the local population.

A Colonial Port City Striving for Food Security

When the European War began in September 1939, the food situation in Hong Kong changed little on the surface. Upon the declaration of war, the colonial government introduced price control of certain European foodstuffs and registered all shipments of imported rice and their whereabouts.[3] Initially, the European War had only a limited impact on the food situation in Hong Kong, as maritime trade in East Asia was little interrupted by German naval activity. However, the fall of France in May of 1940 and the subsequent Japanese occupation of French Indochina in September, deprived Hong Kong of one of the main sources of rice. Furthermore, Hong Kong relied heavily on British Borneo in obtaining firewood, a source easily severed by the Japanese navy.[4] In response to the sudden deterioration of the situation, the colonial government stopped the export of rice and started to build up a rice store for the population.[5] The colonial government also adopted a progressive and interventionist attitude toward the issue of food and nutrition. The Nutrition Research Committee of the government encouraged consumption of foodstuff that were cheaper and more readily available, such as soybean products and fish.[6] Medical officials and academics devised "siege biscuits" (nutritious biscuits that could be stored for a long time) and "siege fish" (salted dry fish) in order to provide the population with cheap and nutritious food when Hong Kong was under siege.[7] The government planned to build storage facilities to provide fish for 1.5 million people for a month.[8]

As the Japanese threat grew in 1941, the colonial government considered how to feed the population when Hong Kong was under siege. In early 1941, the government set up the Food and Firewood Board to determine the amount of food needed in an emergency, imposed a monopoly on import and export of rice, and introduced a fixed price for rice sales.[9] The colonial government also worked with charitable organizations to subsidize rice sales to the urban poor, hoping to alleviate the impact of rising food prices.[10] In September of that year, Hong Kong authorities established communal kitchens responsible for distributing free meals when the city was under siege.[11] According to Maj. Gen. Christopher Maltby, the commander of the Hong Kong garrison, one communal kitchen could distribute five thousand sets of meals in an hour.[12] Personnel who held emergency posts would be fed in designated restaurants that would continue to operate in wartime, including the luxurious Hong Kong Hotel and Café Wiseman.[13]

Japanese forces attacked Hong Kong on December 8, 1941 before many of these preparations were fully in place. Fortunately for Hong Kong residents, the Labour Officer issued a call for kitchen workers to register so that they could be called upon during emergencies.[14] This proved to be of vital importance because, when the war broke out, communal kitchens were already manned and stocked with food. During the first few days of the battle, all communal kitchens on Hong Kong Island operated with few interruptions.[15] After the fall of Kowloon on December 12 and 13, however, the situation deteriorated. When besieging Japanese forces started to shell the north shore of Hong Kong Island and air attacks intensified, residents of Kowloon started to face food shortages, and some were shot when trying to sneak out to find food.[16]

While many of the communal kitchens were located at concealed spots or on hillsides, some were located at government-built fresh-food markets. These were large concrete structures located in urban centers such as Wan Chai and Central, each catering to tens of thousands of locals who lined up for food. While Japanese forces had orders not to attack civilian targets, these markets were occasionally hit by shells or bombs, killing hundreds of residents.[17] The food situation rapidly declined from the evening of December 18 onwards, as Japanese forces landed on the island. Looters started to appear, even as police resorted to shooting looters without trial.[18] On December 24, some of the British and Commonwealth soldiers withdrew to the Wan Chai Fresh Food Market, the strongest building in the area surrounding the city of Victoria. By then, the communal kitchens ceased to operate, and the food distribution system on the island started to fall apart. The next day, the garrison commander surrendered, ending the eighteen-day siege.

The Japanese Attempt to Solve the Food Problem

When Japanese forces entered the city of Victoria on December 28, the rice store of Hong Kong, which had remained largely intact, was seized and shipped away to Japan, together with many other goods. Hong Kong authorities estimated that of the fifty thousand tons of rice and seven thousand tons of flour stored at Kowloon, only five thousand tons and two hundred tons (respectively) were left weeks after the Japanese occupation.[19] Japanese forces initially established a military administration, but Tokyo decided to establish the Hong Kong Occupation Government under the direct control of the General Headquarters (*daihonei*).

Economically, Hong Kong produced few raw materials that Japan needed, although it was one of the transit points for smuggled raw materials such as tungsten. Hong Kong had a sizable industrial sector, but it relied on imported raw materials from different parts of Asia, and, to sustain this sector, Japan had to feed a large population. Occupation forces expected Hong Kong to be self-sufficient in terms of food or that it could satisfy its need through trading with other occupied areas. Thus, one of the first directives received by the new Occupation Government from the Military Affairs Bureau was a reminder of the need for Hong Kong to avoid relying on mainland Japan for food. However, this was a tall order for the occupation authority.

The first problem facing the Japanese authority in Hong Kong in achieving food security without aid from mainland Japan was the lack of shipping. During the first months of the war, most Japanese shipping was used to ferry the invasion forces to different parts of Asia. While the Japanese experienced success on the battlefield, Japanese shipping suffered unexpectedly high losses. After occupying European colonies in Southeast Asia, the Japanese navy had to focus available shipping on carrying resources back to Japan and to supply the garrisons deployed in different parts of Asia. Thus, even if Tokyo was willing to help, Hong Kong received a low priority in receiving shipping tonnage to carry food for the population. After repeated pleas from the metropolitan government at Tokyo, Hong Kong concluded more trade agreements with areas under Japanese control.[20] By then, the sea lanes between Hong Kong and these areas were already severed or precariously maintained by junks. Rice-producing territories such as the French Indochina also suffered from famine, mainly because of Japanese mismanagement.[21]

Another major obstacle was the status of the occupation government and its relationship with the neighboring Japanese authorities. The local authority was encouraged to conclude trade agreements with nearby territories under Japanese control, particularly Canton. However, conflict among the Japanese commanders in China hampered cooperation between the two. The governor-general of Hong Kong envisaged the city as a center for the political work against the Chinese Nationalist Government, but his scheme was in conflict with that of the Japanese high command in China, which saw political work as their exclusive domain.[22] Because of the tension between the Japanese authorities in Hong Kong and Canton over their respective roles, cooperation between them was minimal, even in the economic sphere. It was not until late 1942 that they concluded a formal agreement on trade, and such trade was conducted on an almost barter basis, with Hong Kong exporting mechanical goods in exchange for foodstuffs from Canton. It was only through the insistence of the collaborationist regime in Canton that the Japanese authority allowed Canton to sell rice to Hong Kong.[23] It took until July of 1943, more than one-and-a-half years after the Japanese had captured Hong Kong, for the Japanese to finally reopen the Kowloon–Canton Railway.[24] Even then, the flow of goods between the two places was limited, especially as the Sino–American air forces started to regularly attack the area.

Facing these challenges, the Japanese authority in Hong Kong, with basically unlimited power, relied on population dispersal and rationing to solve the food problem. Many refugees and residents, sensing impending war, left Hong Kong for mainland China. Before the invasion, the Japanese army had already decided to remove the "surplus" population, allowing only those working in key industrial sectors (such as dockyards) to remain.[25] This forceful evacuation was extremely difficult, especially for residents who had to sell most of their belongings. They needed to walk to the border, where they would be searched by Japanese and puppet sentries and have their valuables looted. After crossing the border, they had to walk across bandit-infested territory to larger towns, such as Waichow or Kukong, where help was offered.[26] In a sense, the Japanese movement, or dispersal of the Hong Kong's population, served to weaponize hunger as a tool of war, as it forced the Chinese and the British to take care of the expelled population, further stretching their limited resources. From March of 1942 to the end of the year, only 353,009 Hong Kong residents left. Some of those who left the city also tried to return as the situation in Guangdong was no better. Thus, only 86,310 applied for exit permits in 1943. By the end of 1943, the population of Hong Kong reached 850,000, around the level of the mid-1930s.[27]

Other major policies related to food security were rice rationing and the local administration system. When the Japanese took over Hong Kong, all rice shops were closed, and rice stores seized.[28] The military administration allowed the reopening of rice shops on January 11, 1942, almost three weeks after the fall of Hong Kong. During the interim period, people fed themselves with the help of hawkers selling looted foodstuffs. Some locals received food from Japanese occupation authorities, who used extra food as leverage to solicit cooperation. In the meantime, the military administration established eighteen District Administration Offices (*kuyakusho*) throughout the territory. These offices were manned by Chinese local figures who were responsible for security, hygiene, relief, and rice rationing. All residents of each district were registered and were given ration tickets for rice, salt, sugar, firewood, and matches for starting a cooking fire. Rice shops were organized into government-controlled syndicates and were forced to open and sell rice at a fixed price to those who had the rice ticket. Residents had to wait in line for hours to buy rice, and they were often given poor quality rice or even sand or sawdust-mixed rice. Those who worked for the Japanese in different capacities were given extra, and they often shared with their friends and relatives.[29]

As Gordon King, a Hong Kong University professor who escaped in February 1942, noted: "the queues [for rice] were of prodigious length and after waiting for half a day people would often find that the supply had given out."[30] As there was not enough rice for everyone, the rice sellers stored their best stock for the non-rationing market. Many who obtained extra rice by working for the Japanese also sold their stock in the black market, at rates considerably higher than the ration prices. Gordon King wrote, "on the streets rice could not be purchased for less than $1.80 [per catty, prewar price $0.15]."[31] Other foodstuffs were also in short supply and were sold at exorbitant prices. King continued: "meat and fish [were] at first unobtainable, but later became available in small quantities at prices which were beyond the reach of the ordinary people. The same remarks apply to the supplies of vegetables."[32] The Japanese tried to develop fisheries and agriculture in the New Territories, but only with minimal success.[33] Other Japanese-occupied areas were also reluctant to sell food to Hong Kong.[34]

As the food situation in Hong Kong steadily declined, many of the well-to-do Chinese had left by mid-1943. Some of the Chinese dignitaries and charitable organizations organized the relief effort. Aw Boon Haw, a wealthy overseas Chinese merchant who stayed in Hong Kong, urged Tojo Hideki, the Prime Minister of Japan, to allow him to buy more food for Hong Kong from different parts of Asia, cooperating with eight major Chinese rice merchants in Hong Kong to form the Association for the Maintenance of Food Supply for the Civilians (*man-sik hip-zo wui*). Members of the association pooled their capital and resources to buy food in the nearby areas and resell it at a more affordable price. However, as the Allied air and submarine forces were increasingly active in South China and the South China Sea, Hong Kong found it increasingly difficult to import rice and other foodstuffs, even if the other Japanese authorities in other parts of Asia were willing to comply. Although the planners in

Tokyo had expected to ship 100,000 tons of rice to Hong Kong, between January and December, they only sent 23,768 tons, 2,200 of which were sunk by the Allies. Such an amount was far below what was required as there were still some 600,000 residents living in the city.[35]

In early 1944, Japanese officials asked Hong Kong to provide rationed rice only to those who served directly under the Occupation Government and the military. The idea, however, was opposed by the head of the Civil Administration Department of the Occupation Government, Shirai Kichiji, who argued that such a move would effectively end the civilian administrative apparatus built up by the Japanese since early 1942 and would also tarnish the image of Japan as the liberator of Asians. He particularly mentioned that some of the residents were rounded up by police and left to die on boats in the sea, an act that he argued provided ammunitions for the Allied propaganda efforts.[36] Shirai's plea was ignored, and the Occupation Government announced in April that only the families that worked for the authorities were allotted rice rations.[37] From then on, food price soared, fueled by the collapse in the value of the military script issued by the Occupation Government.

Eyewitness accounts of the period mentioned widespread hunger. Dr. Li Shu Fan, the head of the Hong Kong Sanatorium and Hospital who stayed in Hong Kong until mid-1943, noted that many of the residents in Hong Kong suffered from beriberi because of the lack of vitamin B in their diet. He also suggested that the machine-ground rice sold by the Occupation Government often removed rice hulks that contained much-needed nutrients, especially when the population had little means to maintain a balanced diet and could only rely on rice for subsistence.[38] Residents endured widespread hunger and, as early as in 1942, there were reports concerning cannibalism in Hong Kong among the poor. Oral history records also reveal human flesh removed from bodies on the streets being sold as rabbit or civet meat.[39] Samejima Moritaka, a Japanese priest who was sent to Hong Kong in 1943 to organize a pro-Japanese Christian association, mentions in his memoir people removing flesh from infant bodies.[40] A Japanese military police officer also noted frequent cases of people extracting flesh from bodies.[41] These reports were included in a chart of criminal acts punished by the Japanese authority, for Governor Isogai's private reference. This chart demonstrated that, between 1942 and the end of 1944, cannibalism cases steadily increased from twelve to thirty-seven.[42] From late 1943, intelligence reports demonstrated that a number of people "formerly in good circumstances" killed themselves by "leaping from balconies of tea-houses after partaking of generous refreshments."[43]

Food was also the biggest problem for the more than ten thousand British, Indian, Canadian, Chinese, and other Commonwealth prisoners of war and civilians who were interned in Hong Kong. From the summer of 1942, 4,835 were sent away to Japan; the remainder faced a dwindling food supply. While actual famine did not occur in the prisoner of war camps, many, especially soldiers at Sham Shui Po, suffered from malnutrition and died of malnutrition-related illnesses. For food, non-commissioners and other ranks were forced to work for the Japanese in the expansion of the Kai Tak airdrome.[44] Even the officers who were separately interned at Argyle Street Camp suffered from food shortage, though it was less severe. The Japanese also used better rations to induce the Indian prisoners of war to serve in the Japanese forces, but with only limited effect.[45] As for the civilians of Allied nationalities who were interned at Stanley, they too suffered from food shortage, although some received food parcels from the Chinese and Eurasian residents who stayed outside of the camp, often at considerable risk for those who delivered the parcels. The canteen and the black market of the camp also helped ease the food problem.[46]

Famine of 1945

Throughout 1943–45, the food situation in Hong Kong steadily deteriorated. In May 1944, a tael of rice cost between six and eight yen military script in the black market, against the official price of one-point-five yen. Five months later the respective cost of a tael of rice reached fourteen yen and three yen. During this period, the occupation government could do little but spread misinformation through newspapers, suggesting an improving food situation, for example falsely claiming increased production of foodstuffs or new shipments of rice from other parts of Asia.[47] In December 1944, the occupation government further tightened the food rationing system by only allowing those who worked in Japanese institutions and factories to buy rice at a discounted price (three yen per catty). The price of other commodities, such as peanut cooking oil also increased rapidly.[48] As food allowances were insufficient, those who worked for the Japanese were encouraged to seek parttime work to make ends meet.[49] In anticipation of the imminent starvation, 101,328 people left Hong Kong in December.[50]

A complete collapse of food security came in the Spring of 1945, when the price for a catty of rice reached 145 yen, and then 200 in the subsequent month. Despite the Occupation Government's policy of increasing wages, the situation rapidly declined, and Hong Kong entered a practical state of famine. The government could only respond with more empty promises, such as developing agricultural land near urban areas.[51] In July and August, seventy to eighty dead bodies were found daily in the urban area, most of them succumbed to hunger or illness related to malnutrition.[52]

The Japanese surrender on August 15, 1945 proved to be a blessing for Hong Kong, which would probably have faced a widespread famine throughout the winter of 1945–46 had the war carried on. As early as in the spring of 1945, the British planners who were responsible for retaking Hong Kong had already noted the dangerous food situation. When the British fleet was about to enter Hong Kong, the Supreme Allied Command of Southeast Asia Command (SACSEA) started to gather ships and resources for Hong Kong. The food situation was not immediately dangerous because the merchants were willing to sell their stocks and trade with nearby areas, which restarted within days of the Japanese surrender.[53] The British Military Administration, formed after the British fleet entered Hong Kong on August 30, introduced a new system of price control and rationing for rice. It also hired the urban poor to clean up the city and provide them with a salary to buy food. Forty thousand free meals were also distributed every day in the city.[54]

With the help from the British diplomats in China and the Ministry of Food, Hong Kong was able to buy foodstuffs from different parts of China, including Guangdong, which raised the export price for food in order to stabilize the food market.[55] On September 26, the first shipment of rice, six thousand three hundred tons in total, arrived from Rangoon, Burma, after the Royal Navy cleared the Malacca strait of mines and obstacles.[56] SACSEA also tried to send foodstuffs to Hong Kong from different parts of Asia, including Australia and India. Because of the British effort, within three months after the British takeover, more than eighteen thousand tons of rice reached Hong Kong.[57] Although food shortage and rising food prices sometimes raised concern and criticism, and cases of starvation persisted, the situation throughout the period of military administration was much improved compared to that of Japanese occupation. However, because of the volatile situation in East Asia and Southeast Asia, control of the rice trade and the rationing system was not fully abolished until 1955, a decade after the end of the war.

Conclusion

The experience of Hong Kong during World War II revealed the vulnerability of East Asian port cities in dealing with the problem of food shortages that arose as a result of the disruption of maritime trade. After World War II, Hong Kong became one of the richest societies in Asia. Recovering from its status as a city on the verge of starvation, Hong Kong became, in the words of its tourism authority, the "food capital of Asia."[58] When communist China experienced a widespread famine from 1958 to the 1960s, many in Hong Kong sent parcels of foodstuffs to their relatives in China. The city also fed the millions of refugees who chose to cross the border when China was engulfed by the Cultural Revolution. In that period, there were few physical traces of the hunger experienced by the residents of Hong Kong during the war, but the memory of hunger and privation lingered on, as "six taels four maces" was one of the most commonly remembered catchphrases about the period. The potential danger of Hong Kong's starvation, however, was reimagined in the nationalist narratives about Hong Kong and China. Chinese historical narratives emphasize that mainland China, despite its difficulties, provided food for postwar Hong Kong. As the population of Hong Kong soared, according to this narrative, China also provided Hong Kong with drinking water from the East River. As Cheung Siu-keung mentions, while the trade of food and water (often at higher-than-market cost) is usually described as form of selfless gift, the potential of food (and water) being used as a weapon in Hong Kong has never been missed.[59] In 2019, during the protest against the Extradition Bill, a Chinese academic working in Singapore quoted his joking friend that if the Chinese wanted to stop the protest, they "just need to cut off water to Hong Kong and then everything would be settled."[60]

NOTES

1. The research of this chapter is supported by General Research Fund provided by the Research Grants Council of Hong Kong (project title "The Japanese "Total-State" Experiment in Hong Kong, 1942–1945" Project Number 12600219). For more recent works on Hong Kong history, see: Lau Chi Pang and Chow Ka Kin, *Tunsheng renyu: rishi shiqi xianggangren de jiti huiyi* (Swallowed Voices and Words: Oral History of the Japanese Occupation of Hong Kong) (Hong Kong: Joint Publishing, 2009); Kwong Chi Man, *Chongguang zhilu: riju xianggang yu taipingyang zhanzheng* (Road to Liberation: Japanese Occupation of Hong Kong and the Pacific War) (Hong Kong: Cosmos, 2015).

2. Suzannah Linton, *Hong Kong's War Crimes Trials* (Cambridge: Cambridge University Press, 2014): 115.

3. South China Morning Post (SCMP), 15/7/1939; SCMP, 11/9/1939; SCMP 8/11/1939; SCMP, 13/11/1939; "Prices Board,—Appointment of," *Hong Kong Government Gazette* (GA) 1939, no. 772, 950.

4. Kwong Chi Man, Tsoi Yiu Lun, *Eastern Fortress: A Military History of Hong Kong* (Hong Kong: Hong Kong University Press, 2014): 120–26.

5. SCMP, 5/5/1940; SCMP, 10/6/1940; SCMP, 15/7/1940.

6. SCMP, 11/3/1940; SCMP 31/5/1940.

7. Kerrie MacPherson, "The History of Marine Science in Hong Kong," in *Perspectives on marine environmental change in Hong Kong and Southern China, 1977–2001* (Hong Kong: Hong Kong University Press, 2003): 22–23; Brian Edgar, "The Dark World's Fire: Tom and Lena Edgar in War," https://brianedgar .wordpress.com/tag/geoffrey-herklots/.

8. Anthony Charter, *The First Shall be Last: The War Journal of John Charter and Memoirs of Yvonne Charter, Hong Kong 1940–1945* (Tolworth: Grosvenor, 2018): 52–56.

9. "Essential Commodities Board," GA 1941, No. 169, 199; "Members of the Food and Firewood Control Board," GA 1941, No. 220, 242; "Major R. D. Walker to act as Manager, War Supplies Board," GA 1941, no. 197, 232.

10. George Endacott, *Hong Kong Eclipse* (Hong Kong: Oxford University Press, 1978): 20.

11. Endacott, *Hong Kong Eclipse*, 21.

12. "Hong Kong, 30 November 1941," in "C. M. Maltby Scrapbook," Imperial War Museum Collection, Document 22835.

13. Barbara Anslow, *Tin Hats & Rice* (Hong Kong: Blacksmith, 2018): 24.

14. For the battle of Hong Kong, see: Kwong Chi Man, Tsoi Yiu Lun, *Eastern Fortress*, 161–224.

15. Wang Shaozai "Xianggang lunxuan huiyi (Reminisincences of the Fall of Hong Kong)," *Zhongwai zazhi* (The Kaleidoscope) 35, no. 6, (1984): 79–80.

16. Lin Xin, "Xianggang lunxian mujiji (Witnessing the Fall of Hong Kong)," *Zhongwai zazhi* 34, no. 6, (1983): 147.

17. "E. S. Jones (a Hong Kong Police Office)," Imperial War Museum Collection, Document 26223, 5.

18. Phyllis Harrop, *Hong Kong Incident* (London: Eyre & Spottiswoode, 1943): 79; "E. S. Jones (a Hong Kong Police Office)," Imperial War Museum Collection, Document 26223, 7.

19. "A Brief Report on the Conditions Existing at Hong Kong between the dates 25/12/1941 and 11/5/1942 Submitted by E. J. M. Churn," The National Archives (TNA), CO 980/59.

20. Kwong Chi Man, *Chongguang zhilu*, 130–31.

21. Kwong Chi Man, *Chongguang zhilu*, 131.

22. Kwong Chi Man, *Chongguang zhilu*, 71–72.

23. Jin Xiongbai, *Wang zhengquan de kaichang yu shouchang* (The Rise and Fall of the Wang Jing-wei Regime) (Hong Kong: Chun Chau, 1960): 23–24.

24. Kwong Chi Man, *Chongguang zhilu*, 132.

25. "Dai 23 gun honkon kyūryū gunsei shidō keikaku (The 23rd Army's Plan to

Supervise the Military Administration of Hong Kong)," Rikushi mitsu dainikki (Secret Records of the Ministry of War Concerning China), Japan Centre for Asian Historical Records, Ref: C04123630100, 9.

26. Kwong Chi Man, *Chongguang zhilu*, 175–80.

27. Kwong Chi Man, *Chongguang zhilu*, 175.

28. Yukio Wani, Cheung Wang Yim (tr.), *Suiyue wusheng: yige ribenren zhuixun xianggang rizhan shiji* (Muted in Time: A Japanese's Search for Traces of Japanese Occupation of Hong Kong) (Hong Kong: Arcadia Press, 2013): 35.

29. Chen Junbao; Tse Wing Gwan (ed.), *Chen Junbao riji quanji* (Compilation of the Diary of Chen Junbao), vol. 2 (Hong Kong: Commercial Press, 2004): 65, 68, 70.

30. "Brief Report on Conditions Prevailing in Hongkong during the Period 25th December 1941 to 17th February 1942," 18/3/1942, TNA, FO 371/31671, 7.

31. "Brief Report," 7.

32. "Brief Report," 7.

33. Kwong Chi Man, *Chongguang zhilu*, 127–29.

34. "Waichow Intelligence Summary No. 14," 16/12/1942, ERC, EMR-1B-01, Hong Kong Heritage Project (HKHP).

35. "Shina ni okeru shokuryō jijō (1945)," Gaimushō kiroku (Records of the Ministry of Foreign Affairs), Japan Centre for Asian Historical Records, Ref: B08060396800, 8.

36. "Report with Title (submitted by Shirai Kichiji)," 20/1/10, Gaimushō kiroku (Records of the Ministry of Foreign Affairs), Japan Centre for Asian Historical Records, Ref: B08060396500, 9–13. In fact, the Allies throughout the war did not use this; the official responsible for the act, the head of the police in Hong Kong, was executed.

37. "Extract from Far Eastern Weekly Intelligence Summary No. 68," 28/4/1944, TNA, CO 129/591/4; Wa Kiu Yat Po, 15/3/1944; Zheng Hongtai, Wong Siu-lun, *Xianggang miyeshi* (A History of Rice Business in Hong Kong) (Hong Kong: Joint Publishing, 2005): 114–15.

38. Li Shu Fun, *Xianggang waike yisheng* (A Hong Kong Surgeon) (Hong Kong: Commercial Press, 2019): 204–5.

39. "Interview with Daniel Chan on His Grandparents' Live during the Occupation," 26/5/2019, Author's Collection.

40. Samejima Moritaka, Gong Shusen (tr.), *Xianggang huixiangji: rijun zhanling xia de xianggang jiaohui* (Hong Kong Memoir: The Church in Japanese-Occupied Hong Kong) (Hong Kong: Chinese Christian Literature Council, 1971): 99–101.

41. Nakayama Tokushiro, *Shiki honkon no seikansha* (A Private Note of a Hong Kong Survivor) (Self-printed, 1978): 51.

42. "Reference Material for Governor Isogai (Isogai shiryō), 1945," Hong Kong Museum of History Collection, loaned by KL Leung to Hong Kong Museum of History, 90.

43. "Fortnightly Intelligence Report No. 2," 9/10/1943, TNA, CO 129/590/22.

44. Graham Heywood, *It Won't be Long Now: the Diary of a Hong Kong Prisoner of War* (Hong Kong: Blacksmith, 2015): 91, 102–15.

45. "Military Situation in Hong Kong Based on information received up to 25th October 1942," Personal Papers of Sir Lindsay Tasman Ride, Australian War Memorial Collection, PR82/068/2/34.

46. Geoffrey Emerson, *Hong Kong Internment, 1942 to 1945: Life in the Japanese Civilian Camp at Stanley* (Hong Kong: Hong Kong University Press, 2008): 89–91; Li Shu Fan, *Hong Kong Surgeon*, 186–87.

47. "Fortnightly Intelligence Report No. 2," 16–31/1/1945, The National Archives and Records Administration (NARA), RG 208, Entry 370, Box 386; "Fortnightly Intelligence Report No. 6 & 7," 16/3/1945–15/4/1945, NARA, RG 208, Entry 370, Box 386.

48. "Fortnightly Intelligence Report No. 3," 1–15/2/1945, NARA, RG 208, Entry 370, Box 386.

49. "Fortnightly Intelligence Report No. 6 & 7," 16/3/1945–15/4/1945, NARA, RG 208, Entry 370, Box 386; Chen Junbao; Tse Wing Gwan (ed.), *Chen Junbao riji*, 309.

50. "Reference Material for Governor Isogai (Isogai shiryō), 1945," Hong Kong Museum of History Collection, loaned by KL Leung to Hong Kong Museum of History, 92; "Fortnightly Intelligence Report No. 3," 1–15/2/1945, NARA, RG 208, Entry 370, Box 386.

51. "Fortnightly Intelligence Report No. 8 & 9," 16/4/1945–15/5/1945, NARA, RG 208, Entry 370, Box 386.

52. Zheng Hongtai, Wong Siu-lun, *Xianggang miyeshi*, 118–24.

53. "Memorandum on the Food Situation in Hong Kong from 28/8/1945 to 22/9/1945," Hong Kong Public Records Office (HKPRO), HKRS 211–2–42.

54. "General Report on Hong Kong," HKPRO, HKRS 163–1–76.

55. "C-in-C HK to War Office," 25/10/1945, HKPRO, HKRS 163–1–76; "Chungking to FO," 26/10/1945, TNA, FO 371/46257; "Quarterly Review," HKPRO, HKRS 163–1–179; "General Report on Hong Kong," HKPRO, HKRS 163–1–76.

56. "SACSEA to C-in-C HK," 3/9/1945, TNA, WO 203/1929.

57. "Notes on Rice Position—Hong Kong," 13/11/1945, TNA, WO 203/2447; "ALFSEA to Troopers," 3/12/1945, TNA, WO 203/2447.

58. "A Taste of Southeast Asia," Hong Kong Trade Development Council website, https://hkmb.hktdc.com/en/1X0A8L36/life-style/A-Taste-of-Southeast-Asia.

59. Cheung Siu Keung, "Gushen suoming: zhongguo dui xianggang di shishu ji shiwu gongying (Imprisoning One's Body and Livelihood: China's Food and Water Supplies to Hong Kong)," in Cheung Siu Keung, Leung Kai Chi, Chan Ka Ming (eds.), *Hong Kong, Chengshi, Xiangxiang* (Hong Kong, City, Imagination) (Hong Kong: Infolink Publishing Ltd., 2014): 45–72.

60. "HK Life Necessities Depend on Mainland Resources," Global Times, 21/8/2019, http://www.globaltimes.cn/content/1162118.shtml Accessed 23/5/2020.

CHAPTER 15

Selling Out the Revolution for a Plate of Beans

Social Eating and Violence in Peru's Civil Conflict of the 1980s and 1990s

BRYCE EVANS

The nation of Peru, at the time of this writing home to 33 million people, sits in western South America, at the geographic center of what was once the territory of the Inca, the largest empire in pre-Columbian America. Following independence in 1821, the modern nation-state has undergone development but has also been dogged by conflict, corruption, poverty, and social division. Today, across the country, one of the features of the urban landscape is the *comedor popular* (popular dining room): affordable, female-run communal dining spaces announced by the inviting smell of cooking, a community feel, and a friendly noise and bustle. Social eating in Peru is rooted in the much more ancient tradition of indigenous Andean mutuality, but a major underlying factor behind the growth of modern communal dining in Peru was the largescale rural to urban migration of indigenous people, a phenomenon greatly exacerbated by the country's civil war (c. 1980–2000).

Peru's mass internal migratory movement was accompanied by political turmoil, military intervention and, eventually, devastating civil strife (1980–2000, but ongoing in places at the time of this writing). As violence between Maoist guerrillas and state forces intensified in the 1980s and 1990s, comedores populares and the food they produced became increasingly important spaces. The fear of rural violence intensified the pace of migration and, in the absence of a developed welfare state and wartime food shortages, these female-run dining rooms became vital to the very survival of the country's poorest people. During the bloody conflict—which claimed seventy thousand lives—the women of the comedores populares found themselves in the firing line because such sites were viewed with suspicion by both the government of Alberto Fujimori (who viewed social eating as contrary to its reformist neoliberal agenda) and its Maoist guerrilla antagonists (who viewed the act of feeding people without educating them as not revolutionary enough). The humble yet heroic women of Peru's comedores, denounced by both sides for the perceived crime of serving up plates of rice and beans, are part of a broader women's resistance against a culture of machismo and authoritarianism in Latin America witnessed in the Argentine Mothers of the Plaza Mayor campaign group or the regionwide Ni Una Menos (not one [woman] less) movement. They are also part of a wider transnational phenomenon—commensality in wartime—and victims, as well as resistors, of the exaggerated political tensions attached to this seemingly most inoffensive of human activities. Relying on a range of sources—but in particular oral history interviews with the very women who ran these sites—this chapter relays how, through the ostensibly simple preparation and service of food, the women of the comedores populares were in fact negotiating a route between the twin peaks of government and rebel power.

Commensality in Wartime

Social eating is loaded with meaning. It is here defined as eating with people outside the immediate family unit; a fundamental of human behaviour[1] which many theorists refer to as *commensality*. Although often ostensibly informal, throughout history commensality has also tended to throw up religious or secular parameters and can establish boundaries as well as binding people together.[2] In a more positive light, commensality has been a means through which community cohesion and solidarity has been forged, frequently by people experiencing food insecurity or pursuing forms of justice around food.[3] There are many modern historical examples of large-scale commensality, whether in the form of bottom-up voluntary action or top-down state initiative, but in time of war social eating has tended to take on much greater political significance.

One notable example of wartime social eating, and the debates around it, occurred in early-twentieth-century Europe. During the World Wars of the twentieth century, bottom-up social eating initiatives

Comedor, 1980s. *Image copyright Bryce Evans.*

emerged, chiefly organized by working-class women to protect their communities. These pioneer schemes served as inspiration for wartime governments and many nations launched major social eating programs to combat supply disruption, malnutrition, and price inflation. For example, in Britain during the Second World War (1939–45) the government launched a nationwide network of thousands of "British Restaurants"; similar schemes were rolled out in both Nazi Germany and Fascist Italy.[4] The inspiration for the majority of these schemes came from World War I (1914–18), where state-supported mass feeding experiments were conducted across the European continent.[5] These European examples are important to this study because mass commensality as a wartime activity also witnessed the emergence of attendant political and social anxieties common to the later Peruvian experience. During the Russian Civil War (1917–22) and World War II, the Soviet regime championed communal dining as ideologically desirable, a means of freeing women from "kitchen slavery," challenging the privatized consumption of the capitalist system, and improving for public nutrition; yet it also had to be ideologically conformist, and these sites were typically adorned with propaganda posters and literature. For European conservatives, by contrast, the sight of large numbers of working class people gathering together to dine en masse had alarmingly radical implications, including the threat of revolution, the removal of women from their domestic roles, and the destruction of the family; if communal eating took place at all, they argued, it should do so within firmly patriotic boundaries.[6] Mass commensality in wartime, then, is a politically symbolic act, particularly when carried out on a national scale, with certain political leaders viewing it as ideologically desirable and others viewing it as inherently subversive.

Peru, unlike European countries, did not experience total war in the twentieth century and neither did it experience the consequent development of welfare states afterwards. In the Latin American context, social eating was, and remains, an established social activity, most prominently in the tradition of the fiesta.[7] However, the previously mentioned pace of urbanization in Peru's latter-twentieth-century history would soon transform commensality from an occasional event to a social necessity and would also ensure that large-scale social eating emerged. With this came ideologically opposed attitudes similar to those described above and, similarly, wartime conditions accentuated these divisions. First, though, the conditions underlying Peru's slide toward civil war demand explanation.

Like in Europe, large-scale commensality in Peru grew from organic initiatives. Before the Spanish invasion, the stockpiling of crops and efficient distribution of food from coast to sierra meant that there was no famine in the Incan world: a continuing source of cultural pride in the country to this day. What emerged from the initial Spanish invasion of the sixteenth century, however, was an extractive colonial economy based around the export of mineral resources. Inequalities persisted after independence, with coastal Lima, the colonial capital, remaining the center of power from which a pale-skinned creole elite dictated policy to a large indigenous population mostly located in the Andean highlands.[8] In the 1950s, mass rural-to-urban migration commenced, as postwar shifts in the global agricultural economy caused mass unemployment, pushing people from mountain to coast in search of work, and placing huge strain on embryonic state-welfare networks. In response, the United Nations and the Catholic Church—traditionally the most influential social actor in Peru—established emergency public feeding programs in urban areas, but migration continued apace and outstripped these efforts. Vast *pueblos jovenes* (young towns) soon grew up in the dusty and forbidding desert lands on Lima's furthest edges, lacking basic infrastructure or legal title to land, and populated by impoverished indigenous people.[9]

Statistics illustrate the scale of this demographic shock: in 1940 there were 661,000 people resident in Lima's metropolitan area; at the time of writing this figure stands at over 10 million.[10] In order to sustain their communities, comedores populares soon sprang up at the local level in new slum areas, serving simple plates or rice and beans prepared with basic cooking utensils in large pots.[11] While Peru has a richly eclectic cuisine, plates of rice and beans—*tacu tacu* in Quechua or *frijoles y arroz* in Spanish—are composed of widely available ingredients and are meat-free and therefore inexpensive. At the state level, political turmoil followed in the wake of these demographic pressures and, in 1968, a left-wing military coup installed General Juan Velasco as the president of Peru. Velasco's authoritarian rule sought to elevate the indigenous poor and, among other reforms, delivered democratized land ownership and health and social schemes. Food shortages, however, also emerged toward the end of Velasco's presidency, leading to growing discontent, and in 1975 a right-wing countercoup deposed him; thereafter, many of the gains that Andean migrants had previously won were steadily reversed.[12]

The Coming of the Shining Path and the Civil War

It was against the backdrop of right-wing reaction that a middle-class university professor of philosophy from the south of the country, Abimael Guzmán, came to envision an extremist vision of liberation for the country's poor. Guzmán had demonstrated his solidarity with the indigenous poor by learning Quechua—the ancient language of Peru, which Velasco had elevated to equal linguistic status with Spanish—and became a member of the Peruvian Communist Party. In that party's splits of the 1960s, Guzmán took the Maoist side against the Soviet line and, inspired by Mao Zedong, launched the *Sendero Luminoso* (Shining Path) insurgency from Peru's rural interior.[13] The name was inspired by a quote from the founder of the Peruvian Communist Party, José Carlos Mariátegui, who wrote that Marxism–Leninism was the "shining path to the future." Parenthetically, in contributions to his revolutionary journal *Amauta*, Mariátegui also praised Incan food production and distribution because it was communal rather than privatized.[14] Like Mariátegui, Guzmán imagined an Incan-inspired communism in which all things, including the production, distribution, and consumption of food, would function for the common good rather than private gain; unlike Mariátegui, Guzmán would use brutal methods in pursuit of this goal, inflicting violence not just on rep-resentatives of government but on any workers and peasants who were deemed not to conform to Sendero's rigid dogma.

Peru soon found itself in the midst of a Maoist insurgency, which was announced in 1980 when Shining Path guerrillas burnt ballot boxes in towns in the south, thereby disrupting the first democratic elections in the country since 1964. For the next two decades, state forces and Shining Path guerrillas fought out a protracted civil war, with the government responding to Sendero with their own Argentine-style dirty war of ter-ror perpetrated by commandoes.[15] Because they were located closer to Sendero's rural power base and occupied the bottom rungs of the coun-try's racial and economic pyramid, indigenous people were the most com-mon victims of the violence. The result was ever-greater migration of the indigenous poor to Lima as the rural poor fled the countryside, Sendero's heartland. In pursuing a war tinged not just with utopianism but with a popular millenarianism, Guzmán was not one for hearts and minds and was dismissive of any projects that alleviated poverty, characterizing such measures as "shock absorbers" for the dehumanizing capitalist system.[16] Comedores populares soon found themselves the targets of his ideological condemnation. Some received indirect support through the U.S. Agency for International Development, an example, in Guzmán's eyes, of Yankee imperialist exploitation.[17] The poor indigenous women who led these simple ventures had, according to Sendero's leader, "sold out on the revo-lution for a plate of beans" and were therefore legitimate targets.[18]

The Peruvian economy, meanwhile, was faltering badly. Rejecting the International Monetary Fund (IMF), Alan García (president of Peru from 1985 to 1990) announced protectionist policies that soon led to sharp spikes in the cost of living, hyperinflation, and widespread reversion to the black market. With food queues becoming the new norm, Peru took on the dimensions of a wartime economy. Under these miserable condi-tions and with the state unable to provide a social safety net for its poor, the comedores became vital to survival. As the 1980s became the 1990s, the comedores were feeding approximately 20 percent of all families in Lima alone.[19] In the nation's capital, many comedores received support and blessings from the Bishop of Callao, Ricardo Durand, sometimes availing themselves of donations to the Church from supermarkets and other private enterprises, further exacerbating the scorn with which Sendero viewed them.[20] Garcia's disastrous left-populist policies led to him losing the 1990 election to Alberto Fujimori, a Peruvian of Japanese

Comedor, 2000s.
*Image copyright
Bryce Evans.*

descent and an outsider without a large political base who was a disciple of neoliberalism. Under the presidencies of Fujimori (1990–2000) the poor felt the effects of austerity designed to rescue the economy as well as an escalation of the war against Sendero. Under what was called *Fujishock* austerity, poverty levels increased dramatically.[21] Significantly, Fujimori was influenced by the economist Hernando de Soto, who argued that Peru's path to development lay in market capitalism with proper records of ownership; for de Soto and Fujimori, then, initiatives like the comedores were examples of informal, unrecorded—and therefore inefficient—market activity.[22]

In the midst of these ideological debates, the women of the comedores carried on their day-to-day work, preparing simple dishes of beans and rice for the people of their locales. Positioned between the poles of a dogmatic Maoism and a dogmatic neoliberalism, the women who ran these simple public dining spaces largely avoided any political rhetoric themselves; as one respondent explained, "we simply wanted to feed people."[23] The comedores were run along communal lines, charging very little for simple yet nutritious food and with any profits reinvested to buy food, cooking equipment, and other supplies.[24] This is not to discount the fact that these were highly organized wartime social eating ventures on a scale reminiscent of those in wartime Europe. Yet in achieving food security on a local level, many of the women who volunteered in the comedores shunned identification with either the ideological crusade of the government or that of its Maoist foes; they were simply feeding the people of their communities and meeting a demand that had steadily increased since the war commenced in 1980.[25] In an example of the polarization of the politics of food in wartime, however, comedores populares became the subject of suspicion from both sides in the civil conflict. For the government, they were potentially subversive sites; for the Shining Path, they were not radical enough.

In the Firing Line

1992 would provide several watershed moments in the civil war and catapult the *comedores populares* towards more formal organization and a compact with the government. In April 1992, Fujimori carried out a presidential coup in order to pursue the war against the guerrillas more ardently, suspending the constitution and purging the judiciary. As the government's war on them intensified, the guerrillas were also starting to suffer defeats to local self-defense groups formed in Peru's rural interior. Then came, unexpectedly, what could be considered Fujimori's coup de grace. In September of that year, Guzmán, the mastermind of the rebels' struggle, was captured in a safehouse above a dance studio in Lima, thereby removing Sendero's figurehead.

Women of the comedores, had, over the course of the war, become victims of increased bullying, intimidation, rapes, and other physical violence—most of which came from the belligerent Sendero Luminoso.[26] One of their most prominent voices would also be lost in 1992.

As part of the cycle of violence, María Elena Moyano, a young, prominent Liman community activist from the Villa El Salvador pueblo joven was murdered by the Shining Path at a community barbecue. In a horrific act of gendered violence, the killers then abused her corpse, inserting explosives inside her vagina before blowing her body up.[27] These actions elicited great public sympathy for Moyana and anger toward Sendero; tens of thousands of people attended the funeral of the 33-year-old. Moyano had been the energy behind *Federación Popular de Mujeres de Villa El Salvador* (FEPOMUVES), a federation of women's groups in Lima's sprawling Villa El Salvador shanty town, which administered its network of comedores populares. FEPOMUVES, an early example of women's organization in Peru, was a forerunner of the Central Federation of Women running Community Kitchens (referred to with the even more dizzying acronym, FEMOCCPAALC), the national organization of comedores populares.[28] Moyano was symbolic of how the women active in the community had become stuck in the middle of Peru's civil war. She was heavily critical of the elitism, racism, and disregard of the Peruvian government. Yet the Shining Path—whom she had come to denounce as terrorists and not revolutionaries—hated her because of her embrace of *Vaso de Leche* (glass of milk), a scheme run by the local government that delivered milk to children in Lima's poorest areas.[29] For Moyano, like many of her fellow volunteers, ensuring the basic nutrition of children trumped any ideological objectives. But if she was viewed as a counter-revolutionary by the rebels, she was also eyed uneasily not only by the government, who viewed her as a radical, but also by elements within the Catholic Church, which, one western priest based in Lima confessed, loathed her feminism and quietly breathed a collective sigh of relief when she was murdered.[30] Moyano's murder was a typical maladroit action by Sendero. It would orient the women of the comedores toward the government and the government toward the comedores.

President Fujimori's rise to power was unusual in that it has been characterized as an example of neopopulism. Fujimori, a rank outsider when he ran for President in 1990, lacked the large political party organization typical of institutional Latin American politics.[31] Instead, he was forced to look elsewhere for support bases. Therefore, while cutting spending drastically, Fujimori simultaneously craved the patronage of popular social groups. As a result, Moyano's murder provided the catalyst for a rather odd embrace. In 1992, as the civil war continued and after many years of lobbying for greater state support, the female leaders of the comedores won legal recognition. Fujimori pushed through Law 25307, guaranteeing provision of food for the poor via the comedores and promising to provide them with basic provisions such as rice and cooking oil through the National Food Assistance Scheme. This was seen by some within the movement as a victory; as one respondent put it, "eventually we made Fujimori listen to us."[32] While money had been tight previously, the government was now guaranteeing a basic level of financial support and in the midst of the ongoing civil war, a long-running battle for recognition had been won. According to other volunteers, however, winning state endorsement compromised the independence of the comedores, shifting the women's movement into another arm of a state that fundamentally subjected and excluded them because of their gender and ethnicity.[33]

A war within a war soon developed. In granting financial assistance to the women of the comedores, Fujimori had won their qualified support. While some remained organized on a purely autonomous and localized basis, many were affiliated with the national federation—FEMOCCPAALC—which now gained legal status and wide-ranging consultative powers. In the process, many of the leading women of the comedores transitioned from practical to strategic planning.[34] Simultaneously, Fujimori was buying their support, replicating the way in which European wartime governments came to control feeding initiatives that had previously operated from the bottom up. Yet Fujimori had also, unwittingly, cemented the women's status as operators of a national food justice movement. The latter was outside the President's desired mold. Fujimori, as mentioned, wanted to reorient the Peruvian market toward a North American spirit of rugged individualism. Because the comedores clearly did not conform to his free-market model, his administrations of the 1990s placed pressure on these communal ventures to instead develop into privately owned restaurants. In doing so, Fujimori hoped to gradually erode the state's commitment to provision them.[35] The war against Sendero may have been over, but battles still remained.

Conclusion

Fujimori left the Presidency in 2000, marking the de facto end of Peru's civil war, which had ignited in the 1980s and smoldered on after Gúzman's capture in 1992. At that point, in 2000, more than four thousand kitchens in Lima alone were providing cheap food for a half million of its poorest inhabitants.[36] Two decades later, and on the eve of the two hundredth anniversary of Peru's independence, the country's leading newspaper published a special discussion between historians on the nation's notable moments; in a rare but significant moment of recognition, the "brave women" of the comedores were singled out for praise.[37] Although some comedores transitioned into private ownership as Fujimori desired, the majority did not, affiliating with the national federation, which remains the representative body of bottom-up, communal, and voluntary public feeding schemes. Underlining the persistent politicization of social eating, the achievement of recognition and funding from the state led to a later battle—during the protracted end of the civil war—to assert autonomy. Unsurprisingly, ever since gaining legal entitlement to state support in 1992, the federation has been campaigning to maintain its independent status while also striving to ensure the continuance of basic government assistance.[38] It is a fight which continues to this day.

NOTES

1. See: Angela Meah, "Eating," in Peter Jackson, ed., *Food Words: Essays in Culinary Culture* (Bloomsbury Academic, 2015): 68–72; R. I. M. Dunbar, "Breaking Bread: The Functions of Social Eating," *Adaptive Human Behavior and Physiology*, 3, no. 3 (2015): 198–211.

2. C. Fischler, "Commensality, Society and Culture," *Social Science Information* 50, no. 3–4 (2011): 528–48; C. Chou, S. Kerner, and M. Warmind, eds., *Commensality: From Everyday Food to Feast* (London: Bloomsbury Academic, 2015).

3. A. P. Julier, *Eating Together: Food, Friendship, and Inequality* (Champaign, IL, University of Illinois Press, 2013); M. Blake, "More Than Just Food: Everyday Food Insecurity and Resilient Place Making Through Community Self-Organising," *Sustainability* 11 (2019): 1–22.

4. See: P. J. Atkins, "Communal Feeding in War Time: British Restaurants, 1940–1947," In: I. Zweiniger-Bargielowska, R. Duffett, & A. Drouard, eds., *Food and War in Twentieth Century Europe* (Farnham, England: Ashgate, 2011): 139–53; Frank Trentmann and Fleming Just, eds., *Food and Conflict in the Age of the Two World Wars* (London: Palgrave MacMillan, 2006); Alice Weinreb, *Modern Hungers: Food and Power in Twentieth-Century Germany* (Oxford: Oxford University Press, 2017); Bertram Gordon, "Fascism, the Neo-Right and Gastronomy: A Case in the Theory of the Social Engineering of Taste" in Tom Jaine, ed., *Taste: Proceedings of the Oxford Symposium on Food and Cookery* (London: Prospect, 1988): 82–97; James Vernon, *Hunger: A Modern History* (Cambridge, MA: Harvard University Press 2007).

5. Peter Scholliers, "Restaurants Économiques a Bruxelles Pendant La Grande Guerre," in Caroline Poulaine, ed., *Manger et Boire entre 1914 et 1918* (Dijon: Snoeck, 2014); Hans-Jurgen Teuteberg, "Food Provisioning on the German Home Front 1914–1918," in Ina Zweiniger-Bargielowska, Rachel Duffett and Alain Drouard, eds., *Food and War in Twentieth Century Europe* (London: Ashgate, 2011): 59–72; Bryce Evans, "The National Kitchen in Britain, 1917–1919," *Journal of War & Culture Studies* 10, no. 2 (2017): 115–29.

6. Anna Sorokina, "How the Soviet Union brought Culinary Equality to the Table," Russian Kitchen, January 10, 2018, https://www.rbth.com/russian-kitchen/327231-soviet-union-brought-culinary-equality; for British political anxieties around commensality and class see: Evans, "The National Kitchen in Britain"; L. Margaret Barnett, *British Food Policy during the First World War* (London: Routledge, 1985); John Burnett, *England Eats Out: A Social History of Eating Out in England from 1830 to the Present* (London: Routledge, 2004).

7. C. Giacoman, "The Dimensions and Role of Commensality: A Theoretical Model Drawn from the Significance of Communal Eating among Adults in Santiago, Chile, *Appetite* 107 (2016): 460–70.

8. See: Alfonso Quiroz, *Historia de la corrupción en el Perú* (Lima: Instituto de Estudios Peruanos, 2013); Orin Stark, Carlos De Gregori, and Robin Kirk, eds., *The Peru Reader: History, Culture, Politics* (Durham, NC: Duke University Press, 2005); John Crabtree and Francisco Durand, *Peru: Elite Power and Political Capture* (London: Zed Books, 2017): 8–54.

9. Luis Valcarel, "Tempest in the Andes," in Stark, et al, *The Peru Reader*, 219–22.

10. "Lima cuenta con 9 miliones," *La República*, 17 January 2015.

11. Interview with Vilma Huancan, 12 September 2014.

12. See: Daniel Masterson, *Militarism and Politics in Latin America: Peru from Sánchez Cerro to Sendero Luminoso* (Westport, CT: Greenwood, 1991): 243–99.

13. See Steve Stern, ed., *Shining and Other Paths: War and Society in Peru, 1985–1995* (Durham, NC: Duke University Press, 1998).

14. Berndt Krehoff, "José Carlos Mariátegui y el 'comunismo inkaico,'" http://www .perupolitico.com/?p=1627.

15. Steve Stern, "Beyond Enigma: An Agenda for Interpreting Shining Path and Peru, 1980–1995," in Stern, ed., *Shining*, 5.

16. Isabel Coral Cordero, "Women in War: Impact and Responses," in Stern, ed., *Shining*, 365–66.

17. James Garrett, "Comedores Populares: Lessons for Urban Programming from Peruvian Community Kitchens," (Washington, DC: IFPRI, 2001), mimeo.

18. Cordero, "Women in War," 366; interview with Ester Pisedo Sena, 13 September 2014.

19. Cecilia Blondet and Carmen Montero, *Hoy menú popular: Comedores en Lima* (Lima: Unicef, 1995): 6; Jacqueline Minaya Rodríguez, "Thou Shalt Not Kill with Hunger or Bullets: Soup Kitchens, the Space for Memory and the Notion of Justice in El Agustino Ex Dirigentas" (Proceedings of the University of San Marcos Memory Group, 2013).

20. Interview with Alfredo Garland, 16 August 2019.

21. See: Julio Carrión, *The Fujimori Legacy: The Rise of Electoral Authoritarianism in Peru* (University Park, PA: Penn State University Press, 2006); Peter McKenzie Atack, "Caesarism, Fujimori and the Transformation of Peru into a Neoliberal Order " (PhD dissertation, Carleton University, Canada, 2006).

22. Hernando De Soto, *The Other Path: The Economic Answer to Terrorism* (London: Basic Books, 1989).

23. Interview with Vilma Huancan, 12 September 2014; interview with Maria Julia Montalban Rosalez, 20 September 2014.

24. Florence Babb, *Between Field and Cooking Pot: The Political Economy of Marketwomen in Peru* (Austin: University of Texas Press, 2010).

25. Interview with Maximiliana Jarampa Laurente, 27 September 2014.

26. Cordero, "Women in War," 370.

27. Interview with priest who wishes to remain anonymous, 4 March 2015.

28. Interview with Narda Marquez, 8 September 2014.

29. Diana Milosavich Tupac, ed., *The Autobiography of Maria Elena Moyano: The Life and Death of a Peruvian Activist* (Gainesville, FL: University Press of Florida, 2000): 35–67.

30. Interview with priest who wishes to remain anonymous, 4 March 2015.

31. See: Stéphanie Rousseau, *Women's Citizenship in Peru: The Paradoxes of Neopopulism in Latin America* (Basingstoke: Palgrave, 2009).

32. Interview with Narda Marquez, 8 September 2014.

33. Interview with Estela Cisneros Daura, 8 September 2014.

34. Inga Hajdarowicz, "Does Participation Empower? The Example of Community Kitchens in Lima, Peru," Krytyka.org, 24 September 2013: http://krytyka.org /does-participation-empower-the-example-of-community-kitchens-in -lima-peru/.

35. K. Schroeder, Kathleen, "A Feminist Examination of Community Kitchens in Peru and Bolivia," *Gender, Place & Culture: A Journal of Feminist Geography* 13, no. 6 (2006): 663–68.

36. R. Zibechi, "Lima's Community Kitchens: Combating Hunger and Loneliness," Upside Down World, http://upsidedownworld.org/main/peru-archives-76/1088-limas-community-kitchens-combating-hunger-and-loneliness.

37. *El Comercio*, 22 July 2019. My thanks to Alfredo Garland for this reference.

38. Interview with Julia Castro, 10 September 2014.

CONTRIBUTORS

JUSTIN NORDSTROM is professor of history at Penn State's Hazleton campus, where he teaches U.S. and world history and serves as the campus honors coordinator. His research examines American history through popular texts, including anti-immigrant newspapers, utopian novels, radio transcripts, wartime propaganda posters, and popular cookbooks, demonstrating how media has shaped American identity from the nineteenth century through the present. Nordstrom is the author of *Danger on the Doorstep: Anti-Catholicism and American Print Culture in the Progressive Era* (Notre Dame Press, 2006) and *Aunt Sammy's Radio Recipes: The Original 1927 Cookbook and Housekeeper's Chat* (University of Arkansas Press, 2018).

ERIN STEWART MAULDIN is an environmental historian and assistant professor of history at the University of South Florida. She is author of the award-winning *Unredeemed Land: An Environmental History of Civil War and Emancipation in the Cotton South* (Oxford University Press, 2018) and coeditor of the Wiley-Blackwell *Companion to Global Environmental History* (2012). She serves as coeditor of the book series *Environmental History and the American South* at the University of Georgia Press and is also the book review editor for *Agricultural History*.

MATTHEW RICHARDSON is curator of social history at Manx National Heritage on the Isle of Man. His abiding interest throughout his working life has been British military history in the nineteenth and twentieth centuries, an interest founded in family history research into forebears who served in the South African War, World War I, and World War II. He is the author of numerous published works covering aspects of these conflicts and has curated several major exhibitions exploring the material culture of warfare, both from the battlefields and home fronts.

KARLINE McLAIN is professor of religious studies at Bucknell University, where she teaches courses on the religions of South Asia. Her area of expertise is religion in colonial and postcolonial India, and a persistent interest in religion, public culture, and pluralism underlies her diverse projects.

Her first book, *India's Immortal Comic Books: Gods, Kings, and Other Heroes* (Indiana University Press, 2009), received the Edward Cameron Dimock, Jr. Prize from the American Institute of Indian Studies for its contribution to the Indian humanities. Her second book, *The Afterlife of Shirdi Sai Baba: Competing Visions of a Global Saint* (University of Washington Press, 2016), explores the many interpretations of Shirdi Sai Baba across hagiography, ethnography, film, and history. She is currently at work on a book titled *Gandhi's Ashrams: Residential Experiments for Universal Wellbeing*, which studies the intentional communities founded by Mahatma Gandhi in India and South Africa.

MOHD AHMAR ALVI is assistant professor of English at Aligarh Muslim University, Aligarh, India. For his doctoral research, he is looking at the interface of food studies and Dalit studies, where the central thesis explores how Dalit writers use their foodways to document resistance against Brahmanical and majoritarian notions of taste, cuisine, pure food, and prohibition of beef. Alvi has been awarded a grant jointly by Literary Observer Publishing House (St. Petersburg, Russia) and European University (St. Petersburg, Russia) to present a paper titled "Consuming Fear: A Case Study of Fear-based Food Politics in India" at the international conference Anthropology of Fear at European University.

JING SUN is a PhD candidate in modern Japanese history at the University of Pennsylvania. She received a broad, international education in China, Japan, South Korea, and the United States. Her research interests include food, war and society, history of medicine in Japan and East Asia, and world history. She is working on a dissertation titled "Nurturing a Robust Society: Japan in the Making of the Global Science of Nutrition 1869–1951," which explores political, economic, and sociocultural development in modern Japan and the world through the prism of nutrition science. Her long-term goal is to rethink the modern experience by examining food and society in Japan and the world from the late nineteenth through the mid-twentieth century.

LESLIE A. PRZYBYLEK is senior curator at the Senator John Heinz History Center in Pittsburgh, Pennsylvania, where she researches popular culture, technology, and foodways of the nineteenth and twentieth centuries. Przybylek has wrestled with issues of regional history and identity on both sides of the Mississippi River, including Western Arkansas and Kansas City, Missouri, where she previously served as curator of humanities exhibitions with Mid-America Arts Alliance and *NEH on the Road*, engaging small and mid-size museums across the country with NEH-funded humanities scholarship. A public historian devoted to encouraging people to think critically about the history of local communities, Przybylek has curated more than forty exhibitions, including multiple projects focused on World War II and its home-front impact. She is the author of numerous articles in publications such as *Western Pennsylvania History*, *Pennsylvania Magazine of History and Biography*, *Repast*, and *Craft Beverages and Tourism, Volume 1 / The Rise of Breweries and Distilleries in the United States*.

YVONNE TAN is currently pursuing an MA in Southeast Asian studies and has a chapter titled "Piratical Headhunters yang semacam Melayu dan Cina: Creating the Native Other in the Mat Salleh Rebellions (1894–1905)" forthcoming in *Race and Colonial Wars in the Nineteenth Century* edited by Farish Noor and Peter Carey (Amsterdam University Press, 2021). She also coedits a zine called *Students in Resistance*, committed to exploring underdiscussed topics in Malaysia's political discourse. Her research interests include postcolonial historiographies, spectrality in national myths, social movements, and cultural theory.

CHRISTOPHER MENKING is associate professor of history at Tarrant County College in Fort Worth, Texas. His dissertation and subsequent research examines U.S. Army logistics during the U.S.–Mexico War and how the war influenced South Texas. He published an article, "Brazos Santiago: The Forgotten Gateway of Texas, 1836–1874," in 2017 in the journal *Military History of the West*. His current projects include creating two monographs from his dissertation and a project called "Songs for the Dead: Music from the United States–Mexico War Era" to showcase period music from the U.S. and Mexico in both a concert and a digital repository online.

CHRISTOPHER S. ROSE is a social historian of medicine, focusing on the nineteenth and twentieth century Middle East. He has taught in the School of Behavioral and Social Sciences at St. Edward's University in Austin, Texas. He has also taught in the Department of History and the Department of Middle Eastern Studies at the University of Texas at Austin. Prior to pursuing his doctorate, he was director of outreach and public programming at the University of Texas's Center for Middle Eastern Studies. An active public historian, he founded the podcast *15 Minute History* and served as cohost for eight years. He is also a past president of the Middle East Outreach Council.

EVAN P. SULLIVAN is an instructor of history at SUNY Adirondack and earned his PhD at the University at Albany, focusing on disability and the senses in World War I American rehabilitation. He specializes in the intersections of gender, disability, the senses, and modern war. Sullivan is a regular writer at *Nursing Clio*, where he writes on topics such as the histories of nursing, hospitals, disability, and alternative medicine.

CAROL HELSTOSKY is an associate professor of history and chair of the history department at the University of Denver, where she teaches classes in modern European history and food history. She is the author of several works in food history, including *Garlic and Oil: Food and Politics in Modern Italy*, *Pizza: A Global History*, and *Food Cultures of the Mediterranean*, and the editor of *The Routledge History of Food*. She is finishing a book-length study on the history of the art market in late nineteenth- and early twentieth-century Italy. Her current research project is a cross-cultural culinary history of meatlessness, an examination of the history of culinary creativity in societies that have consumed little or no meat.

NEL DE MÛELENAERE is a historian of nineteenth- and twentieth-century Europe, and assistant professor at the Social and Cultural Food Studies (FOST) research group of the University of Brussels (VUB). Her research examines the experiences and impact of female American relief workers in Belgium and France and living standards of Belgian families during and after World War I and the development of home economics and nutritional science. In 2019, she was the BAEF Cabeaux-Jacobs postdoctoral fellow at Cornell University, which awarded her the Dean's Fellowship in the History of Home Economics. Her dissertation explored forgotten militarization processes in Belgian society between 1890 and 1914 and was published by Leuven University Press in 2019. She has previously worked as scientific coordinator for National movements and Intermediary Structures in Europe (NISE) and the Centre for Historical Research and Documentation on War and Contemporary Society (CegeSoma).

BREANNE ROBERTSON is an art historian of nineteenth- and twentieth-century American art and an education specialist at the National Archives and Records Administration (NARA). Her research focuses on issues of national identity, race, and cross-cultural exchange. Prior to joining NARA's museum staff, she taught art history and American studies at Wesleyan University, worked as a military historian at Marine Corps University, and held fellowships at the Georgia O'Keeffe Museum, Crystal Bridges Museum of American Art, Dumbarton Oaks Library and Museum, and Smithsonian American Art Museum. Her publications include *Investigating Iwo: The Flag Raisings in Myth, Memory and Esprit de Corps* (Marine Corps History Division, 2019) and art historical essays on religious history paintings, social studies textbooks, and New Deal–era mural art. She is currently completing a monograph on Pan-Americanism and art under the Good Neighbor Policy.

KWONG CHI MAN is an associate professor in the history department of Hong Kong Baptist University. He specializes in the military and naval history of modern East Asia, particularly from the Sino-Japanese War (1894–95) to the 1970s. He has published *Eastern Fortress A Military History of Hong Kong, 1840–1970* (coauthored) and *War and Geopolitics in Interwar Manchuria*. His works can also be found in *Modern Asian Studies*, *War in History*, and *Journal of Military History*.

BRYCE EVANS is associate professor of history at Liverpool Hope University. He is the author of five books and numerous academic articles. His latest monograph, *Food and Aviation in the Twentieth Century: The Pan American Ideal* (Bloomsbury, 2021), is the first academic study of food and aviation.

INDEX

Italic page numbers indicate photographs or illustrations.

defoliants, 134
Delpar, Helen, 223
dentures, 47
Department of Hawkers and Petty
 Traders (DHPT), 139
Department of the Interior, U.S., 232
De Waal, Alex, 12
Dewey, John, 5
Dharasana Salt Works (Gujarat, India),
 69–70
dietitians, 183–84, 186
Diner, Hasia, 10
disability, and veterans' rehabilitation,
 177–86
disease
 in Boer War, 46
 in Egypt during WWI, 170
 livestock (*See* animal disease)
District Administration Offices (Hong
 Kong), 246–47
District War Executive Committee, 133
doctrine of improvement, 26
Domino Theory, 131
Duffett, Rachel, 185
Durand, Ricardo, Bishop of Callao, 260
Dyer, Reginald, 67

East River, 251
Eating for Victory (Bentley), 113
Eden, Ashely, 85
Egypt
 rinderpest in, 29–30
 in WWI and aftermath, 161–72
Egyptian Gazette, 166
Egyptian Labor Corps (ELC), 164
Egyptian Revolution (1919), 162, 171–72
Eisenhower, Dwight, and administration,
 131
Emergency Food Denial Organization, 135
emergency rations, 47
Encephelartos altensteinii (Hottentot's
 bread), 52
epizootics, 22–24, 28, 30, 33, 34
Eritrea, 30
Ethiopia, 30
ethnic Chinese, in Malaya, 131, 132, 136
ethnic cookbooks, in U.S. during WWI,
 195–200
Evans, Bryce, 255–64

Evolution of Corn, The (Houser), 228–29,
 228–30

famine, 11–12, 94, 168, 193, 251
famine of 1945, 242, 249–50
farm worker programs, 235
fascism, 194, 200–204. *See also* Nazism
*Federación Popular de Mujeres de Villa El
 Salvador* (FEPOMUVES), 262
Federal Territories Ministry (Malaysia),
 140
Fibber McGee and Molly (radio show), 121
films. *See* propaganda films
Finch, Martha, 10
Flaviviridae, 23
Food Across Borders (anthology), 149
Food and Firewood Board (Hong Kong),
 243
food autarky
 in Italy, 200–201
 in Japan, 91–102
food denial, 133–35, 140
food inequality, 215–16
Food in the Civil War Era (Veit), 149
food rationing. *See* rationing
food relief, in Belgium after WWI, 207–17
food riots (Italy, 1919), 200
Foods America Gave the World, 226
food shortages
 in Peru, 256, 259
 in WWI-era Belgium, 213
 in WWI-era Europe, 177
Food Will Win the War (film), 237
"Food Will Win the War" poster, 5, *8*, *9*
foraging, 151
forced migration, 242, 246
Fort Bayard hospital, 184
Fort McHenry hospital, 180–86
Fort McPherson hospital, 185
Fort Ontario hospital, 185
"Four Minute Men," 5, 7
Foust, Edmond C., 235
France, 192
Franco-Prussian War (1871), 29
Freedmen's Bureau, 28
free-market capitalism, in Peru, 261, 264
Frémont, John, 150
French West Africa, rinderpest in, 30
"Friday's feast," 196

fruit
in Belgian children's diet, 212
in Egypt during WWI, 166
in Mexican markets, 154
and WWI-era food economy in U.S.,
195, 200, 201, 203
Fujimori, Alberto, 256, 260–64
"Fujishock" austerity, 261

Gandhi, Kasturba, 64, 70
Gandhi, Mohandas K. "Mahatma," 57–71
salt and empire in India, 65–70
sugar and empire in South Africa,
58–65
and vegetarianism, 85–86
García, Alan, 260
Gates, Paul, 21
gaurakshini sabhas (cow protection
societies), 79, 80, 82
gender roles. *See* women
General Hospital Number 1 (New York
City), 183
General Hospital Number 11 (Cape May,
New Jersey), 182–83
Gent, Edward, 130
Germany
and Pan-Americanism in WWII, 221
sharecropping in colonies, 35
social eating during WWII, 257
substitutions in diet during WWI, 192
vegetarianism in, 203
and Treaty of Versailles, 10
Gibson, George, 154
Gimson, Franklin, 138
Give Us This Day (Australian propaganda
film), 121
globalization, 28–29, 242
goats, 80
Goldberg, Ellis, 163
Good Neighbor Policy, 221–38
Gow, Kenneth, 178
Graham, Sylvester, 151
Grain that Built a Hemisphere, The (film),
234–35
Great Britain
and black market for meat during
WWII, 109, 110, 112–17, 121, 122
and food in Hong Kong during
famine of 1945, 242

social eating during WWII, 257
substitutions in diet during WWI, 192
Great Depression, 221, 230
Greater East Asian Co-Prosperity Sphere,
101, 102
Greene, Ann, 21
Green Giant niblets, 226, *227*
Guadalupe Hidalgo, Treaty of, 150
Guardian (London), 133–34
guerilla warfare, Malayan Emergency
and, 130–39
Guha, Ramachandra, 59
Gurney, Sir Henry, 136
Guzmán, Abimael, 259–60, 262, 264

halla, 129
Hamilton, George, 229
hardtack biscuits, 47
Harrison, Grace Clergue, 196
Harvey, Sir Paul, 171
hawkers and hawking. *See* street hawking
Hawkers Inquiry Commission, 138–39
Hayato Ōtani (Ishikawa Shingo), 92–93
Haynes, Edward, 80
Helstosky, Carol, 191–204
Henaut, Stephane, 11
Hercules Hygienic Supply House
(Chicago, Illinois), 194
Hind Swaraj (Indian Home Rule)
(Gandhi), 62–63
Hindus and Hinduism, 61, 66, 75–86
Hiroda Cabinet, 95
Hobhouse, Emily, 43, 49–51
hog cholera, 21–29
Home on the Range (USDA film), 119
Hong Kong
and famine of 1945, 249–50
food during wartime (1938–1946),
241–51
Japanese attack on (December 8,
1941), 244
Hong Kong Occupation Government,
244–45, 248
Hoover, Herbert, 207, 209, 213
hospitals, rehabilitation of WWI-era
veterans in, 177–86
Hottentot's bread *(Encephelartos
altensteinii)*, 52
House of Correction (Bombay, India), 76

victory gardens in WWI, 178
visual culture of corn in WWII,
234–38
U.S. Agency for International
Development, 260
U.S. Army
and hog cholera, 21, 24
during U.S.–Mexico war, 149–53
veterans' disability and rehabilitation
in WWI, 177–86
U.S. Army General Hospital No. 9
(Lakewood, New Jersey), 180–81,
183, 184
U.S. Army Hospital (Oteen, North
Carolina), 184
U.S. Army Medical Department, 183
U.S. Capitol Building, 224
U.S. Food Administration (USFA),
7, 10, 178
U.S. Office of Inter-American Affairs, 234
United States Department of Agriculture
(USDA), 22, 25–27
U.S.–Mexico War (1846–1848), 147–57, 221
Unto This Last (Ruskin), 60

Vaal River, 45
Vancouver Sun, 116
Vaso de Leche (glass of milk), 263
vegetarian cookbooks, 198–99
vegetarianism, 70
Gandhi and, 61
in India, 75–86
during WWI, 194–95
Veit, Helen Zoe, 149
Velasco, Juan, 259
Verandah riots (Singapore, 1888), 129
Versailles, Treaty of, 10
Versailles Conference, 171
veterans, rehabilitation in WWI, 177–86
Victoria (queen of England), 47
Victoria, Hong Kong, 244
victory gardens, 178
Viljoen, Ben, 49
Villa El Salvador (Lima, Peru), 262
vitamin B, 248
vitamin C, 212
Vivekananda, Swami, 78

Voices in the Kitchen (Abarca), 149
voluntarism, in WWI, 178

Wakatsuki Cabinet, 93
Wallace, Henry A., 225–26, 230
Waller, Richard, 28
Walt Disney Studio, 234
Wampanoag Indians, 223
Wan Chai Fresh Food Market (Victoria,
Hong Kong), 244
Wartime Prices and Trade Board
(WPTB) (Canada), 116–18
Watts, Michael, 11–12
Wauters, Joseph, 213
wheat
in Belgian children's diet, 211–12
in Egypt during WWI, 161, 164,
167–72
wheat flour, 96, 99
Wheeler, Candace, 223
White, Sir George, 44
"White Areas" (during Malayan
Emergency), 138
Whitehead, Ann, 32
Wilson, W. H., 169–70
Wilson, Woodrow, 4, 5
Windsor, Ontario, 122
Windsor Star, 116
women
and black-market meat during
WWII, 119–22, *120*
and Peruvian comedores populares,
255–64, *257*, *261*
Women's Land Army, 235
Woolton, Lord (Frederick James
Marquis), 115
World War I
culinary nationalism in U.S., 191–204
Egypt in, 161–72
food propaganda campaigns and
posters, 4–10, *6*, *8*, *9*
Gandhi's service to Britain in, 65
impact on Belgian children's diet,
212–16
and Japanese attempts at food
autarky in Manchuria, 92
and salt tax, 67